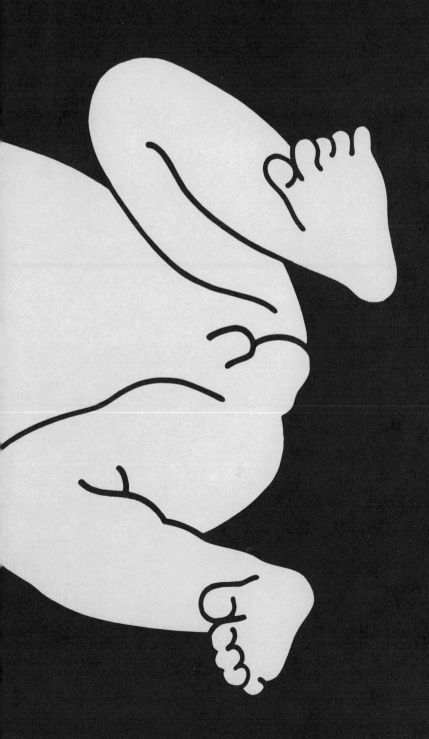

Human Body

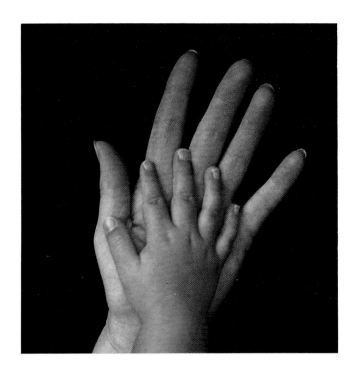

TIME-LIFE
ALEXANDRIA, VIRGINIA

CONTENTS

1

The Mysteries of Human Life

There are thousands of mysteries contained in the human body. What makes muscles grow? Where does sweat come from? What causes goose bumps? How does food get digested? This book provides the answers to those and many other questions about the human body and how it does what it does.

But to scientists learning about the body, every answer seems to raise a dozen more questions. One of the most intriguing areas is explored in this chapter on reproduction and development.

A human being—that complicated collection of brains and bones, blood and organs, thoughts and feelings and knowledge—starts out as a single cell. After it is fertilized, the cell is called a zygote, and it divides and develops into groups of cells, forming the parts that will one day make up a complete baby. This growth and development process takes approximately 266 days from fertilization. In that time, the fetus will grow to an average weight of 7 pounds, or two billion times that of the original fertilized egg.

Controlling this whole process, and dictating everything from the shape of a child's fingernails to his or her aptitude for music, is the spiraling cord of chemicals known as deoxyribonucleic acid, or DNA. How DNA makes up genes and chromosomes, and how these tiny structures that are present in every cell really work, may be the ultimate mystery of the human body.

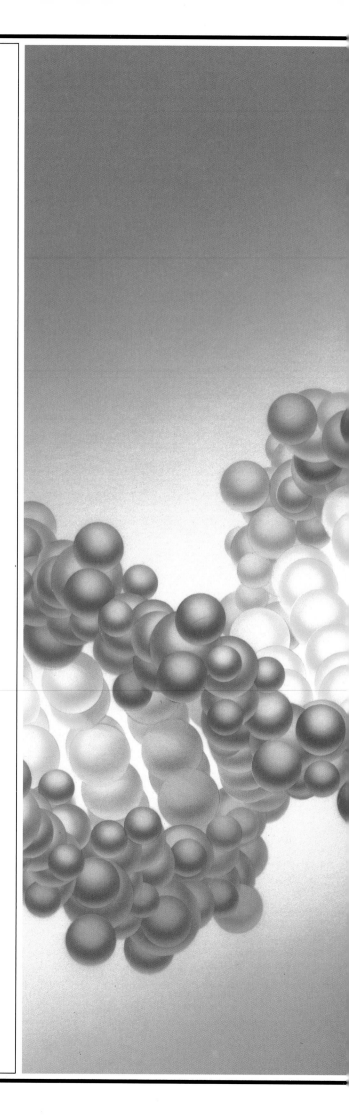

Molecules of DNA form a twisted chain in the nucleus of each human cell. Invisible to the naked eye, these chemicals determine all of a person's inherited characteristics.

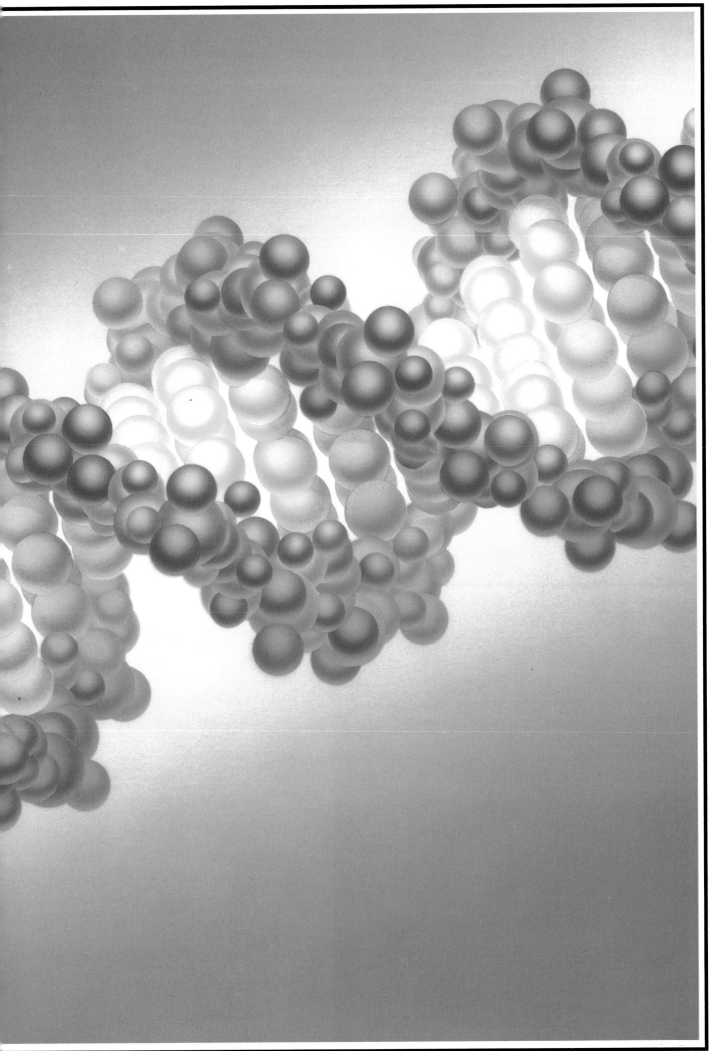

What Is the Human Body Made Of?

The human body is made of tiny building units called cells, each about 1/1000 of an inch wide. An adult body contains about 75 trillion cells—if they could be laid end to end, they would form a chain 1,180,000 miles long.

Cells group together to form tissues. Tissues are divided into four different types: epithelial, connective, nerve, and muscle. A mass of tissue that has a specific form and function is called an organ, such as the heart, kidneys, etc. When organs work together to perform a particular job in the body, they form an organ system, such as the digestive system or the nervous system.

Muscular and skeletal systems

Digestive system

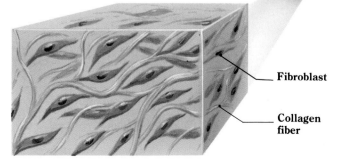

A covering for the body inside and out

Epithelial tissue, which is made up of one or more layers of cells, forms the skin and lines the spaces that are inside the body.

The inner layer of skin cells covering this hand grows out as the harder outer layer wears away.

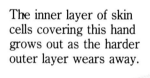

Epidermis

Dermis

Holding the body together

Connective tissue supports the body and allows the organs to do their work. It is formed from specialized cells interwoven with tiny fibers.

Formed from connective tissue, veins carry blood cells in a fluid called plasma.

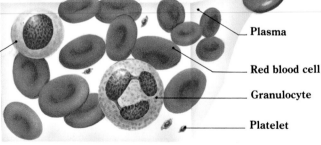

Lymphocyte

Plasma

Red blood cell

Granulocyte

Platelet

The trachea's hairlike cilia remove foreign matter; the small intestine's villi absorb nutrients.

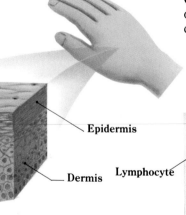

Trachea

Mucus-secreting cells

Small intestine

Cilia

Villi

Loose connective tissue lies under the epidermis, or the upper layer of skin.

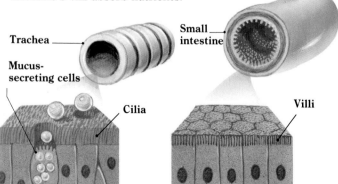

Fibroblast

Collagen fiber

Working together for a common purpose

Organ systems, especially the oxygen-bearing cardiovascular and respiratory systems, work closely together.

Cardiovascular system   **Nervous system**

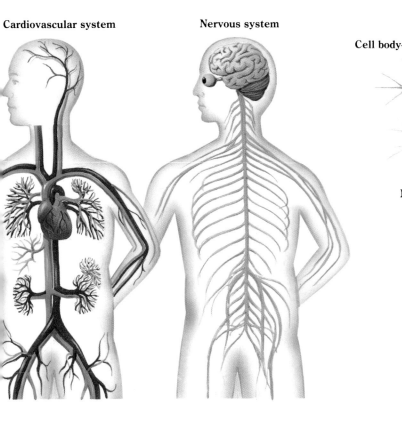

The body's communications network

This motor nerve cell *(below)* is part of the body's nervous system, which includes the brain, the spinal cord, and nerves throughout the body.

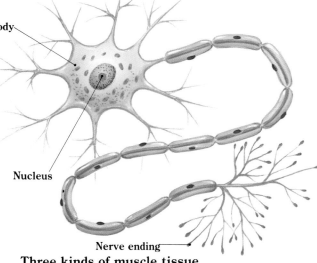

Cell body

Nucleus

Nerve ending

Three kinds of muscle tissue

Smooth muscle occurs in and around the internal organs; skeletal muscle is primarily involved in movement. Cardiac muscle pumps the heart.

Visceral (smooth) muscle

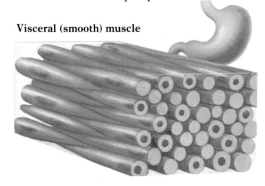

Trachea

Cartilaginous tissue, which is softer and more flexible than bone, can be found in the larynx, trachea, nose, and ears.

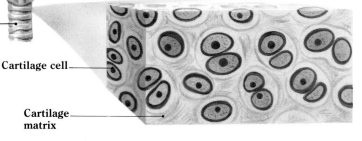

Cartilage cell

Cartilage matrix

This osseous, or bony, tissue, the main element in bones, is made of hard cells able to support the body.

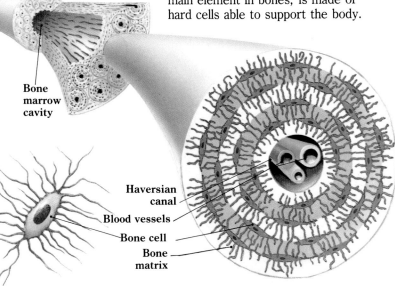

Bone marrow cavity

Haversian canal

Blood vessels

Bone cell

Bone matrix

Skeletal (striated) muscle

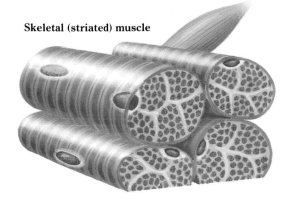

Cardiac muscle

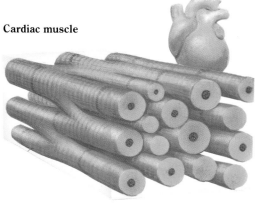

How Are New Human Cells Formed?

Although cells may vary in shape or size according to the tissue to which they belong, all cells have certain things in common. For example, contained within the membrane of almost every cell is a nucleus, which is surrounded by cytoplasm. The nucleus and the cytoplasm together are called protoplasm.

In addition, all cells reproduce in roughly the same way through cell division. The most common type of cell division, illustrated below, is called mitosis. In this sequence, the original cell, or parent cell, divides to produce two daughter cells. The process, which in humans could take as little as a few minutes or as much as a few hours to complete, will produce exact replicas of the original cell.

Division and multiplication

A cell's chromosomes contain its genetic material, the molecules that dictate the cell's structure and functions. When cells divide in mitosis, this material is duplicated within the daughter cells. The illustrations below show four chromosomes (there are actually 46 in a human cell) during division.
1. Centrioles duplicate as chromatids in the nucleus change to become individual chromosomes.
2. Centrioles separate and form spindles.
3. Chromosomes align as the nucleus disappears.
4. Each chromosome divides to form a new chromosome.
5. Migration of the chromosomes is complete, and cytoplasm begins to constrict.
6. A new nucleus is formed in each of the two daughter cells.

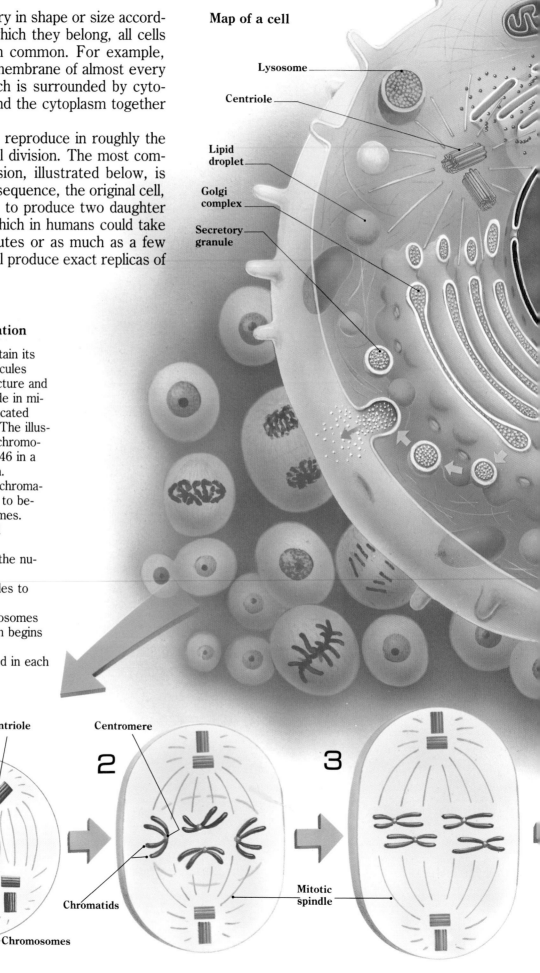

Map of a cell

Lysosome

Centriole

Lipid droplet

Golgi complex

Secretory granule

Centriole

Centromere

1

2

3

Parent cell

Chromatids

Chromosomes

Mitotic spindle

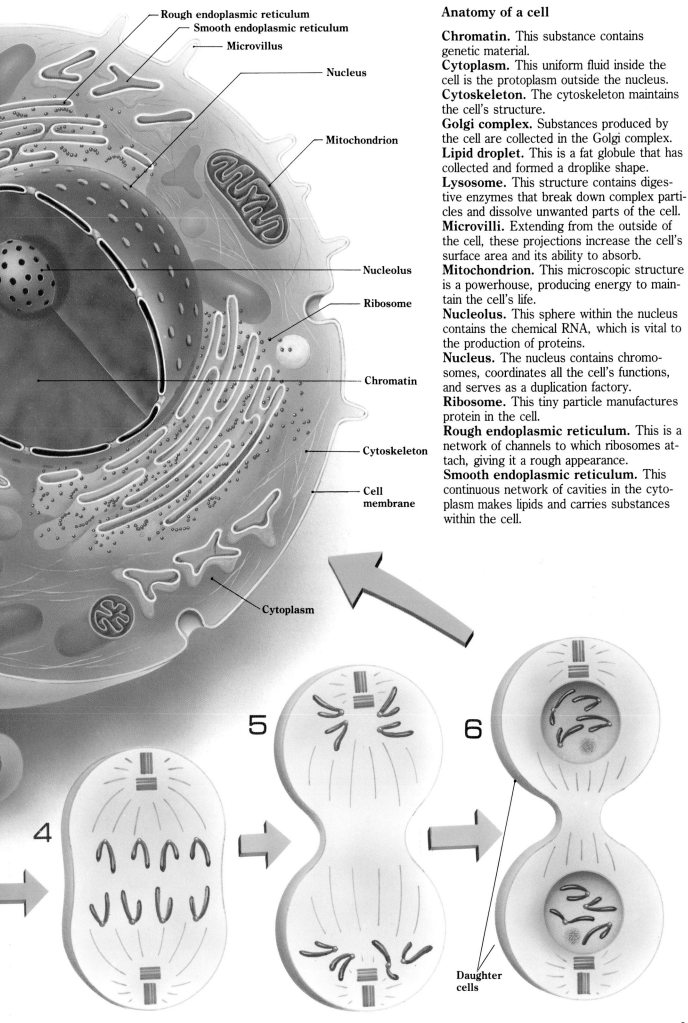

Rough endoplasmic reticulum
Smooth endoplasmic reticulum
Microvillus
Nucleus
Mitochondrion
Nucleolus
Ribosome
Chromatin
Cytoskeleton
Cell membrane
Cytoplasm

Anatomy of a cell

Chromatin. This substance contains genetic material.

Cytoplasm. This uniform fluid inside the cell is the protoplasm outside the nucleus.

Cytoskeleton. The cytoskeleton maintains the cell's structure.

Golgi complex. Substances produced by the cell are collected in the Golgi complex.

Lipid droplet. This is a fat globule that has collected and formed a droplike shape.

Lysosome. This structure contains digestive enzymes that break down complex particles and dissolve unwanted parts of the cell.

Microvilli. Extending from the outside of the cell, these projections increase the cell's surface area and its ability to absorb.

Mitochondrion. This microscopic structure is a powerhouse, producing energy to maintain the cell's life.

Nucleolus. This sphere within the nucleus contains the chemical RNA, which is vital to the production of proteins.

Nucleus. The nucleus contains chromosomes, coordinates all the cell's functions, and serves as a duplication factory.

Ribosome. This tiny particle manufactures protein in the cell.

Rough endoplasmic reticulum. This is a network of channels to which ribosomes attach, giving it a rough appearance.

Smooth endoplasmic reticulum. This continuous network of cavities in the cytoplasm makes lipids and carries substances within the cell.

4

5

6

Daughter cells

What Is DNA and What Does It Do?

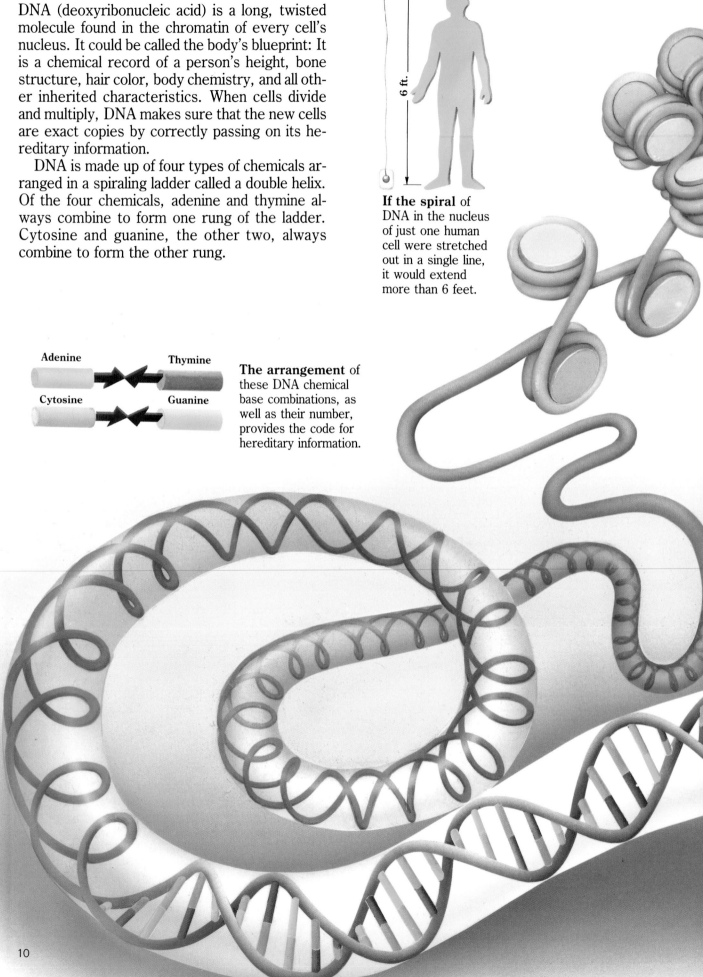

DNA (deoxyribonucleic acid) is a long, twisted molecule found in the chromatin of every cell's nucleus. It could be called the body's blueprint: It is a chemical record of a person's height, bone structure, hair color, body chemistry, and all other inherited characteristics. When cells divide and multiply, DNA makes sure that the new cells are exact copies by correctly passing on its hereditary information.

DNA is made up of four types of chemicals arranged in a spiraling ladder called a double helix. Of the four chemicals, adenine and thymine always combine to form one rung of the ladder. Cytosine and guanine, the other two, always combine to form the other rung.

6 ft.

If the spiral of DNA in the nucleus of just one human cell were stretched out in a single line, it would extend more than 6 feet.

Adenine   Thymine

Cytosine   Guanine

The arrangement of these DNA chemical base combinations, as well as their number, provides the code for hereditary information.

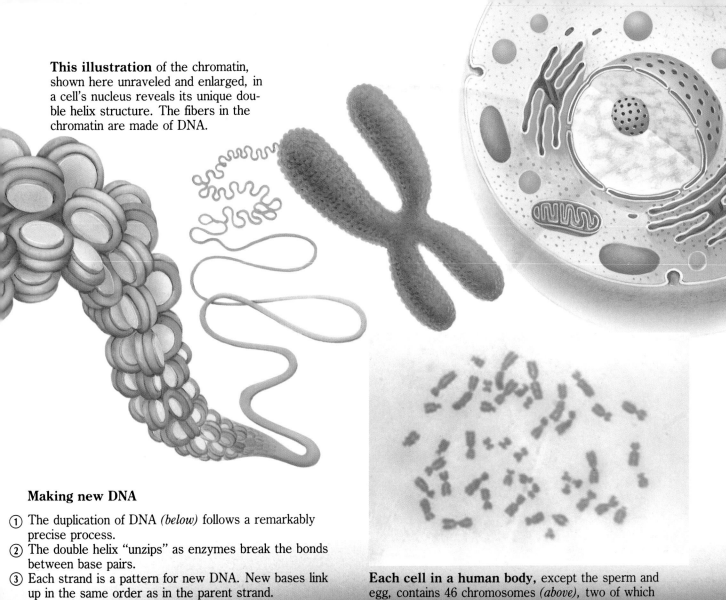

This illustration of the chromatin, shown here unraveled and enlarged, in a cell's nucleus reveals its unique double helix structure. The fibers in the chromatin are made of DNA.

Making new DNA

① The duplication of DNA *(below)* follows a remarkably precise process.

② The double helix "unzips" as enzymes break the bonds between base pairs.

③ Each strand is a pattern for new DNA. New bases link up in the same order as in the parent strand.

The completed duplication produces two strands, both derived from the parent strand and both with the same codes as the parent. In this way, DNA is able to hand down information from cell to cell.

Each cell in a human body, except the sperm and egg, contains 46 chromosomes *(above)*, two of which determine gender. Except for identical twins, no two people have chromosomes with the same DNA code.

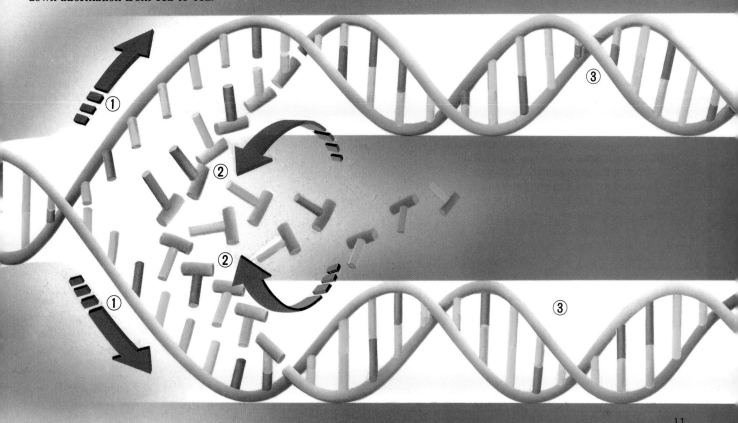

How Does Human Life Begin?

The nine-month journey leading to a baby's birth begins when a sperm cell from a man fertilizes an egg cell, or ovum, from a woman. The newly fertilized egg cell, which combines its 23 chromosomes with those of the sperm in order to make a complete set of 46, will begin dividing and reproducing within 24 hours of fertilization. By the time the egg reaches the mother's uterus, it has divided five or six times and resembles a fluid-filled ball. The ball then attaches itself to the wall of the uterus, where it draws nourishment from the mother's blood.

Within the next three weeks, the various organs of the body will begin to develop. Directed by the DNA blueprint, the cells continue dividing rapidly until what started out as a single egg cell has become the more than six trillion cells of a newborn baby. During the nine months of pregnancy, the fetus lives in a fluid-filled bag called the amniotic sac, which protects it until birth.

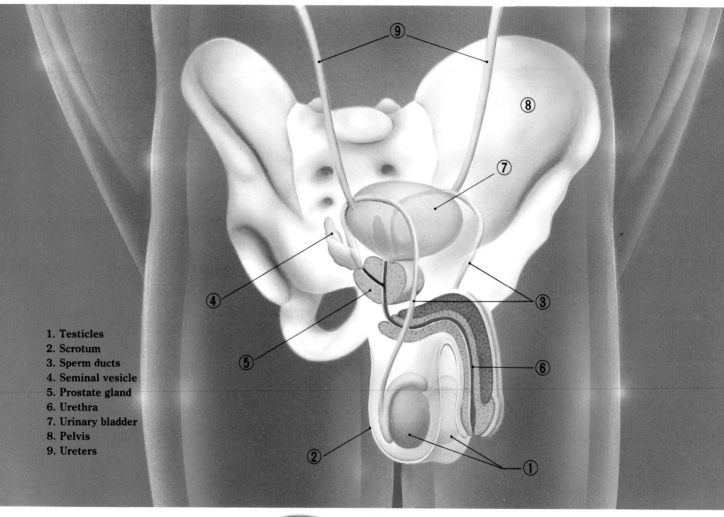

1. Testicles
2. Scrotum
3. Sperm ducts
4. Seminal vesicle
5. Prostate gland
6. Urethra
7. Urinary bladder
8. Pelvis
9. Ureters

One in 300 million

Sperm produced in the testicles travel through the sperm duct and mix with fluids from the seminal vesicle and the prostate gland to become semen. The semen passes through the urethra and is ejected from the penis during sexual intercourse. Ejaculation releases up to 300 million sperm, only one of which will fertilize the egg.

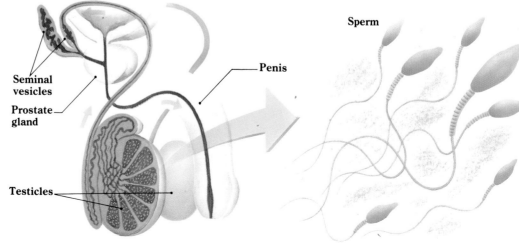

Seminal vesicles

Prostate gland

Testicles

Penis

Sperm

12

The male and female pelvis

Seen from the top, the difference between the male pelvis and female pelvis is clear. The female pelvis, through which a baby passes, is broader and more shallow, making it perfect for carrying and delivering a baby.

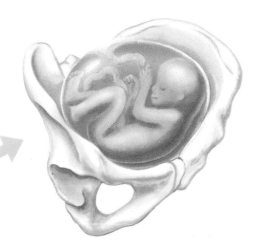

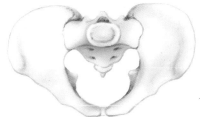

Male pelvis

Female pelvis

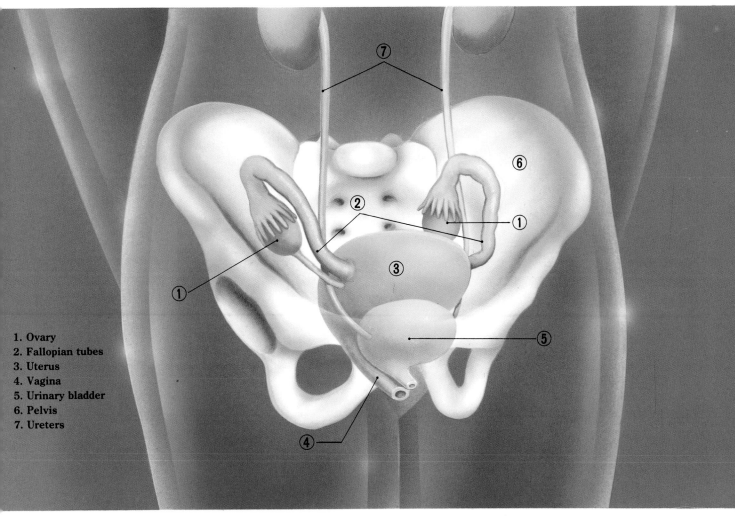

1. Ovary
2. Fallopian tubes
3. Uterus
4. Vagina
5. Urinary bladder
6. Pelvis
7. Ureters

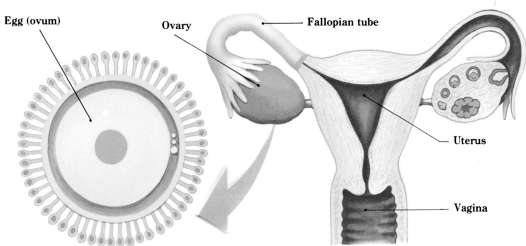

Egg (ovum)

Ovary

Fallopian tube

Uterus

Vagina

Delivering the egg

The ovaries, located at the end of the fallopian tubes leading to the uterus, develop the egg. About every 28 days, one ovary releases a mature egg into the fallopian tube, where it may be fertilized by a sperm. If the egg is not fertilized within 24 hours, it will die and be flushed from the body.

How Are Egg and Sperm Cells Made?

The egg, which is made from cells called oocytes in the ovaries, and the sperm, which is made from cells called spermatocytes in the testicles, are different from the rest of the cells in the body. The other cells reproduce through a process called mitosis *(pages 8 and 9)*. Reproductive cells, as the egg and the sperm are called, divide by means of meiosis.

In meiosis, each reproductive parent cell divides twice to form four daughter cells. Each of the reproductive daughter cells contains only 23 chromosomes, or half the number found in other human cells. Because of this, when the sperm and the unfertilized egg combine chromosomes, the resulting fertilized egg will contain a total of 46 chromosomes. This allows the new egg to divide and reproduce in the same way as non-reproductive cells.

Forming sperm cells

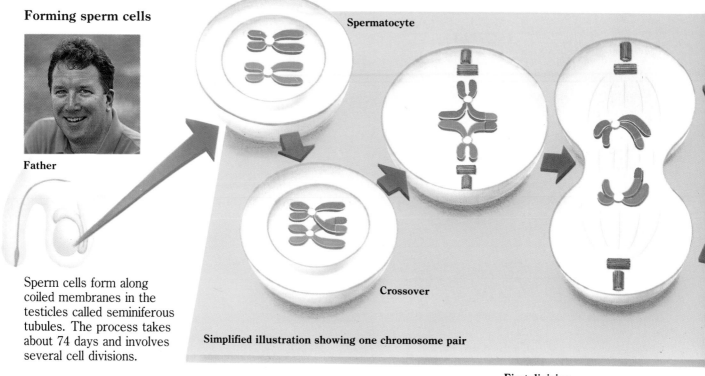

Father

Sperm cells form along coiled membranes in the testicles called seminiferous tubules. The process takes about 74 days and involves several cell divisions.

Spermatocyte

Crossover

Simplified illustration showing one chromosome pair

First division

Oocyte

Carrying eggs

At birth, a human female has between 200,000 and 400,000 eggs in her ovaries. By the time she reaches sexual maturity, also called puberty, that number will have dwindled to about 10,000. Of those, about 400 will be released at the rate of about one every 28 days.

Mother

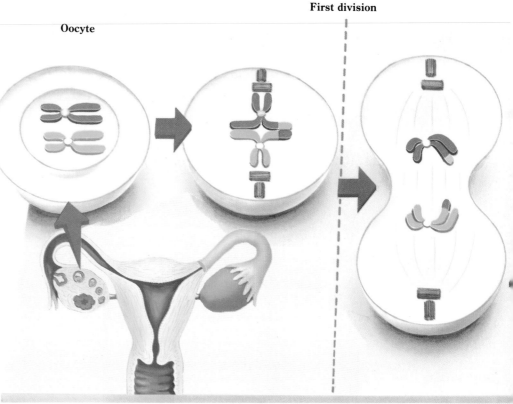

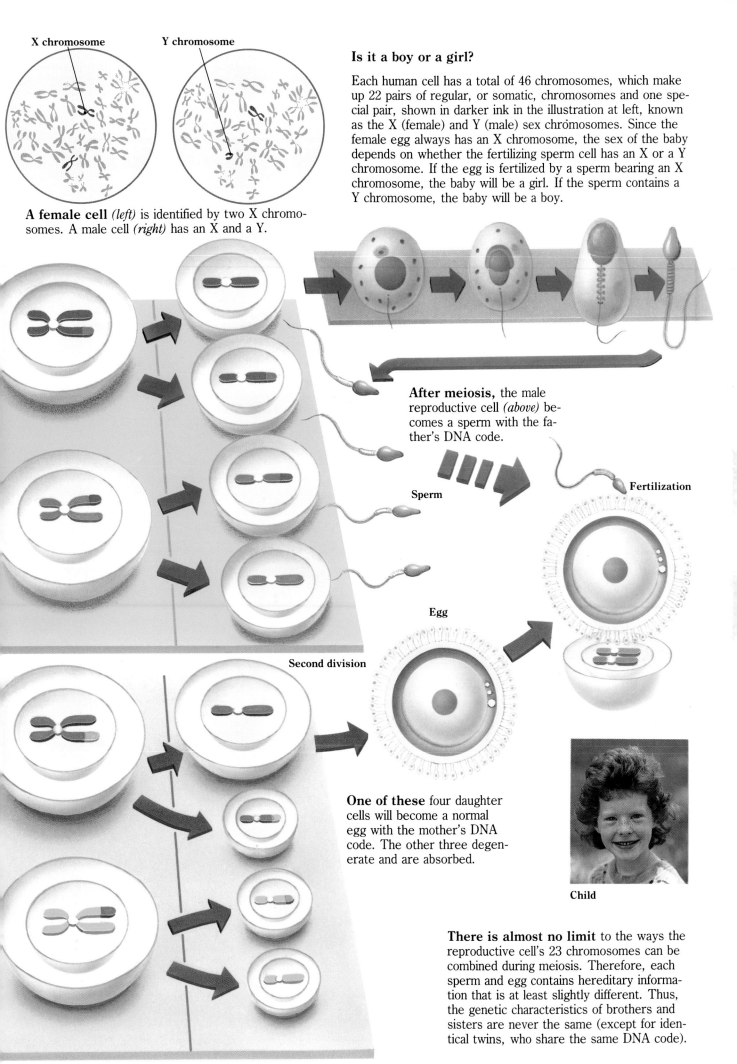

X chromosome **Y chromosome**

A female cell *(left)* is identified by two X chromosomes. A male cell *(right)* has an X and a Y.

Is it a boy or a girl?

Each human cell has a total of 46 chromosomes, which make up 22 pairs of regular, or somatic, chromosomes and one special pair, shown in darker ink in the illustration at left, known as the X (female) and Y (male) sex chromosomes. Since the female egg always has an X chromosome, the sex of the baby depends on whether the fertilizing sperm cell has an X or a Y chromosome. If the egg is fertilized by a sperm bearing an X chromosome, the baby will be a girl. If the sperm contains a Y chromosome, the baby will be a boy.

After meiosis, the male reproductive cell *(above)* becomes a sperm with the father's DNA code.

Sperm

Egg

Second division

Fertilization

One of these four daughter cells will become a normal egg with the mother's DNA code. The other three degenerate and are absorbed.

Child

There is almost no limit to the ways the reproductive cell's 23 chromosomes can be combined during meiosis. Therefore, each sperm and egg contains hereditary information that is at least slightly different. Thus, the genetic characteristics of brothers and sisters are never the same (except for identical twins, who share the same DNA code).

What Is Fertilization?

Before a sperm fertilizes an egg, several things must happen. First, the sperm must make its way from the vaginal canal through the uterus and enter the fallopian tube. There, in the widest part of the tube, it encounters a mature egg that has been released from the ovary. A single sperm penetrates and shares its chromosomes with the egg. Thus fertilized, the egg, which is now called a zygote, continues its development and becomes a multicelled ball called the blastocyst, which eventually will become attached to the wall of the uterus.

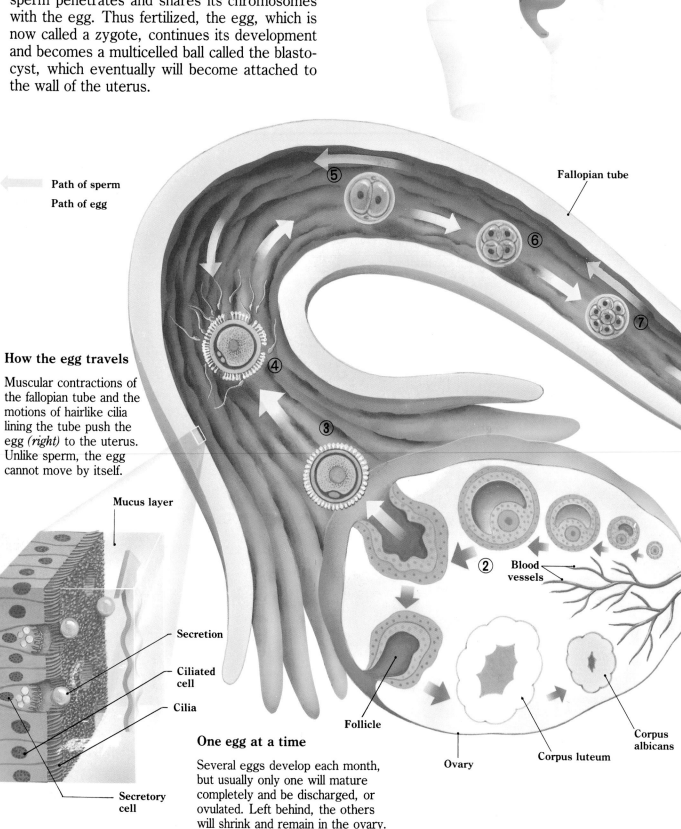

Uterus

Fallopian tube

Path of sperm

Path of egg

How the egg travels

Muscular contractions of the fallopian tube and the motions of hairlike cilia lining the tube push the egg *(right)* to the uterus. Unlike sperm, the egg cannot move by itself.

Mucus layer

Secretion

Ciliated cell

Cilia

Secretory cell

Blood vessels

Follicle

Ovary

Corpus luteum

Corpus albicans

One egg at a time

Several eggs develop each month, but usually only one will mature completely and be discharged, or ovulated. Left behind, the others will shrink and remain in the ovary.

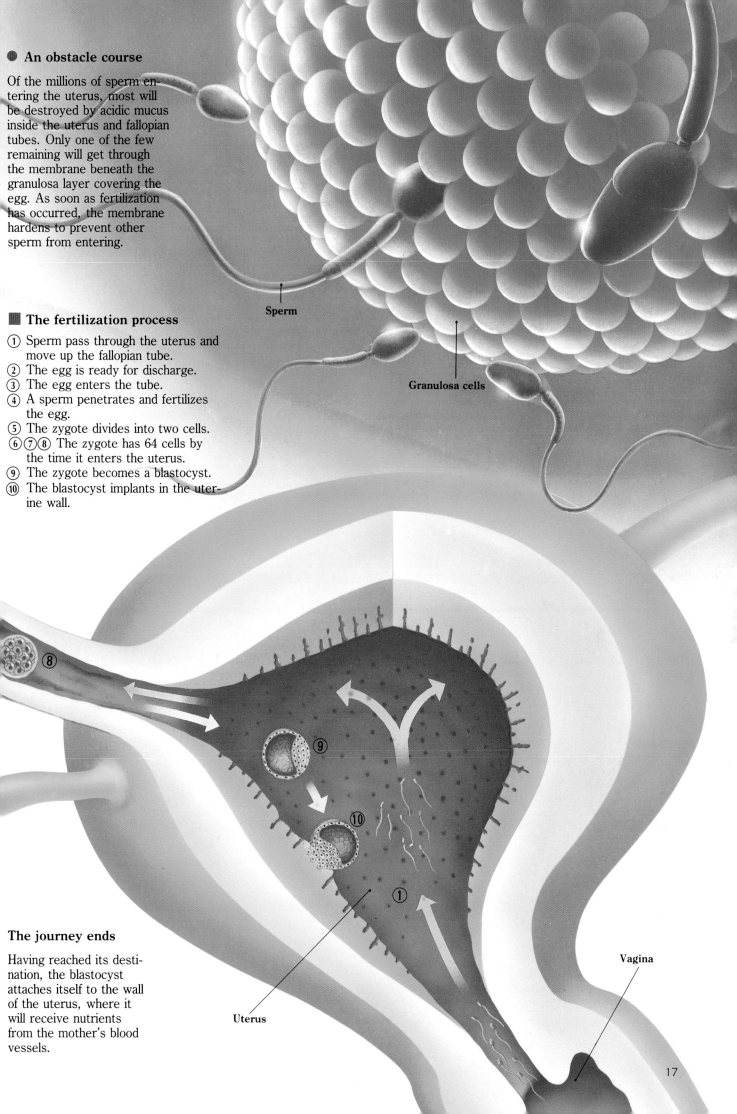

● An obstacle course

Of the millions of sperm entering the uterus, most will be destroyed by acidic mucus inside the uterus and fallopian tubes. Only one of the few remaining will get through the membrane beneath the granulosa layer covering the egg. As soon as fertilization has occurred, the membrane hardens to prevent other sperm from entering.

■ The fertilization process

① Sperm pass through the uterus and move up the fallopian tube.
② The egg is ready for discharge.
③ The egg enters the tube.
④ A sperm penetrates and fertilizes the egg.
⑤ The zygote divides into two cells.
⑥⑦⑧ The zygote has 64 cells by the time it enters the uterus.
⑨ The zygote becomes a blastocyst.
⑩ The blastocyst implants in the uterine wall.

Sperm

Granulosa cells

The journey ends

Having reached its destination, the blastocyst attaches itself to the wall of the uterus, where it will receive nutrients from the mother's blood vessels.

Uterus

Vagina

17

How Does a Baby Grow in the Womb?

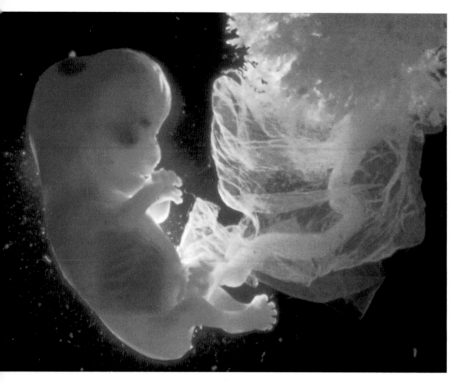

Once the multicelled ball known as the blastocyst has attached itself to the uterus, the placenta begins to form between the blastocyst and the uterine wall. A spongy, disk-shaped organ, the placenta will process food, oxygen, and waste products for the fetus.

Within two weeks of fertilization, the blastocyst has developed into an embryo. In 30 days the arms begin to form, and at about 50 days, the fingers start to appear. Shortly thereafter, legs and feet develop. Around the ninth week, the sex can be identified, and the embryo is considered a fetus.

A 10-week-old fetus

How a fetus develops

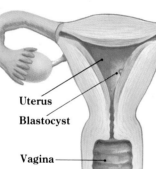

Uterus
Blastocyst
Vagina

30 days
35 days
40 days
45 days
7 weeks

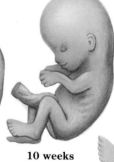

10 weeks
12 weeks

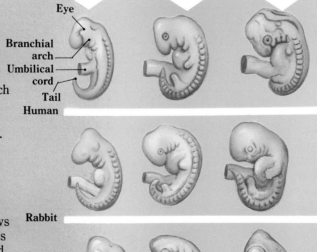

● **Very distant cousins**

In their early stages, these three different creatures look very much alike. Thirty days after fertilization, the human embryo looks like a fish. It even has a gill-like breathing slit called the branchial arch. This is also found in the rabbit and the lizard. Some people believe this shows that vertebrates (animals with backbones) evolved from fishlike creatures and once lived in a watery environment.

Eye
Branchial arch
Umbilical cord
Tail
Human

Rabbit

Lizard

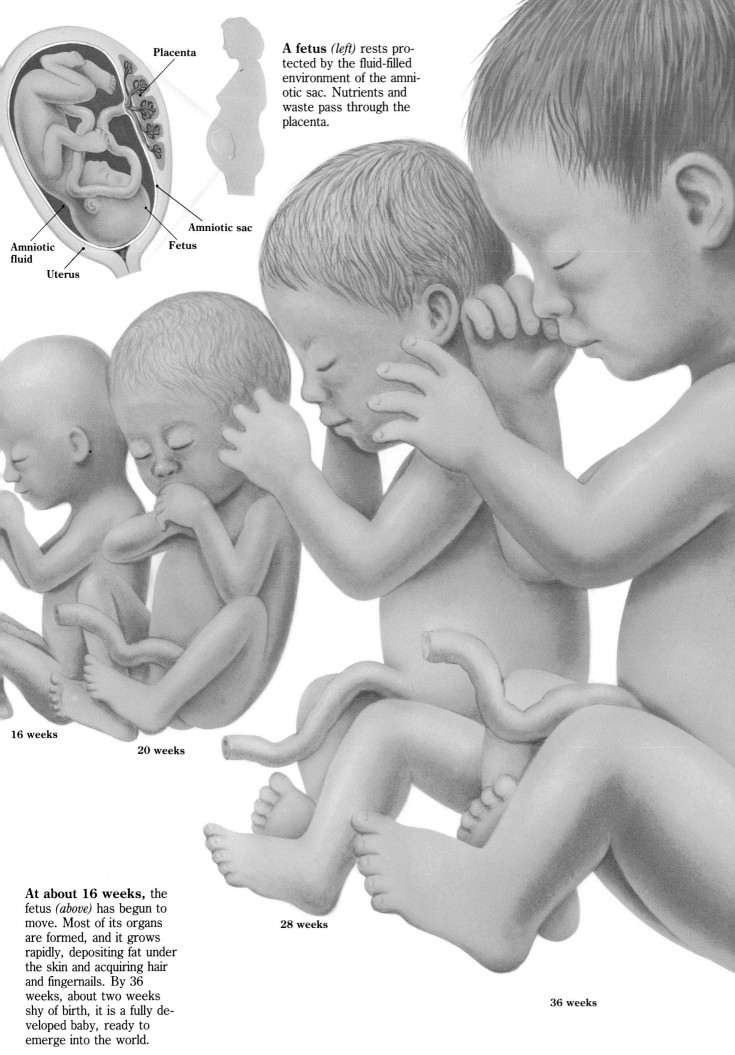

Placenta

Amniotic sac

Amniotic
fluid

Fetus

Uterus

A fetus *(left)* rests protected by the fluid-filled environment of the amniotic sac. Nutrients and waste pass through the placenta.

16 weeks

20 weeks

28 weeks

36 weeks

At about 16 weeks, the fetus *(above)* has begun to move. Most of its organs are formed, and it grows rapidly, depositing fat under the skin and acquiring hair and fingernails. By 36 weeks, about two weeks shy of birth, it is a fully developed baby, ready to emerge into the world.

How Does a Fetus Get Its Food?

Pregnant woman

Although a fetus receives all of its nutrients and oxygen from its mother's blood supply, its blood never mixes directly with the mother's. Instead, the fetus makes its own blood, which passes through the umbilical cord to the placenta.

The bottom of the placenta is embedded in the wall of the uterus. Blood vessels extend from the placenta into the tissue of the uterus in fingerlike projections called chorionic villi. Next to these, in the intervillous space, are blood vessels from the mother. Through a thin layer of tissue called the trophoblast, mother and fetus exchange nutrients, gases, and waste. Food and oxygen from the mother filter through the trophoblast into the fetus's veins, and waste passes from the fetus to the mother's blood to be eliminated.

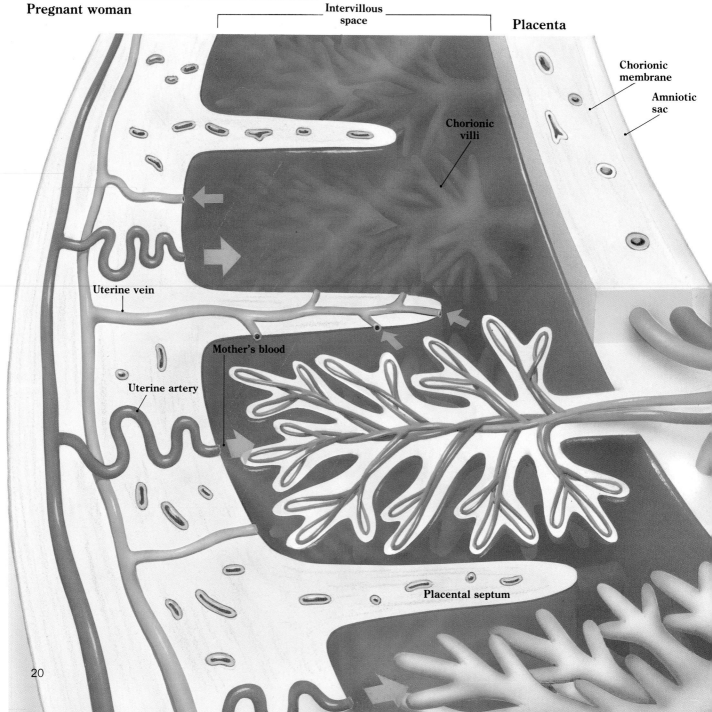

Intervillous space

Placenta

Chorionic membrane

Amniotic sac

Chorionic villi

Uterine vein

Mother's blood

Uterine artery

Placental septum

A protective barrier

A thin but very effective barrier called the trophoblast separates the blood of a mother and a fetus. Nutrients, oxygen, and antibodies pass through the barrier into the fetus's blood, and the wastes from the fetus pass out into the uterine vein. Some harmful substances in the mother's blood, such as bacteria, are screened out. However, expectant mothers must still be extremely careful since there are certain drugs and chemicals, such as nicotine and alcohol, that can pass through the membrane and harm the fetus.

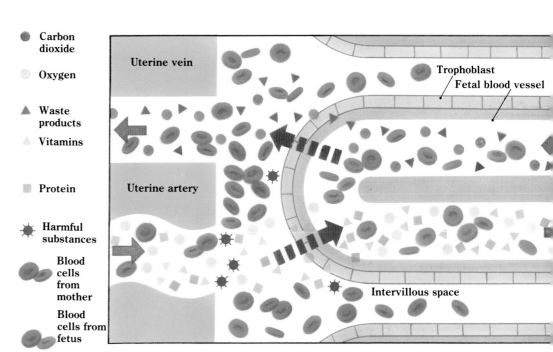

- ● Carbon dioxide
- ○ Oxygen
- ▲ Waste products
- △ Vitamins
- ■ Protein
- ✴ Harmful substances
- Blood cells from mother
- Blood cells from fetus

Uterine vein

Trophoblast
Fetal blood vessel

Uterine artery

Intervillous space

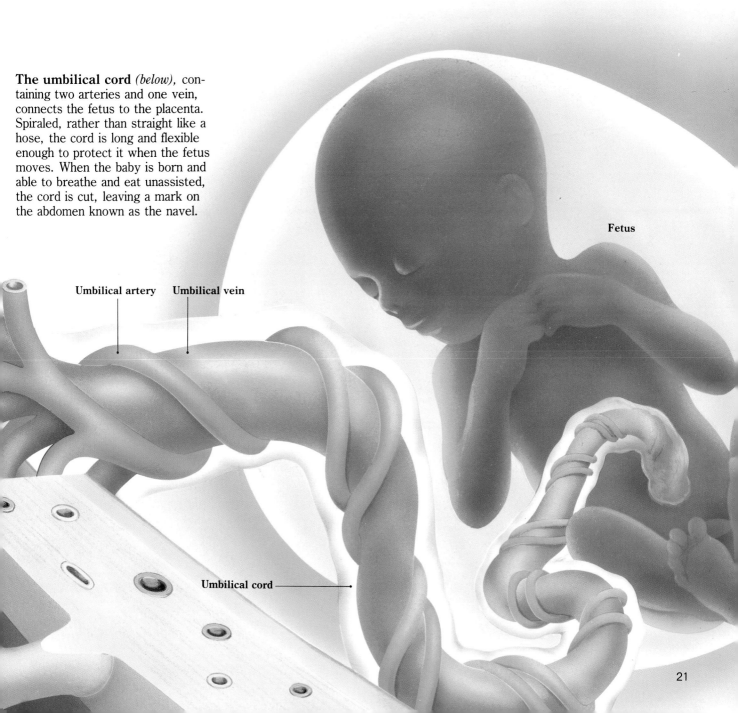

The umbilical cord *(below),* containing two arteries and one vein, connects the fetus to the placenta. Spiraled, rather than straight like a hose, the cord is long and flexible enough to protect it when the fetus moves. When the baby is born and able to breathe and eat unassisted, the cord is cut, leaving a mark on the abdomen known as the navel.

Fetus

Umbilical artery   Umbilical vein

Umbilical cord

Why Are Some People Born Twins?

Identical twins develop from a single egg.

Twins, siblings born at the same time, come in two varieties: identical and fraternal. Identical twins are the product of a single fertilized egg that unexpectedly divided at an early stage of its development. Although they develop as separate embryos, identical twins share the same genetic code.

Fraternal twins are created when two eggs released at the same time are fertilized by different sperm. Since their genetic codes come from different egg-sperm DNA combinations, they resemble each other no more than any other brothers or sisters. Other multiple births, such as triplets, quadruplets, or even quintuplets, depend on the number of eggs ovulated and on the abnormal splitting of the egg early in embryonic development.

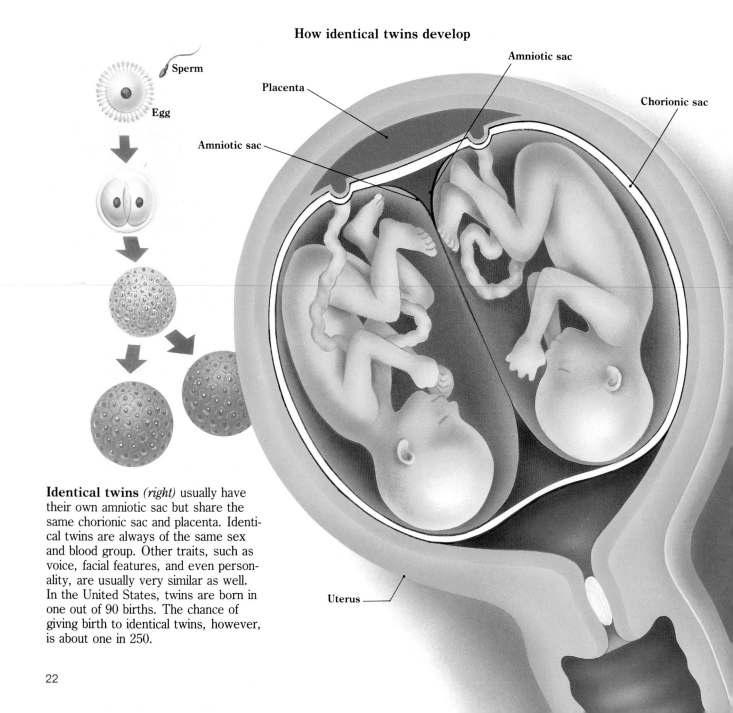

How identical twins develop

Sperm

Egg

Placenta

Amniotic sac

Amniotic sac

Chorionic sac

Uterus

Identical twins *(right)* usually have their own amniotic sac but share the same chorionic sac and placenta. Identical twins are always of the same sex and blood group. Other traits, such as voice, facial features, and even personality, are usually very similar as well. In the United States, twins are born in one out of 90 births. The chance of giving birth to identical twins, however, is about one in 250.

Multiple births

Sometimes babies are born three, four, or even five at a time, producing triplets, quadruplets, and quintuplets. These rare multiple births have several possible causes. In the case of these quadruplets *(right)*, the possibilities include the following: Four eggs are ovulated and fertilized; two eggs are ovulated and fertilized, then divide; or three eggs are ovulated and fertilized, and one of them divides *(below)*.

Three eggs, four offspring

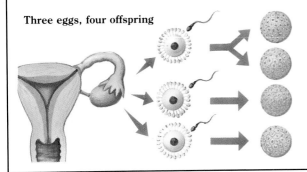

Quadruplets occur in about one out of 650,000 births.

How fraternal twins develop

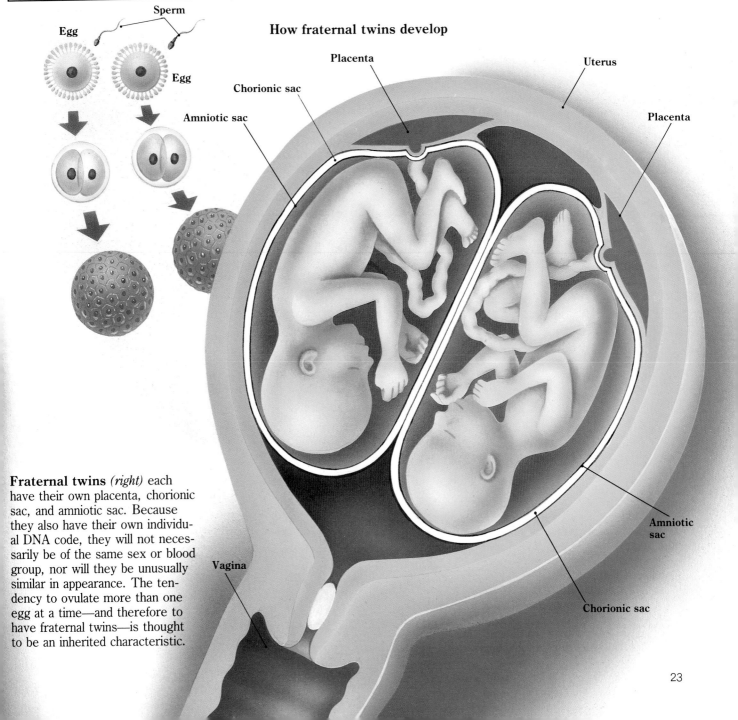

Fraternal twins *(right)* each have their own placenta, chorionic sac, and amniotic sac. Because they also have their own individual DNA code, they will not necessarily be of the same sex or blood group, nor will they be unusually similar in appearance. The tendency to ovulate more than one egg at a time—and therefore to have fraternal twins—is thought to be an inherited characteristic.

Sperm

Egg

Egg

Placenta

Chorionic sac

Amniotic sac

Uterus

Placenta

Amniotic sac

Chorionic sac

Vagina

How Does the Brain Develop?

Because the brain controls the body's most complicated functions, it is one of the first organs to develop before birth. Three weeks after fertilization of the egg occurs, the neural tube begins to form. Its upper end swells and three bumps appear. The first will become the cerebrum, the seat of intelligence and the senses, and the thalamus, the message relay center. The second bump will turn into the midbrain, a collection of nerve fibers that serve as a bridge to connect all the different parts of the brain. The third bump will develop into the cerebellum, which controls the movement of the muscles; the pons, which connects nerves to different parts of the brain; and the medulla oblongata, which controls the separate functions of breathing, blood circulation, and digestion. Most of the basic brain divisions are shaped by the eleventh week.

Development of the brain

3 weeks

4 weeks

7 weeks

15 weeks

6 months

Central sulcus

Exterior sulcus

Brain area

In the third week of pregnancy, the brain (*enlarged above*) is 1/25 of an inch long. As the months go by, the brain adds neurons at a rate of up to 250,000 a minute.

The growth of nerve cells

The nerve cells in the cerebral cortex, the thin outer layer of the cerebrum, are highly developed before birth. After birth, the brain grows primarily through the branching of formed nerve fibers, peaking in young adulthood and degenerating with age.

Cross section

Cerebral cortex

| Embryo | Fetus | Infancy | Age 20 | Age 40 | Age 60 |

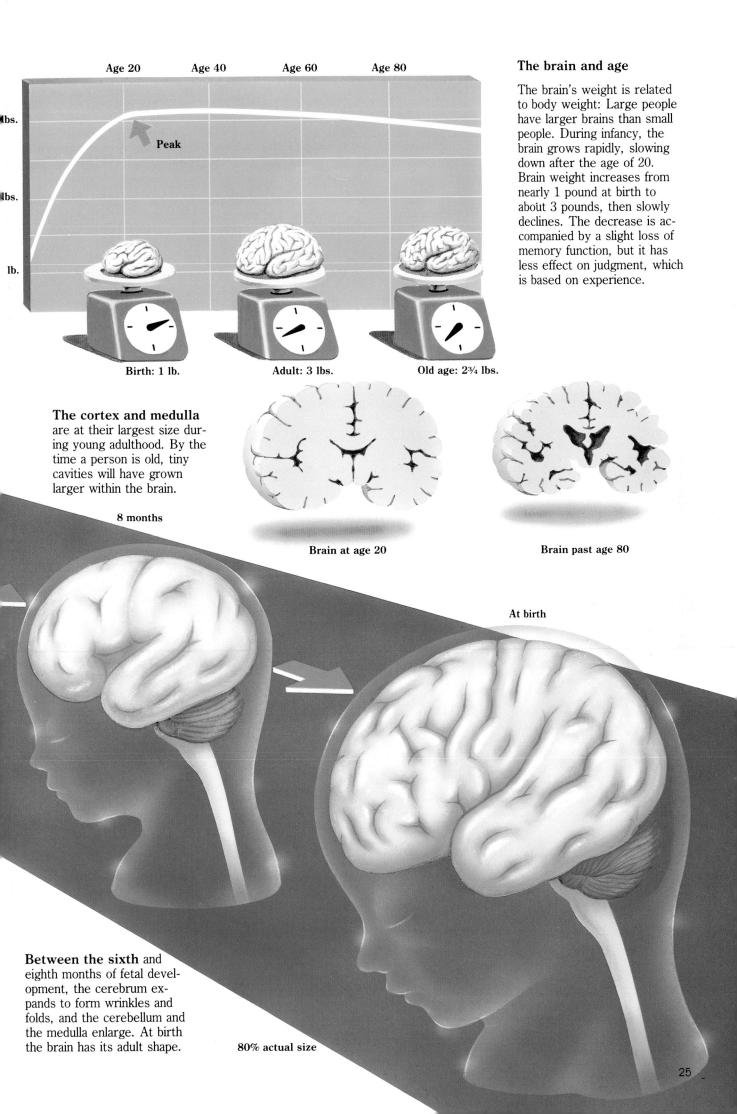

Age 20   Age 40   Age 60   Age 80

The brain and age

The brain's weight is related to body weight: Large people have larger brains than small people. During infancy, the brain grows rapidly, slowing down after the age of 20. Brain weight increases from nearly 1 pound at birth to about 3 pounds, then slowly declines. The decrease is accompanied by a slight loss of memory function, but it has less effect on judgment, which is based on experience.

lbs.

lbs.

lb.

Peak

Birth: 1 lb.

Adult: 3 lbs.

Old age: 2¾ lbs.

The cortex and medulla are at their largest size during young adulthood. By the time a person is old, tiny cavities will have grown larger within the brain.

8 months

Brain at age 20

Brain past age 80

At birth

Between the sixth and eighth months of fetal development, the cerebrum expands to form wrinkles and folds, and the cerebellum and the medulla enlarge. At birth the brain has its adult shape.

80% actual size

25

Why Do Baby Teeth Fall Out?

Baby teeth, or milk teeth, fall out because they are sized for a child's jawbone. As the jawbone grows, the teeth become too small by comparison. Permanent teeth must develop in order to fill up the available space.

Milk teeth begin to appear between six and eight months after birth, and by the age of two years and four months all 20 of them are usually in place. The replacement of the smaller and weaker milk teeth begins with the growth of a first permanent molar at about the age of six. The last of the 32 adult teeth, the third molar or wisdom tooth, may not come in at all. If the jawbone is already crowded with teeth, the arrival of a wisdom tooth can prove to be an extremely uncomfortable experience.

Milk teeth and permanent teeth

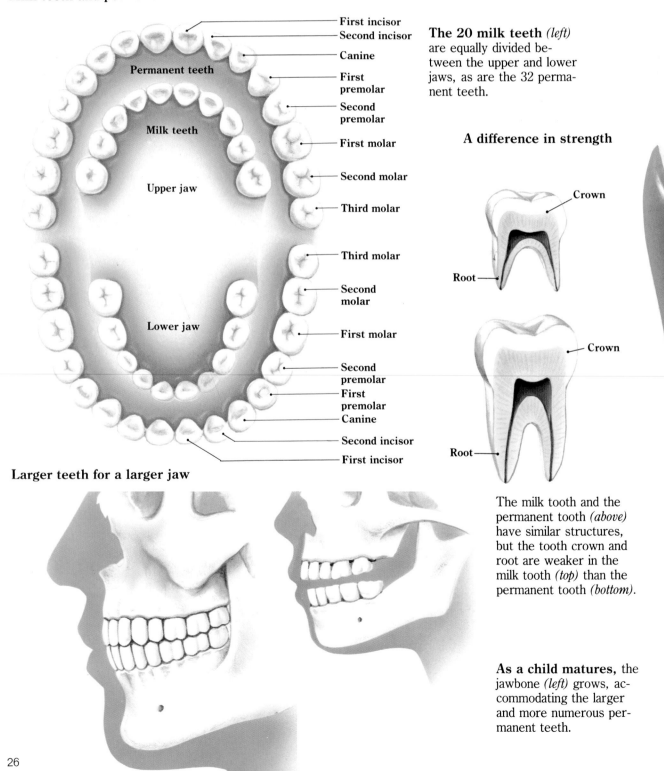

First incisor
Second incisor
Canine
First premolar
Second premolar
First molar
Second molar
Third molar

Permanent teeth
Milk teeth
Upper jaw

Third molar
Second molar
First molar
Second premolar
First premolar
Canine
Second incisor
First incisor

Lower jaw

Larger teeth for a larger jaw

The 20 milk teeth *(left)* are equally divided between the upper and lower jaws, as are the 32 permanent teeth.

A difference in strength

Crown
Root

Crown
Root

The milk tooth and the permanent tooth *(above)* have similar structures, but the tooth crown and root are weaker in the milk tooth *(top)* than the permanent tooth *(bottom)*.

As a child matures, the jawbone *(left)* grows, accommodating the larger and more numerous permanent teeth.

Pushed out from below

Permanent teeth *(below)* begin to develop inside the gums as soon as the first milk teeth appear. As a permanent tooth grows, it cuts away the root of the milk tooth. When its root is completely eroded, the milk tooth falls out and is replaced by the permanent tooth.

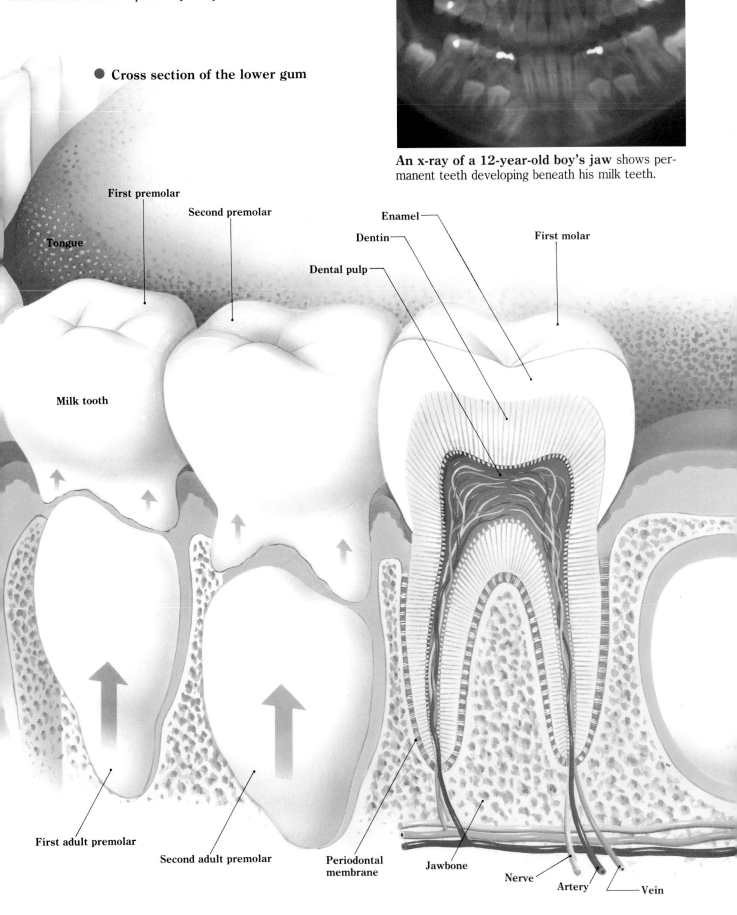

An x-ray of a 12-year-old boy's jaw shows permanent teeth developing beneath his milk teeth.

● **Cross section of the lower gum**

Tongue

First premolar

Second premolar

Enamel

Dentin

Dental pulp

First molar

Milk tooth

First adult premolar

Second adult premolar

Periodontal membrane

Jawbone

Nerve

Artery

Vein

What Is In Vitro Fertilization?

When a woman's fallopian tubes are blocked (which can happen for a variety of reasons), her only hope of becoming pregnant may be in vitro fertilization. In vitro (Latin for "in glass") refers to a procedure in which a mature egg is removed from a woman's ovary, fertilized outside her body, and then placed in her uterus to develop into a normal fetus.

The birth of Louise Brown in Bristol, England, in 1978 marked the first successful in vitro fertilization. Now, the procedure is regularly done around the world.

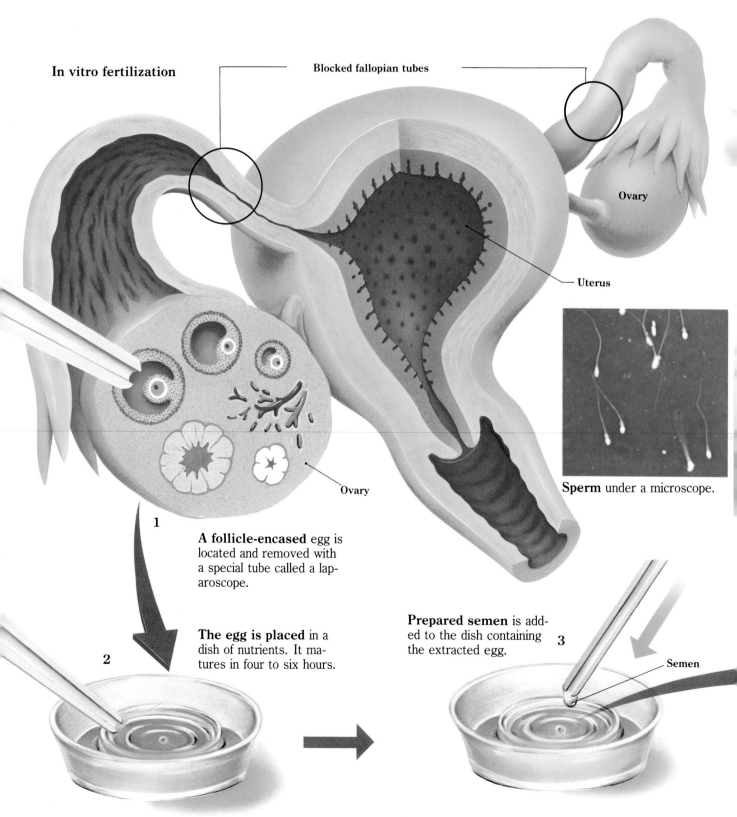

In vitro fertilization

Blocked fallopian tubes

Ovary

Uterus

Ovary

Sperm under a microscope.

1 A follicle-encased egg is located and removed with a special tube called a laparoscope.

2 The egg is placed in a dish of nutrients. It matures in four to six hours.

3 Prepared semen is added to the dish containing the extracted egg.

Semen

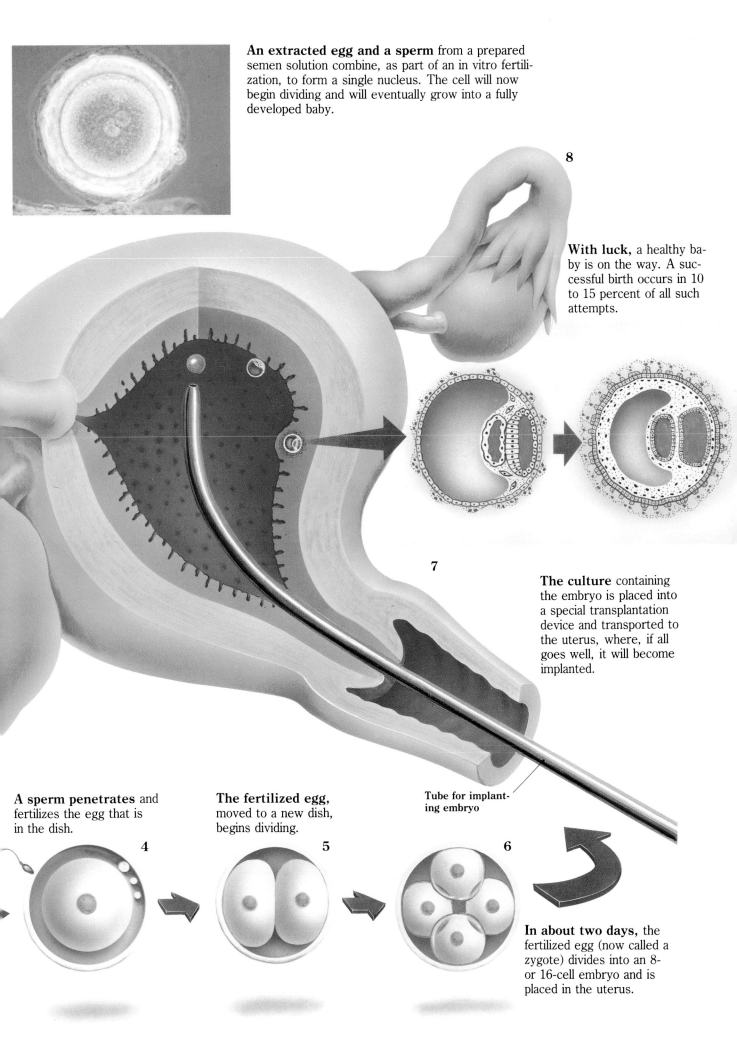

An extracted egg and a sperm from a prepared semen solution combine, as part of an in vitro fertilization, to form a single nucleus. The cell will now begin dividing and will eventually grow into a fully developed baby.

8

With luck, a healthy baby is on the way. A successful birth occurs in 10 to 15 percent of all such attempts.

7

The culture containing the embryo is placed into a special transplantation device and transported to the uterus, where, if all goes well, it will become implanted.

A sperm penetrates and fertilizes the egg that is in the dish.

4

The fertilized egg, moved to a new dish, begins dividing.

5

Tube for implanting embryo

6

In about two days, the fertilized egg (now called a zygote) divides into an 8- or 16-cell embryo and is placed in the uterus.

2
Your Super Structure

The framework of the human body—the skeleton, the muscles, and the skin—is a strong yet flexible construct. The 206 bones that make up the adult skeleton support the body and work with the muscles and nerves to move the body's various parts. Specialized bones protect vital internal organs: The skull, for example, encases the brain, while the ribs and sternum shield the heart and lungs. In addition to serving as a fortress, the bones function as a factory: Marrow inside the bones produces essential blood components known as platelets, red blood cells, and white blood cells.

The muscles, too, have different roles. Skeletal muscles—muscles attached to the skeleton—are striated, or banded, whereas muscles of the internal organs are smooth. A third muscle type, called cardiac muscle, is found only in the heart.

To contract, a muscle needs energy; it gets this from a chemical called adenosine triphosphate, or ATP, which is released in the muscle cells. Half the energy produced by ATP is in the form of heat. That's why shivering—a series of uncontrollable muscle contractions—keeps the body warm.

The third element of the framework, the skin, has two main jobs: to interpret the outside world and to protect the body. As a sensory organ, the skin registers pain, touch, and temperature. And through a hardening process called keratinization, the skin manufactures such natural defenses as fingernails, toenails, and hair.

A seemingly simple action—at right, the release of a ball—demands interaction of bones, muscles, and skin. While the bones and muscles of the hand and forearm create leverage and thrust, the skin provides feedback in the form of sensory information.

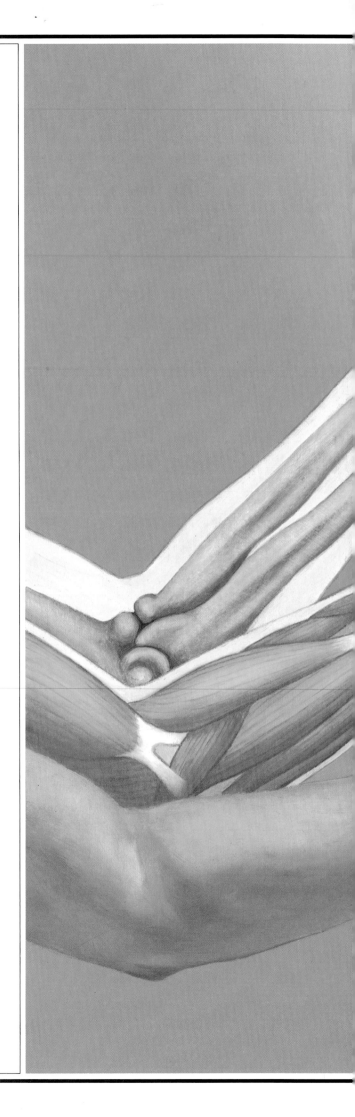

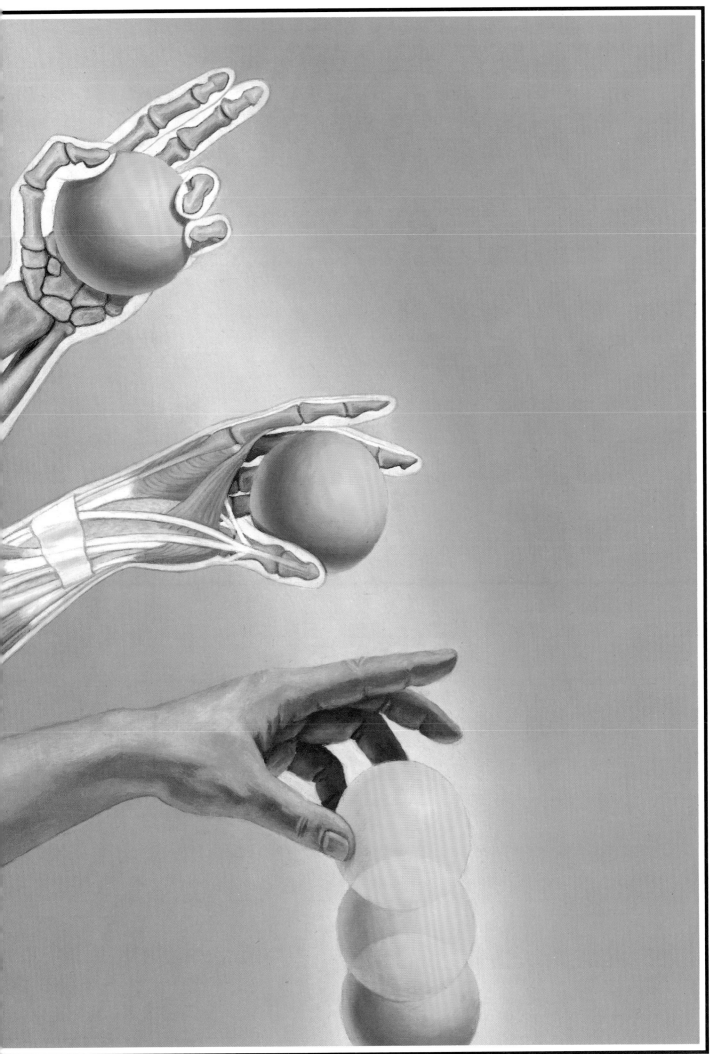

How Many Bones Are in the Body?

Babies are born with 350 soft bones, but many of the bones fuse together as the baby grows. For this reason, a typical adult skeleton comprises only 206 bones; together these weigh some 20 pounds. The smallest bone, found in the middle ear, is one-tenth of an inch long. The biggest bone—the femur—represents about 25 percent of the body's height. The skull, seemingly a single bone, is in fact 29 bones.

Bones are classified according to shape. Bones can be long, short, flat, or irregular. The spine consists of 26 vertebrae.

The skull

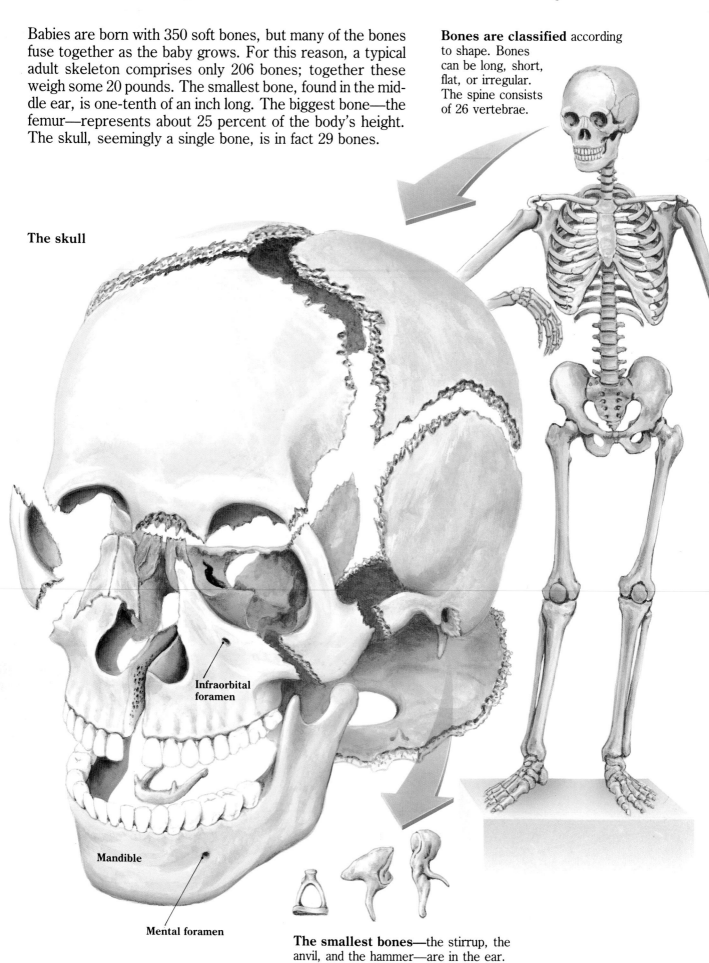

Infraorbital foramen

Mandible

Mental foramen

The smallest bones—the stirrup, the anvil, and the hammer—are in the ear.

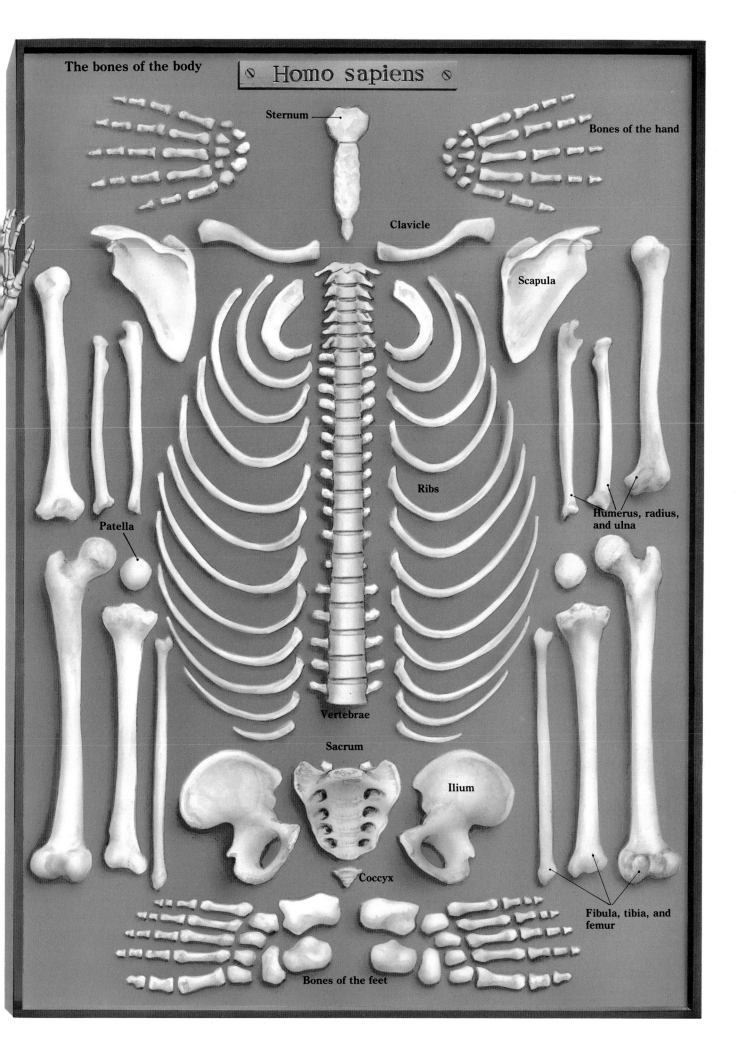

The bones of the body

Homo sapiens

Sternum

Bones of the hand

Clavicle

Scapula

Ribs

Humerus, radius, and ulna

Patella

Vertebrae

Sacrum

Ilium

Coccyx

Fibula, tibia, and femur

Bones of the feet

33

How Do Bones Grow?

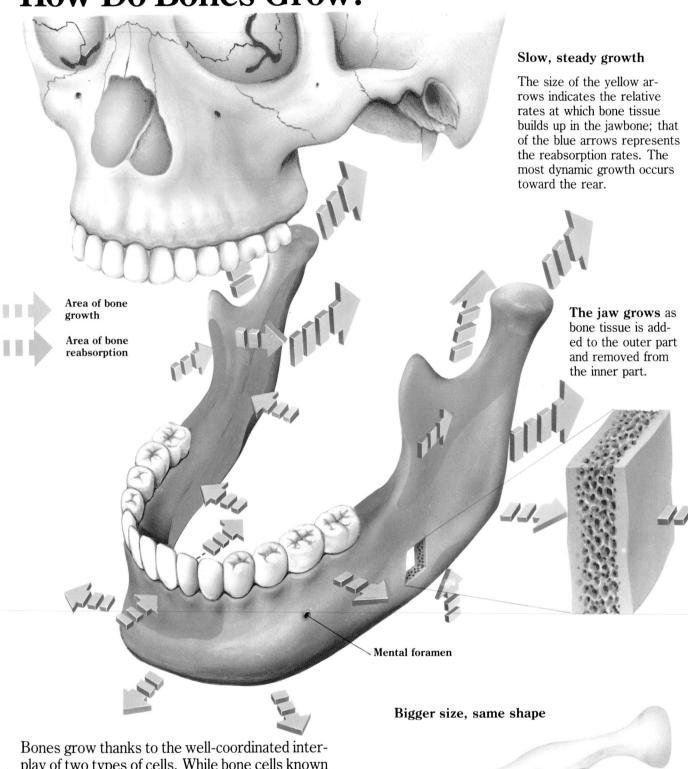

Slow, steady growth

The size of the yellow arrows indicates the relative rates at which bone tissue builds up in the jawbone; that of the blue arrows represents the reabsorption rates. The most dynamic growth occurs toward the rear.

Area of bone growth

Area of bone reabsorption

The jaw grows as bone tissue is added to the outer part and removed from the inner part.

Mental foramen

Bigger size, same shape

As the body grows, bones get bigger but retain their basic shape. Here, an infant's jawbone *(blue outline)* is compared with an adult's.

Bones grow thanks to the well-coordinated interplay of two types of cells. While bone cells known as osteoblasts deposit newly formed tissue in some areas of the bone, their counterparts—called osteoclasts—dissolve and then reabsorb the bone tissue in other areas.

The osteoblasts produce new bone tissue slightly faster than the osteoclasts dissolve the old, so bones keep their basic shape as they get bigger. The human jawbone, for example, begins with the contour shown in blue at right; when fully grown *(white contour, right)*, it has roughly the same shape but is almost twice the size.

The ebb and flow of bone growth

A growing jawbone *(below)* gains tissue in the areas marked by the yellow arrows and loses it in the areas marked by the blue arrows. Beginning around age six, the baby teeth *(center)* make way for the permanent teeth *(right)*.

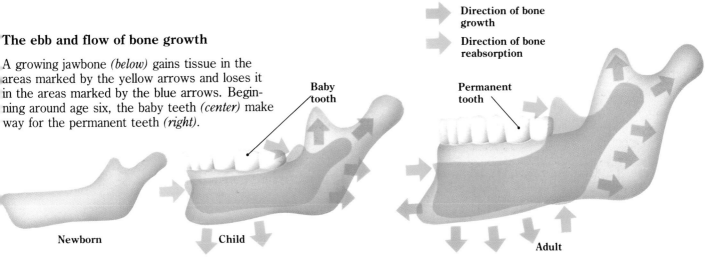

Direction of bone growth

Direction of bone reabsorption

Baby tooth

Permanent tooth

Newborn

Child

Adult

The process of bone growth

The process of bone growth is like that of building a brick wall from one side and chipping it away from another. Specialized osteoblasts called osteocytes secrete a bone matrix that hardens into bone tissue. The osteoclasts, meanwhile, erode the bone from a different side.

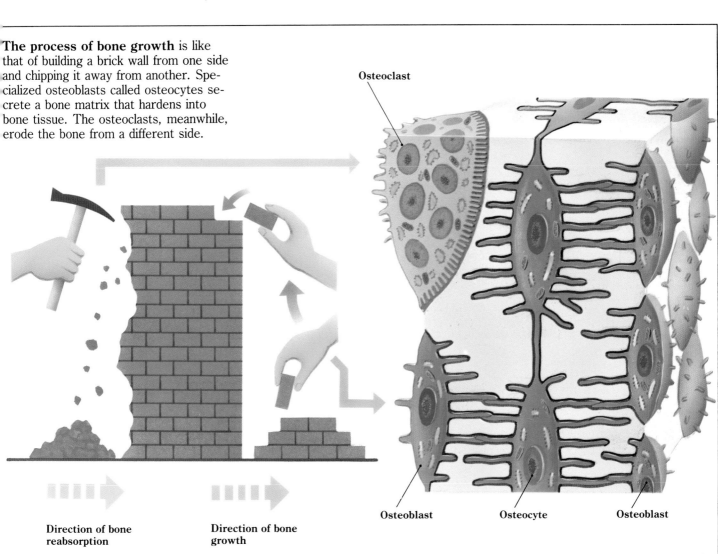

Osteoclast

Direction of bone reabsorption

Direction of bone growth

Osteoblast

Osteocyte

Osteoblast

Where elite bones meet

A newborn baby's skull has two soft spots at the top *(near right)*. These made the skull flexible enough to pass safely through the narrow birth canal. The bones grow closer together *(center)*; by 18 months, the soft spots will have vanished. Only thin juncture lines, called sutures *(far right)*, remain in the adult skull.

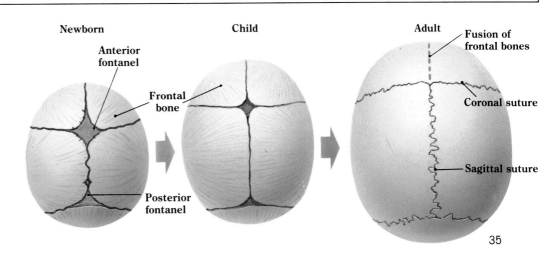

Newborn

Child

Adult

Anterior fontanel

Frontal bone

Posterior fontanel

Fusion of frontal bones

Coronal suture

Sagittal suture

How Do Muscles Exert Force?

Muscles exert force by contracting, or making themselves shorter. The voluntary contractions of various skeletal muscles—so called because both ends of the muscle are attached to the skeleton—keep the body erect, enable it to bear and exert forces, and cause it to move.

Above all, muscle contraction requires energy. The body extracts this energy from the nutrients in food and stores it in a special chemical, adenosine triphosphate (ATP), for later use. The energy stored in the ATP is released whenever a nerve instructs a muscle to contract.

A skeletal muscle consists of many long, cylindrical fibers. Each of these fibers is in turn filled with long bundles of even smaller fibers, called myofibrils. How the myofibrils help a muscle to contract is explained below.

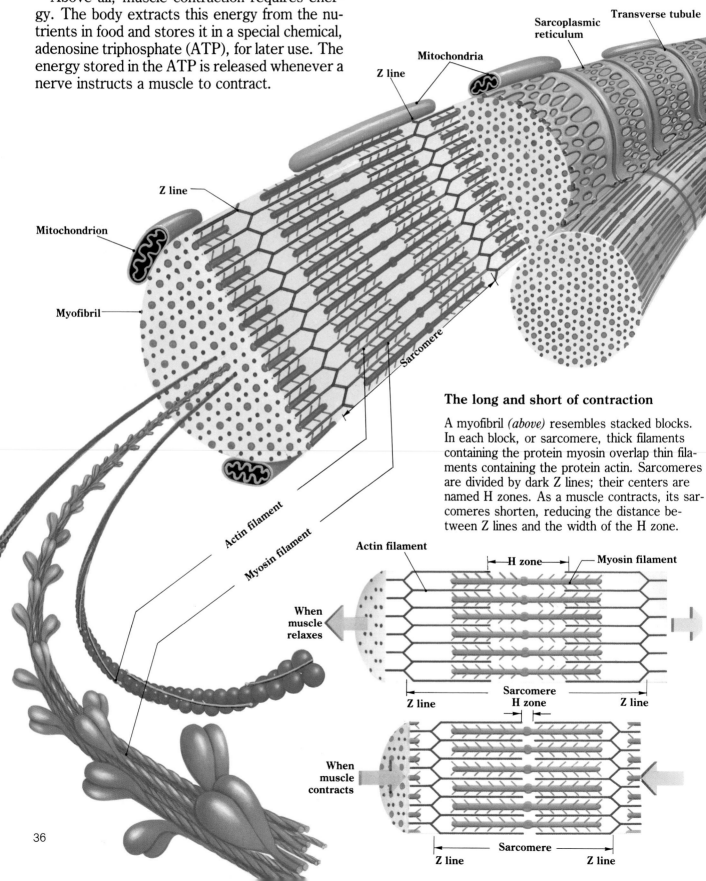

Mitochondria
Sarcoplasmic reticulum
Transverse tubule
Z line
Z line
Mitochondrion
Myofibril
Sarcomere
Actin filament
Myosin filament

The long and short of contraction

A myofibril *(above)* resembles stacked blocks. In each block, or sarcomere, thick filaments containing the protein myosin overlap thin filaments containing the protein actin. Sarcomeres are divided by dark Z lines; their centers are named H zones. As a muscle contracts, its sarcomeres shorten, reducing the distance between Z lines and the width of the H zone.

Actin filament
H zone
Myosin filament
When muscle relaxes
Sarcomere
Z line
Z line
H zone
When muscle contracts
Sarcomere
Z line
Z line

The anatomy of a hair

The hair root, buried in the skin, is surrounded by the hair follicle. Blood vessels attached to the hair papilla supply the hair bulb with nutrients for growth. The hair is connected to a tiny erector muscle that makes the hair stand up *(pages 44-45)*. The sebaceous gland secretes an oil, sebum, that protects the skin and waterproofs the hair.

Light brown hair

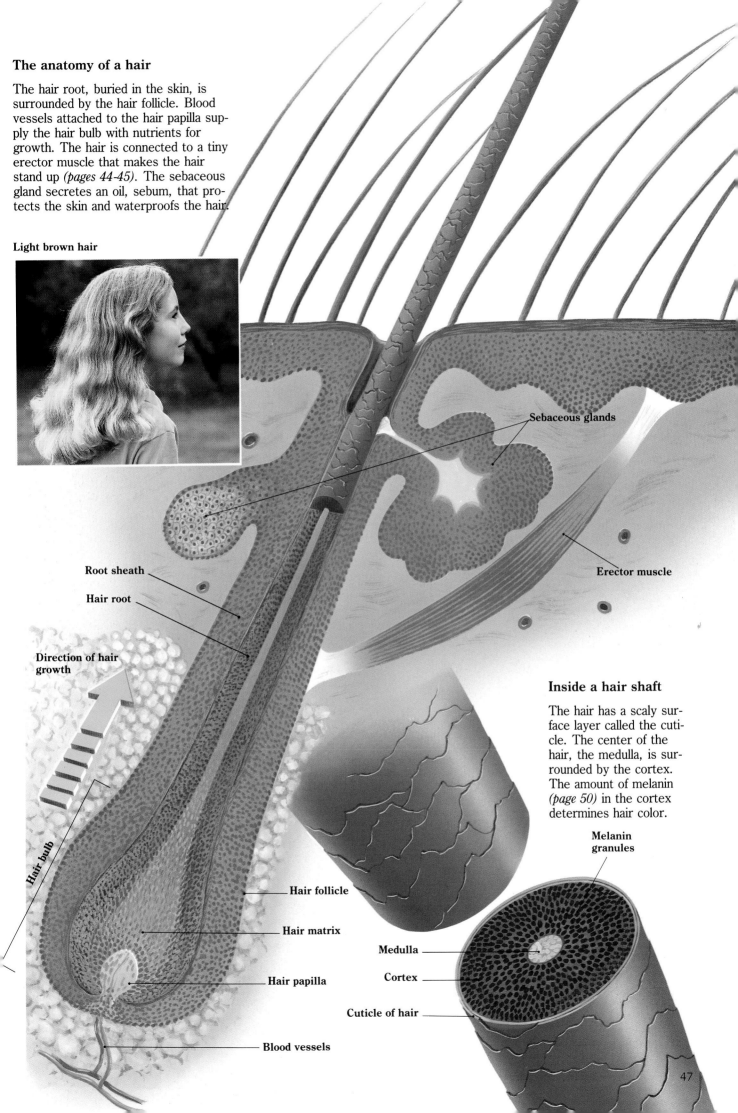

Sebaceous glands

Erector muscle

Root sheath

Hair root

Direction of hair growth

Inside a hair shaft

The hair has a scaly surface layer called the cuticle. The center of the hair, the medulla, is surrounded by the cortex. The amount of melanin *(page 50)* in the cortex determines hair color.

Melanin granules

Hair bulb

Hair follicle

Hair matrix

Hair papilla

Medulla

Cortex

Cuticle of hair

Blood vessels

47

How Does a Cut Heal?

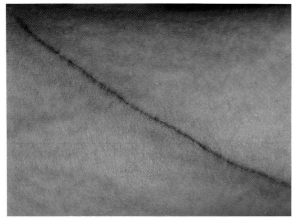

A scratch wound

In its ability to mobilize many different types of cells to protect and heal itself after an injury, the human body is a truly remarkable machine.

When a cut on the skin reaches as deep as the dermis—the skin layer below the epidermis—blood vessels are broken and blood flows into the cut. A protein in the blood called fibrin quickly forms long fibers, which weave together in a tangled mesh, or clot, that halts bleeding. This clot will dry into a scab.

As the blood clots, white blood cells move into the wound, attacking germs and disposing of damaged cells. Cells at the base of the epidermis and in the dermis divide repeatedly, forming new tissue to rebuild the damaged area. Gradually, the cut heals.

The healing process

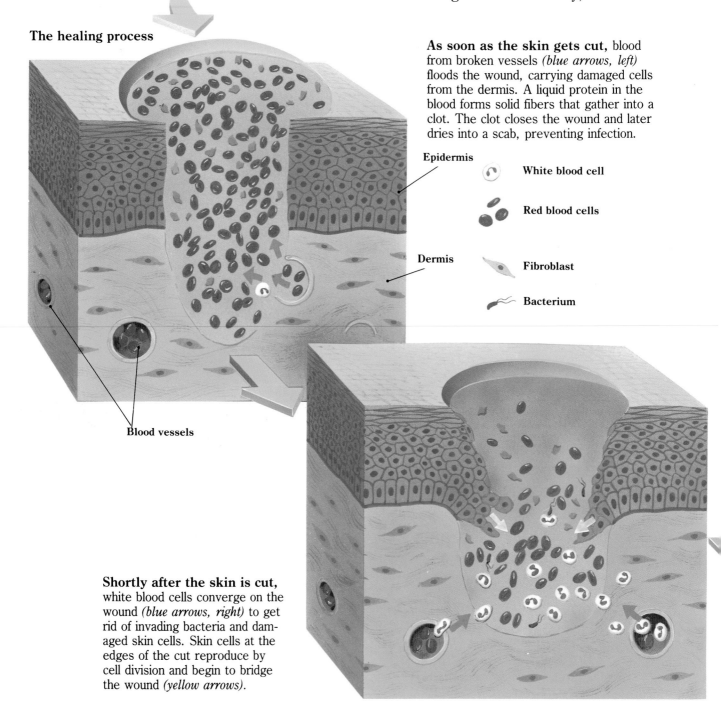

As soon as the skin gets cut, blood from broken vessels *(blue arrows, left)* floods the wound, carrying damaged cells from the dermis. A liquid protein in the blood forms solid fibers that gather into a clot. The clot closes the wound and later dries into a scab, preventing infection.

Epidermis

Dermis

White blood cell

Red blood cells

Fibroblast

Bacterium

Blood vessels

Shortly after the skin is cut, white blood cells converge on the wound *(blue arrows, right)* to get rid of invading bacteria and damaged skin cells. Skin cells at the edges of the cut reproduce by cell division and begin to bridge the wound *(yellow arrows).*

Healing is complete after six or seven days. New blood vessels develop in the dermis. The scab falls off, revealing the new skin below.

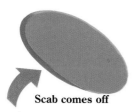

Scab comes off

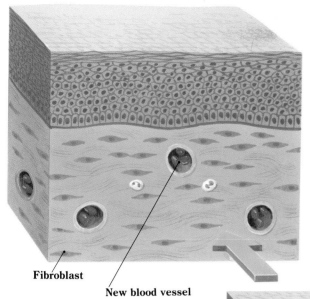

Fibroblast

New blood vessel

Regeneration by communication

In a laboratory experiment, a thin slice of glass and a thin sheet of cellophane were inserted in living skin. Unable to penetrate the nonporous glass, the skin cells did not regenerate; instead, they grew around the obstruction. Able to penetrate the porous cellophane, however, the skin cells regenerated normally. The experiment suggests that skin cells must be able to "communicate" with one another if the body is to repair damaged skin.

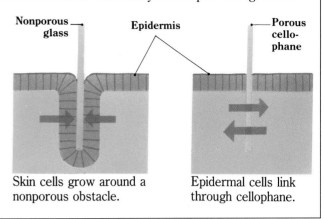

Nonporous glass   Epidermis   Porous cellophane

Skin cells grow around a nonporous obstacle.

Epidermal cells link through cellophane.

Four or five days later, the bridge of epidermal cells has thickened into a new layer of skin. The fibroblasts continue to form connective tissue.

Within two or three days, the epidermal cells have formed a thin bridge beneath the scab. In the deeper, dermal layer, fibroblasts—special cells that manufacture fibers of connective tissue—begin to rebuild the damaged skin tissues. The white blood cells continue cleaning up the area.

Why Does Skin Come in All Colors?

Skin color varies because each individual has a different mix of pigments in his or her skin. A pigment is a substance whose presence in the cells of a tissue gives that tissue its characteristic color. Melanin, for example, is a blackish-brown pigment; the more melanin in the skin, the darker the skin's color.

In addition to coloring skin, melanin protects it from harmful ultraviolet (UV) rays of the sun. In the world's tropical regions, where the sun's light is most intense, evolution has favored the development of races with higher pigment quantities: The larger amount of melanin provides greater protection from the sun. At higher latitudes, where sunlight is less intense, races evolved with lower melanin content and thus lighter skin.

Although UV rays can cause sunburn and even skin cancer, limited exposure is in fact beneficial to growth. How UV rays affect the skin is explained at right.

The chemistry of a suntan

Ultraviolet rays in sunlight stimulate skin cells known as melanocytes to produce granules of the pigment melanin. As the melanin granules penetrate the surrounding cells, they darken the skin. Soles and palms contain no melanocytes, so they do not tan.

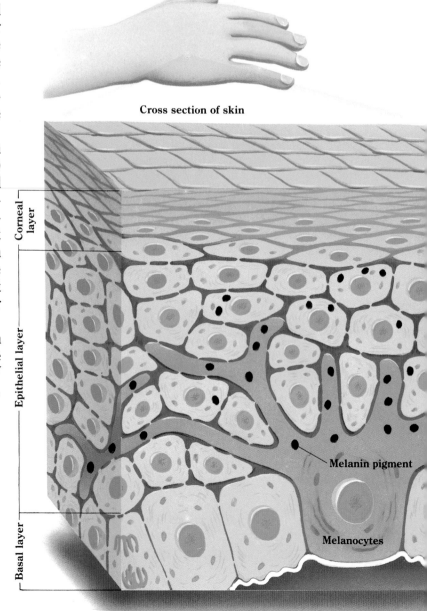

Cross section of skin

Corneal layer

Epithelial layer

Basal layer

Melanin pigment

Melanocytes

Skin color and environment

Skin color, dictated by the amount of melanin in the skin, evolved to provide a balance between preventing cancer and permitting the synthesis of vitamin D. In latitudes with much direct sunlight, the black African race developed a high level of melanin; in latitudes with less sunlight, the Asiatic race developed less melanin, and the Caucasian race the least.

 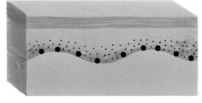

 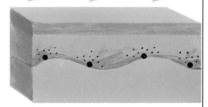

The black African race has high melanin levels, a protection against intense sunlight.

The Asiatic race has a lower amount of melanin, resulting from exposure to less sunlight.

The Caucasian race has low levels of melanin, the effect of exposure to weak sunlight.

Prolonged exposure to the sun's ultraviolet rays is believed to cause skin cancer. Brief exposure to UV rays, however, prompts the body to produce vitamin D, which in turn stimulates bone growth. Judicious doses of sunlight are therefore crucial to a child's development.

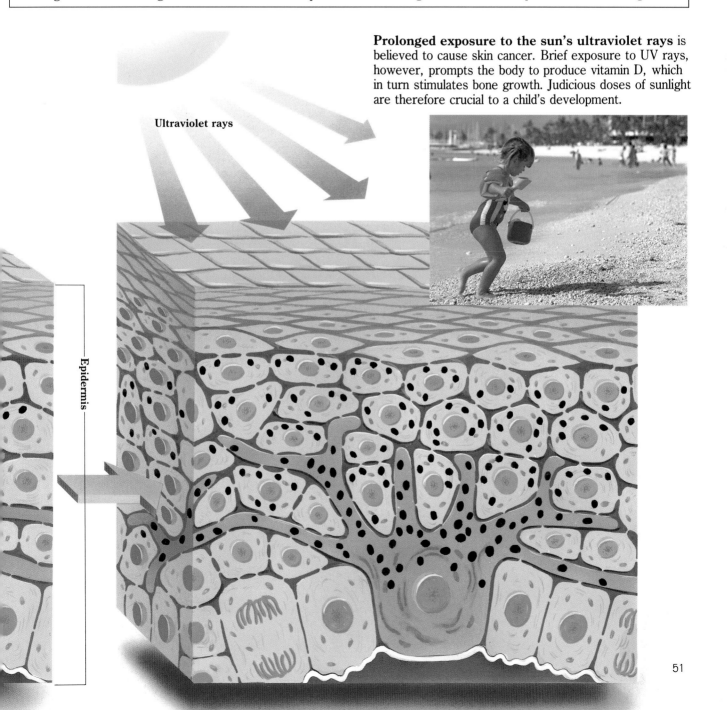

Ultraviolet rays

Epidermis

3
Respiration and Circulation

For all its beautiful design, without energy the human body would be no more than motionless flesh. To keep its systems running, therefore, the body produces energy by burning carbohydrates, proteins, and fats inside its cells through a process that is known as oxidation.

Cells need oxygen to make oxidation work; after they use the oxygen to burn fuel, they give off carbon dioxide. This exchange of gases is called respiration. The word *respiration* usually refers to breathing, or external respiration; structures such as the lungs and trachea that are involved in external respiration are called respiratory structures. However, every cell in the body is also involved in internal respiration—the exchange of oxygen and carbon dioxide.

Transporting these gases is the role of the circulatory system—the heart *(right)*, the blood, and the network of vessels through which the heart pumps blood. The circulatory system delivers oxygen from the air and nutrients from food to the cells and takes away their waste products. The bloodstream also carries the cells that defend the body against infections, as well as the chemicals, or hormones, produced by glands to regulate the body's workings.

This chapter examines the body's respiratory and circulatory systems, describing how they help to supply the body with the elements it needs for health.

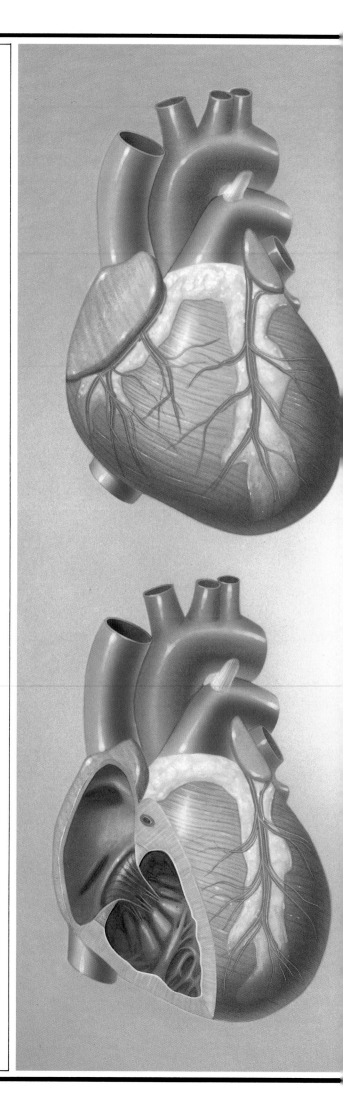

At the center of the circulatory system is the heart. The top three pictures, from left to right, show the human heart from the front, top, and back. At bottom are views into valves in the left and right sides of the heart.

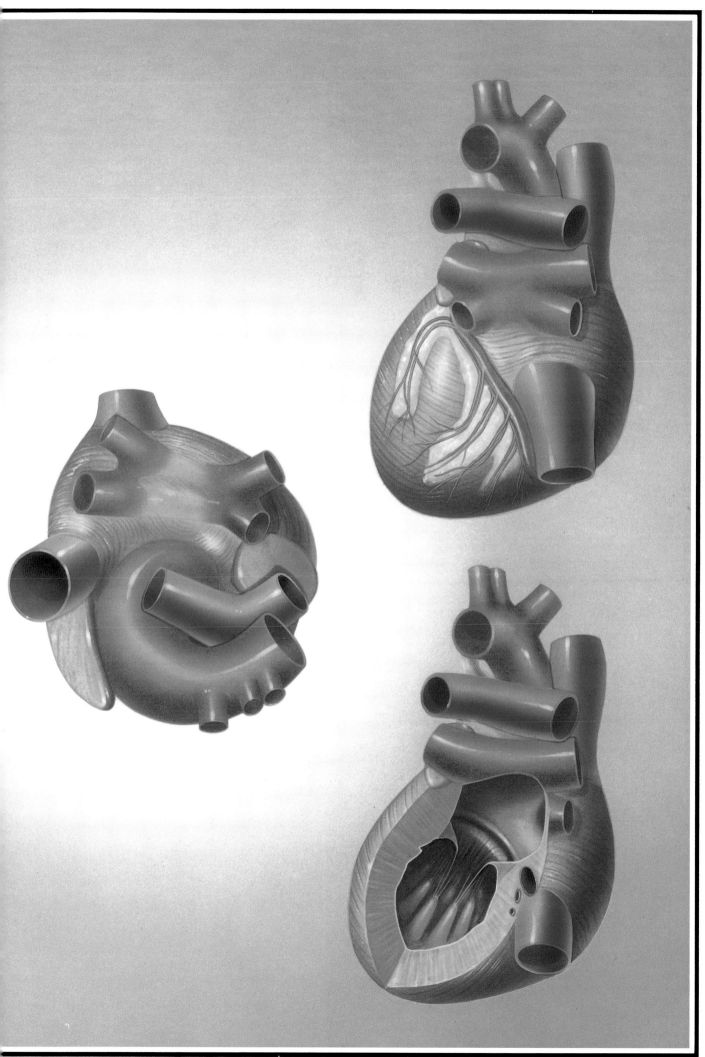

53

How Do People Breathe?

Breathing—taking air into the lungs and forcing it back out—is normally done automatically and involuntarily. The lungs are in the chest cavity, enclosed by the ribs and walled off from the abdomen by the diaphragm, a dome-shaped, muscular partition. Since lungs cannot move by themselves, breathing depends on movements of the diaphragm and the muscles of the chest wall between the ribs. When these muscles contract, they enlarge the chest cavity, causing the air pressure to decrease. This makes the lungs expand and pull in air; when the muscles relax, the chest contracts and the air rushes out.

Air's pathway into the body

Entering through the nose or mouth, air passes into the windpipe, or trachea, at the top of the throat. The trachea carries the air to the lungs; there it branches to form smaller bronchial tubes. The tubes branch repeatedly, reaching many tiny air sacs, or alveoli.

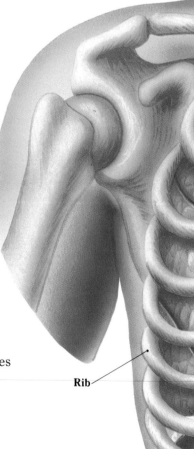

Esophagus—

Right lung

Rib

Rib movements in breathing

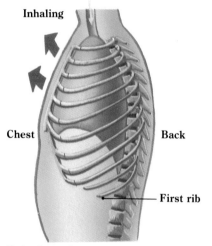

Inhaling

Chest   Back

First rib

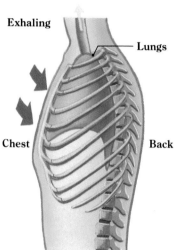

Exhaling

Lungs

Chest   Back

Inhaling. The diaphragm and intercostal, or "between-rib," muscles contract, pulling the ribs upward. This broadens the chest, drawing air into the lungs.

Exhaling. The contracted muscles relax, letting the ribs fall slightly and narrowing the chest. Air is forced out of the lungs.

How the diaphragm moves

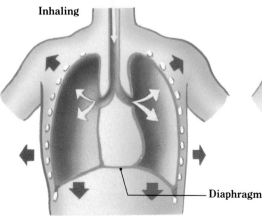

Inhaling

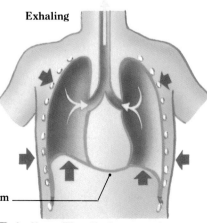

Exhaling

Diaphragm

Inhaling. As the rib cage expands *(arrows, above),* the diaphragm contracts downward, enlarging the chest cavity.

Exhaling. The diaphragm relaxes and is pressed up by the abdominal organs. The chest narrows, driving air out of the lungs.

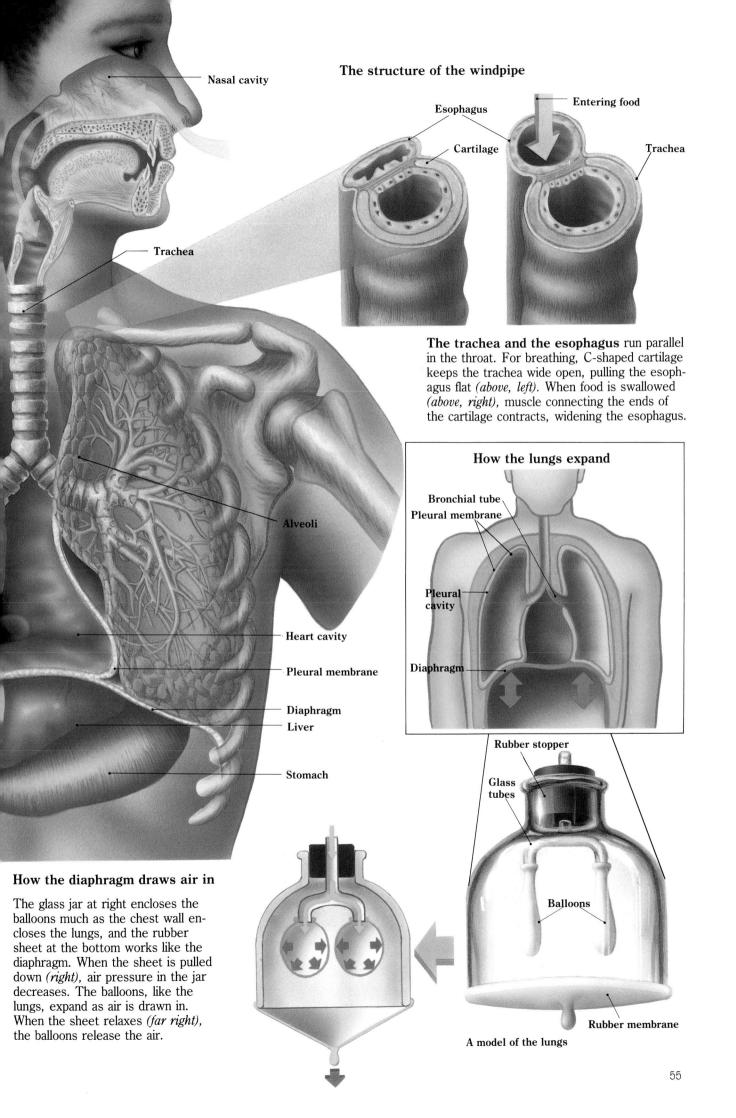

Nasal cavity

The structure of the windpipe

Esophagus

Entering food

Cartilage

Trachea

Trachea

The trachea and the esophagus run parallel in the throat. For breathing, C-shaped cartilage keeps the trachea wide open, pulling the esophagus flat *(above, left)*. When food is swallowed *(above, right)*, muscle connecting the ends of the cartilage contracts, widening the esophagus.

Alveoli

How the lungs expand

Bronchial tube
Pleural membrane

Pleural cavity

Diaphragm

Heart cavity

Pleural membrane

Diaphragm

Liver

Rubber stopper

Glass tubes

Stomach

Balloons

How the diaphragm draws air in

The glass jar at right encloses the balloons much as the chest wall encloses the lungs, and the rubber sheet at the bottom works like the diaphragm. When the sheet is pulled down *(right)*, air pressure in the jar decreases. The balloons, like the lungs, expand as air is drawn in. When the sheet relaxes *(far right)*, the balloons release the air.

Rubber membrane

A model of the lungs

55

Why Does the Body Need Oxygen?

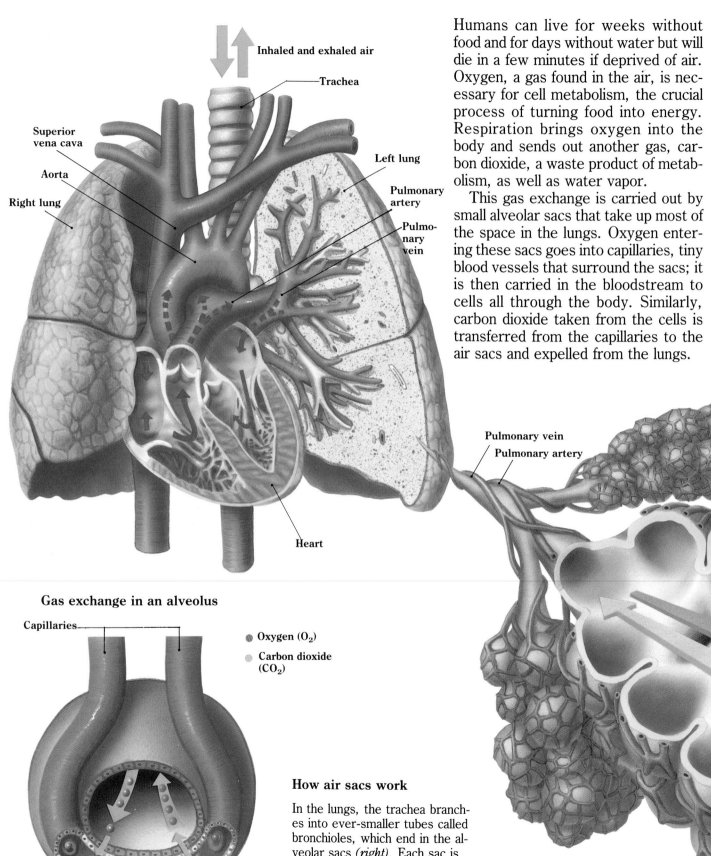

Inhaled and exhaled air

Trachea

Superior vena cava

Aorta

Right lung

Left lung

Pulmonary artery

Pulmonary vein

Heart

Pulmonary vein
Pulmonary artery

Gas exchange in an alveolus

Capillaries

- Oxygen (O$_2$)
- Carbon dioxide (CO$_2$)

Red blood cells

Red cells give up CO$_2$ and receive O$_2$.

Humans can live for weeks without food and for days without water but will die in a few minutes if deprived of air. Oxygen, a gas found in the air, is necessary for cell metabolism, the crucial process of turning food into energy. Respiration brings oxygen into the body and sends out another gas, carbon dioxide, a waste product of metabolism, as well as water vapor.

This gas exchange is carried out by small alveolar sacs that take up most of the space in the lungs. Oxygen entering these sacs goes into capillaries, tiny blood vessels that surround the sacs; it is then carried in the bloodstream to cells all through the body. Similarly, carbon dioxide taken from the cells is transferred from the capillaries to the air sacs and expelled from the lungs.

How air sacs work

In the lungs, the trachea branches into ever-smaller tubes called bronchioles, which end in the alveolar sacs *(right)*. Each sac is made up of small pouches, or alveoli, which are covered by capillaries. The picture at left shows an alveolus (the singular form of *alveoli)*. Inhaled oxygen enters the air sac, then passes through the thin walls of the alveoli to red blood cells in the surrounding capillaries. As the red blood cells lose their carbon dioxide and gain oxygen, their color changes from bluish to red.

Where the oxygen goes

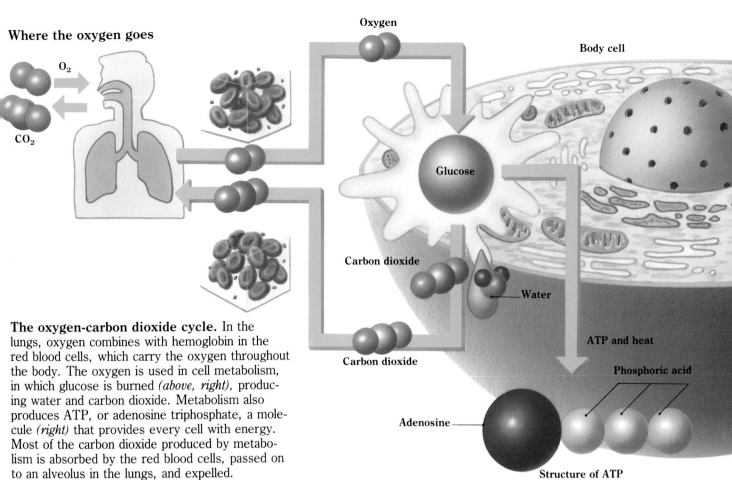

The oxygen-carbon dioxide cycle. In the lungs, oxygen combines with hemoglobin in the red blood cells, which carry the oxygen throughout the body. The oxygen is used in cell metabolism, in which glucose is burned *(above, right),* producing water and carbon dioxide. Metabolism also produces ATP, or adenosine triphosphate, a molecule *(right)* that provides every cell with energy. Most of the carbon dioxide produced by metabolism is absorbed by the red blood cells, passed on to an alveolus in the lungs, and expelled.

Structure of ATP

Inside an alveolar sac

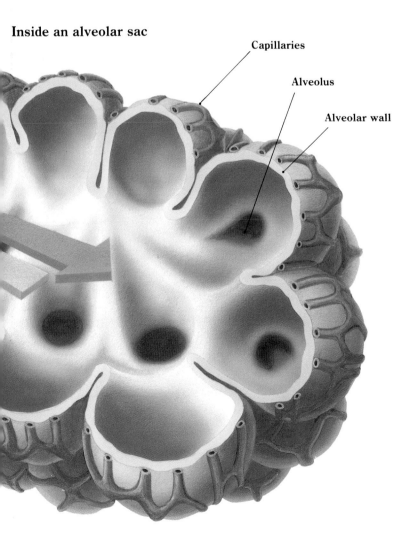

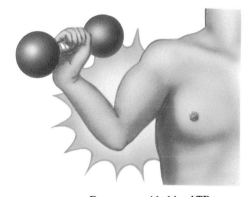

Energy provided by ATP

	Inhaled air (mmHg)	Exhaled air (mmHg)
Nitrogen N_2	596.0 (78.42%)	565.0 (74.34%)
Oxygen O_2	158.0 (20.79%)	116.0 (15.26%)
Carbon dioxide CO_2	0.3 (0.04%)	32.0 (4.22%)
Water H_2O	5.7 (0.75%)	47.0 (6.18%)
Total	760.0 (100%)	760.0 (100%)

The air entering the lungs contains more oxygen, and the air leaving contains more carbon dioxide, measured in millimeters of mercury (mmHg).

Where Does the Voice Come From?

A cutaway view of the head

The vocal cords

Seen through the mouth, the larynx, at the top of the throat *(below)*, stands open at the entrance to the windpipe, or trachea. During swallowing, the epiglottis covers the larynx entrance, keeping food out of the trachea.

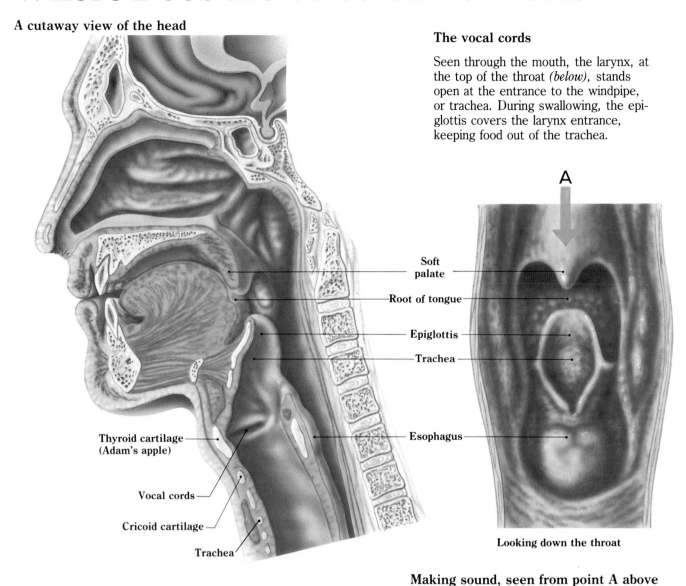

Soft palate

Root of tongue

Epiglottis

Trachea

Esophagus

Thyroid cartilage (Adam's apple)

Vocal cords

Cricoid cartilage

Trachea

Looking down the throat

The larynx. The vocal cords *(right)*, at the top of the trachea, are two membranes right behind the Adam's apple.

Making sound, seen from point A above

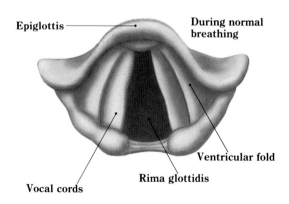

Epiglottis

During normal breathing

Ventricular fold

Rima glottidis

Vocal cords

The voice is the sound produced by air passing between the vocal cords, amplified and shaped by the mouth and nose. The vocal cords are two folded, elastic membranes found in the larynx, or voicebox, near the top of the trachea. Shaped like a triangular box, the larynx is made up of nine pieces of cartilage, linked by muscles and ligaments. When the muscles controlling the vocal cords are relaxed, air passes between them without making a sound. But when the vocal cords are taut, air exhaled from the lungs makes them vibrate, generating sound.

Many other parts of the body besides the larynx work together to turn vocal sounds into speech. The muscles of the ribs, the diaphragm, and many of the muscles of the neck, face, lips, and tongue are also involved in producing words. The brain coordinates the movements of these muscles; it also sends orders to the ribs and the diaphragm to make sounds softer or louder by varying air pressure.

How vocal sound is made

A cutaway view of the trachea *(below)* reveals the vocal cords. To create a sound, the lungs force air through the closed membranes, making them vibrate.

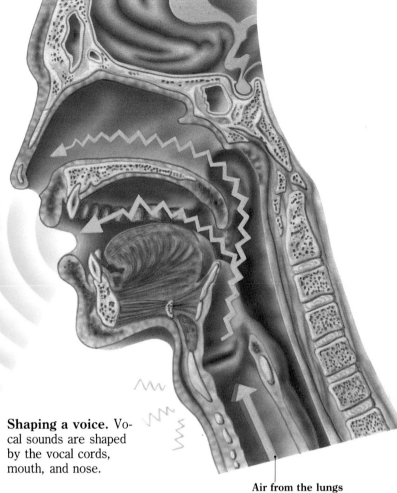

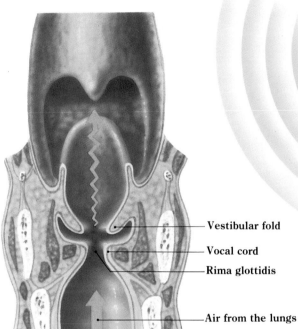

Vestibular fold

Vocal cord

Rima glottidis

Air from the lungs

Cutaway of trachea

Shaping a voice. Vocal sounds are shaped by the vocal cords, mouth, and nose.

Air from the lungs

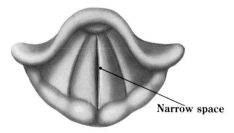

While speaking

Narrow space

While whispering

Wider space

During breathing *(left),* the vocal cords are wide apart. To make a sound, the cords are almost closed, as shown in the top illustration above; they open a little wider *(bottom)* for a whisper.

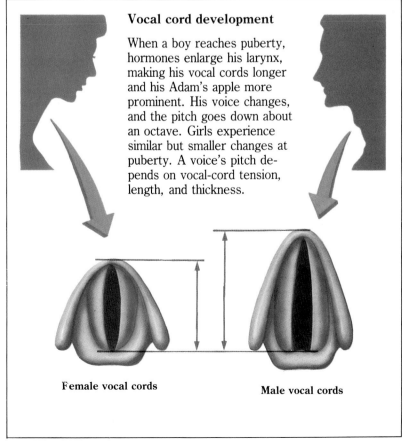

Vocal cord development

When a boy reaches puberty, hormones enlarge his larynx, making his vocal cords longer and his Adam's apple more prominent. His voice changes, and the pitch goes down about an octave. Girls experience similar but smaller changes at puberty. A voice's pitch depends on vocal-cord tension, length, and thickness.

Female vocal cords

Male vocal cords

How Does the Heart Keep Beating?

The human heart beats without stopping for an average of 70 years, pumping a total of about 180 million quarts of blood through the body. This impressive performance is made possible by a special kind of muscle that exists in the heart alone. It is called the myocardial, or heart, muscle, and it combines the properties of two other kinds of muscle found elsewhere in the body, striated muscle and smooth muscle. Striated muscles, like those found in the arms and legs, are voluntary muscles; they move quickly and on command but also tire quickly. Smooth muscles, like those in the stomach and intestines, are involuntary; they cannot be moved at will and are tireless. The heart muscle is both involuntary and striated. It lets the heart beat at an even pace, but it can rapidly change that pace when needed.

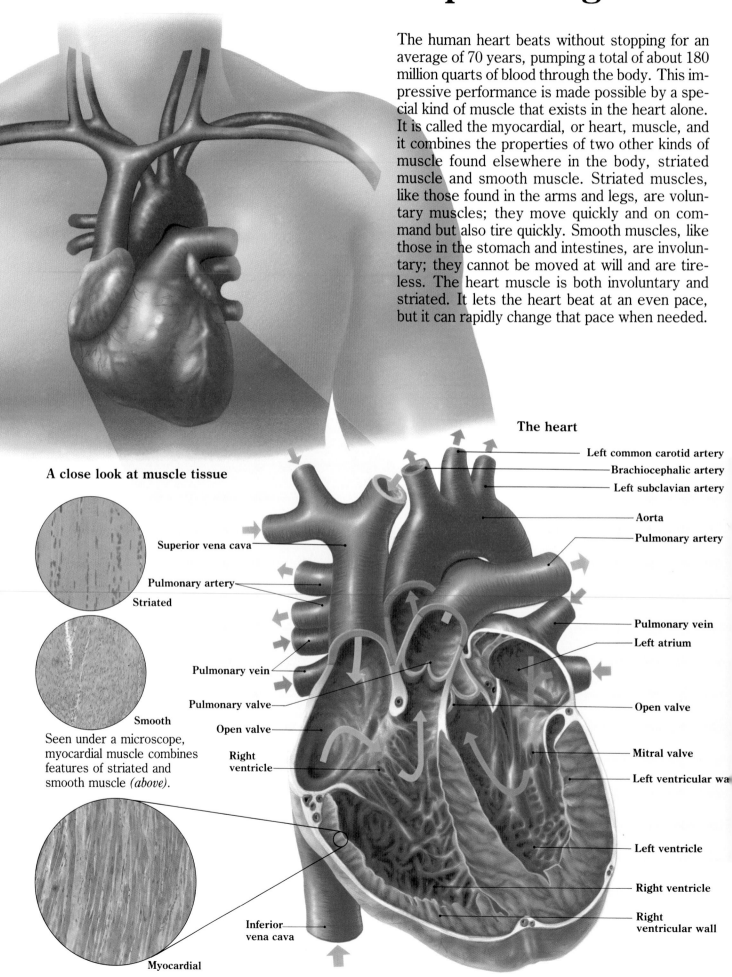

A close look at muscle tissue

Striated

Smooth

Seen under a microscope, myocardial muscle combines features of striated and smooth muscle *(above)*.

Myocardial

The heart

Left common carotid artery
Brachiocephalic artery
Left subclavian artery
Aorta
Pulmonary artery
Superior vena cava
Pulmonary artery
Pulmonary vein
Left atrium
Pulmonary vein
Pulmonary valve
Open valve
Open valve
Mitral valve
Right ventricle
Left ventricular wa
Left ventricle
Right ventricle
Inferior vena cava
Right ventricular wall

A pump that changes speed

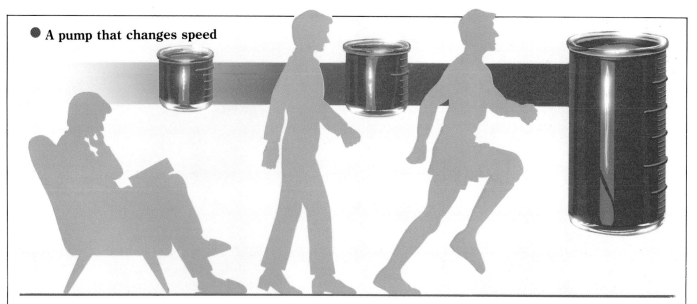

When a person rests, the heart beats 60 to 80 times and pumps 5 to 6 quarts of blood a minute. Mild exercise raises the beat to 100 to 120 times a minute and the blood flow rate to 7 to 8 quarts a minute. Strenuous exercise increases the beat to up to 200 times a minute, moving 30 quarts of blood a minute.

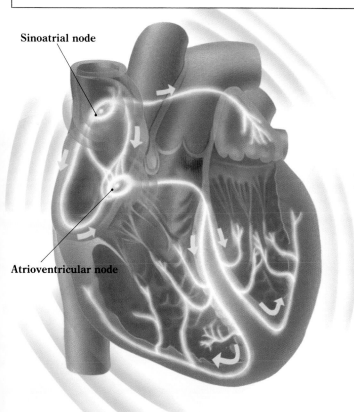

Sinoatrial node

Atrioventricular node

How the pacemaker works

The heart's natural pacemaker, the sinoatrial node, is embedded in the wall of the heart. It sends electrical impulses through heart muscle *(arrows, left),* causing the muscle to relax and contract. When the muscle relaxes, the chambers inside the heart fill with blood. When the muscle contracts, it squeezes the blood out of one chamber and into another. Eventually the blood is forced out of the heart and into the arteries.

Following the route of blood

Relaxing and contracting as regularly as the ticking of a metronome, the heart takes in used blood and supplies it with fresh oxygen. The blood enters the heart at the right atrium and then passes into the right ventricle. From there it is pumped into the lungs through the pulmonary artery and, refreshed with oxygen, returns to the heart through the pulmonary veins. It reenters the heart at the left atrium, passes into the left ventricle, and finally exits the heart through the aorta.

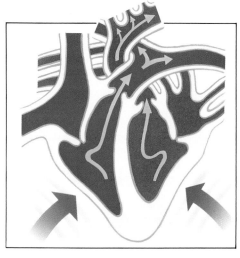

How Do Veins and Arteries Differ?

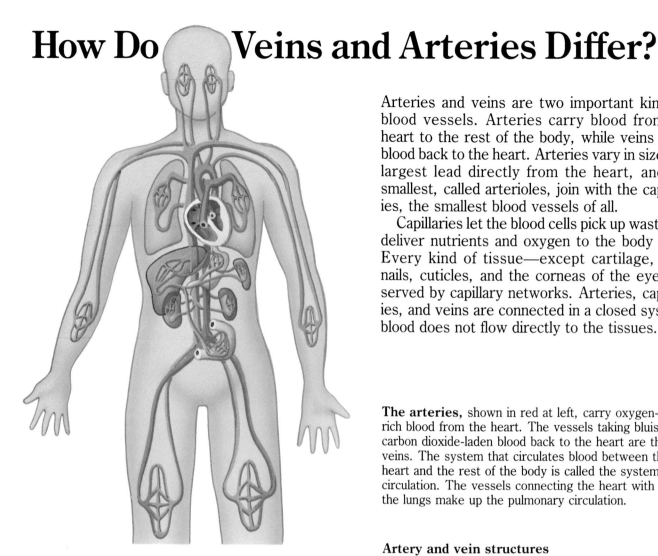

Arteries and veins are two important kinds of blood vessels. Arteries carry blood from the heart to the rest of the body, while veins carry blood back to the heart. Arteries vary in size; the largest lead directly from the heart, and the smallest, called arterioles, join with the capillaries, the smallest blood vessels of all.

Capillaries let the blood cells pick up waste and deliver nutrients and oxygen to the body cells. Every kind of tissue—except cartilage, hair, nails, cuticles, and the corneas of the eyes—is served by capillary networks. Arteries, capillaries, and veins are connected in a closed system; blood does not flow directly to the tissues.

The arteries, shown in red at left, carry oxygen-rich blood from the heart. The vessels taking bluish carbon dioxide-laden blood back to the heart are the veins. The system that circulates blood between the heart and the rest of the body is called the systemic circulation. The vessels connecting the heart with the lungs make up the pulmonary circulation.

Artery and vein structures

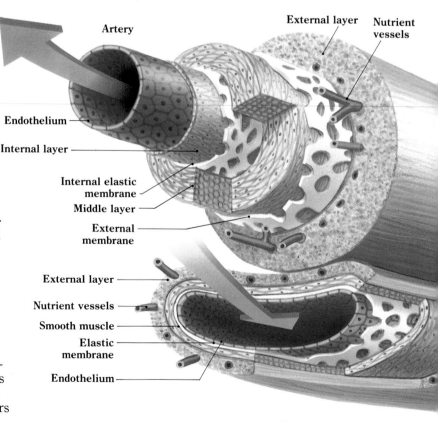

Blood-vessel cross sections

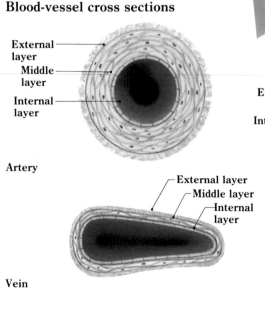

External layer
Middle layer
Internal layer

Artery

External layer
Middle layer
Internal layer

Vein

Arteries and veins have three layers, but because an artery *(top)* must contain the pressure of blood pumped from the heart, its walls are thicker and more elastic. Inner layers are fed by the blood within the vessel; outer layers are served by built-in small blood vessels *(right)*. Veins *(right, bottom)* have valves that keep blood from flowing back to the capillaries.

Three kinds of capillaries

Capillaries, the tiniest blood vessels, have walls only one cell thick. As seen in the illustrations below, many capillaries are so narrow that blood cells must travel through them in single file. Continuous capillaries *(top),* found in muscle tissue, let fluids in and out at the joints between cells in their walls. Fenestrated ("windowed") capillaries *(middle)* are more porous; found in the kidneys, endocrine glands, and intestines, they permit more fluids to enter and leave the bloodstream. Sinusoids *(bottom)* are enlarged capillaries found in the bone marrow, spleen, and liver, where their cell-size openings allow blood cells to enter and leave the bloodstream.

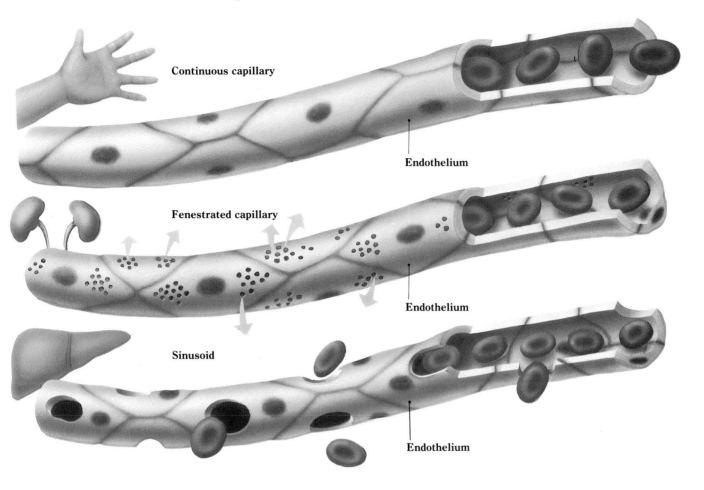

Continuous capillary

Endothelium

Fenestrated capillary

Endothelium

Sinusoid

Endothelium

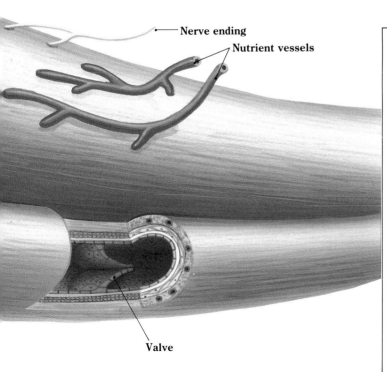

Nerve ending

Nutrient vessels

Valve

How veins keep blood moving

Because the heart's action is so far away, veins need help in moving blood back toward the heart. Curiously enough, many veins get that help from neighboring arteries, as seen below. With each heartbeat, the artery *(center)* swells, squeezing the parallel veins; inside the veins, one-way valves open and close to keep blood moving.

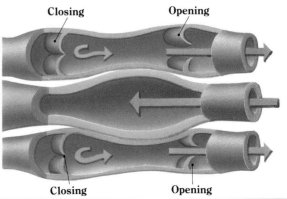

Closing   **Opening**

Closing   **Opening**

Why Is Blood Red?

The color of blood comes from its red blood cells, which contain an iron-bearing red pigment, hemoglobin. Hemoglobin bonds easily with oxygen and transports it throughout the body. Blood's redness varies with the amount of oxygen in it; blood is brightest when its hemoglobin is fully loaded with oxygen.

Blood also contains white blood cells, which engulf and remove disease-causing agents and combat infection. Platelets are the third kind of blood cell; they help form clots to stop bleeding. All these cells are called the formed elements of blood, and they circulate in the blood's liquid component, blood plasma.

The blood that circulates in the body normally accounts for about 7 percent of body weight—the percentage is lower in small children and higher in pregnant women.

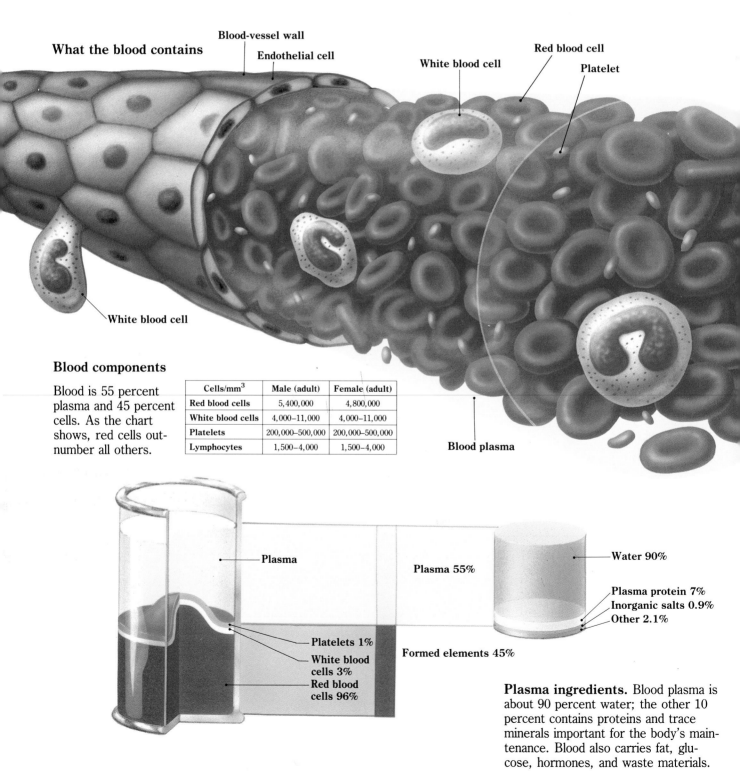

What the blood contains

Blood-vessel wall
Endothelial cell
White blood cell
Red blood cell
Platelet
White blood cell
Blood plasma

Blood components

Blood is 55 percent plasma and 45 percent cells. As the chart shows, red cells outnumber all others.

Cells/mm³	Male (adult)	Female (adult)
Red blood cells	5,400,000	4,800,000
White blood cells	4,000–11,000	4,000–11,000
Platelets	200,000–500,000	200,000–500,000
Lymphocytes	1,500–4,000	1,500–4,000

Plasma
Plasma 55%
Water 90%
Plasma protein 7%
Inorganic salts 0.9%
Other 2.1%
Platelets 1%
White blood cells 3%
Red blood cells 96%
Formed elements 45%

Plasma ingredients. Blood plasma is about 90 percent water; the other 10 percent contains proteins and trace minerals important for the body's maintenance. Blood also carries fat, glucose, hormones, and waste materials.

Blood cells seen through a scanning electron microscope

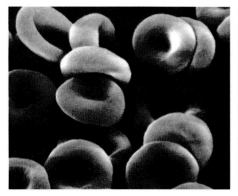

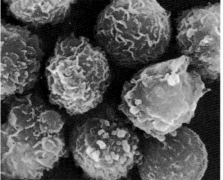

Disk-shaped and concave on both sides, red blood cells have no nuclei. They live about 120 days.

White blood cells have nuclei and can move. They change shape when active and squeeze through capillary walls.

Colorless, irregular, and small, these platelets are entangled with strands of fibrin in a developing blood clot.

What the red blood cells do

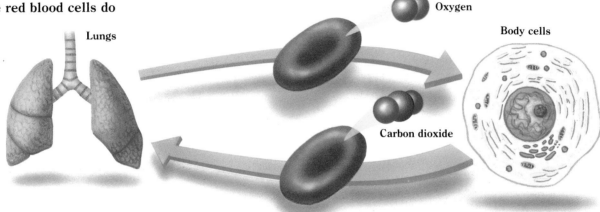

Lungs

Oxygen

Body cells

Carbon dioxide

What the white blood cells do

Meeting a disease germ *(below),* a white blood cell called a neutrophil moves to engulf and devour the bacterium. White cells also promote healing of injuries.

Red cells pick up oxygen in the lungs *(above, left)* by means of their hemoglobin, which bonds easily with oxygen. They deliver oxygen to other cells *(above)* and collect carbon dioxide.

White cell ingests bacterium

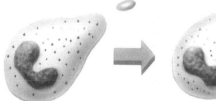  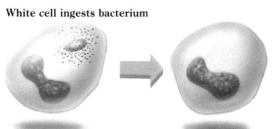

What the platelets do

Red blood cell

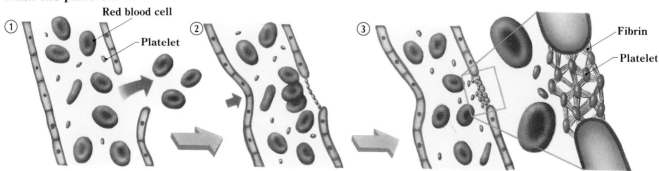

① Platelet ② ③ Fibrin Platelet

Platelets stop the loss of blood from a damaged blood vessel by following the steps shown above.
1. Platelets gather where a blood vessel is injured and red cells are flowing out.
2. The first platelets to arrive form a plug across

the opening, dying in the process. They release chemicals that convert fibrinogen to fibrin.
3. Fibrin forms a mesh of needlelike fibers that trap platelets and other blood cells, creating an insoluble clot *(enlarged above, right).*

65

Where Is Blood Made?

Cross section of bone

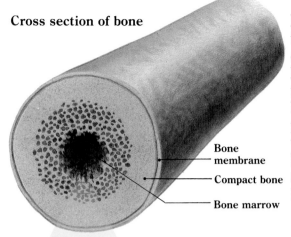

Bone
membrane

Compact bone

Bone marrow

Magnified view
of bone marrow

Most blood cells are produced in the bone marrow, the living tissue at the center of certain bones. Some white blood cells, however—the lymphocytes—come primarily from the lymph glands, spleen, and thymus. In a newborn baby, all of the bone marrow is involved in the production of blood cells, but as the baby grows up, some bone marrow shuts down production. By adulthood only the skull, ribs, breastbone, vertebrae, hipbones, and ends of the long bones produce blood cells. Each kind of blood cell has a specific life span, and when one blood cell is lost, it is automatically replaced by another one like it.

Production of blood cells

Active, blood-cell-producing bone marrow *(below)* is honeycombed with chambers in which precursor cells mature into various kinds of blood cells—red, white, or platelets. The mature cells *(below, right)* slip into sinusoid capillaries *(below and page 63)* to join the bloodstream. An adult's marrow produces enough red cells for a pint of blood each week.

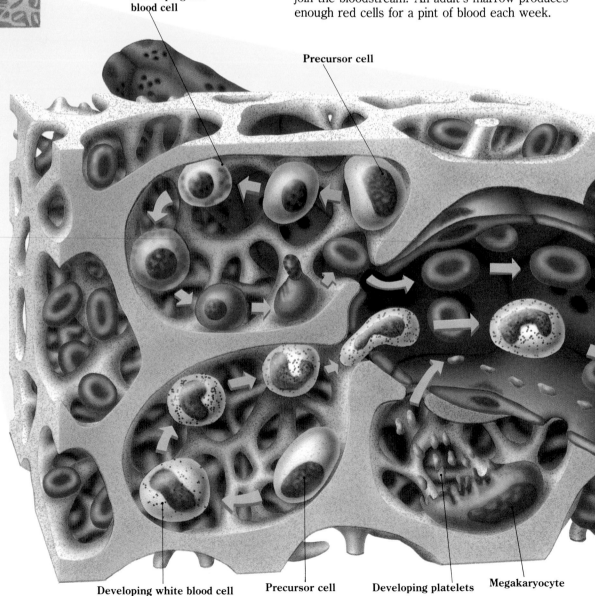

Developing red
blood cell

Precursor cell

Developing white blood cell   Precursor cell   Developing platelets   Megakaryocyte

Blood cells from precursor cells

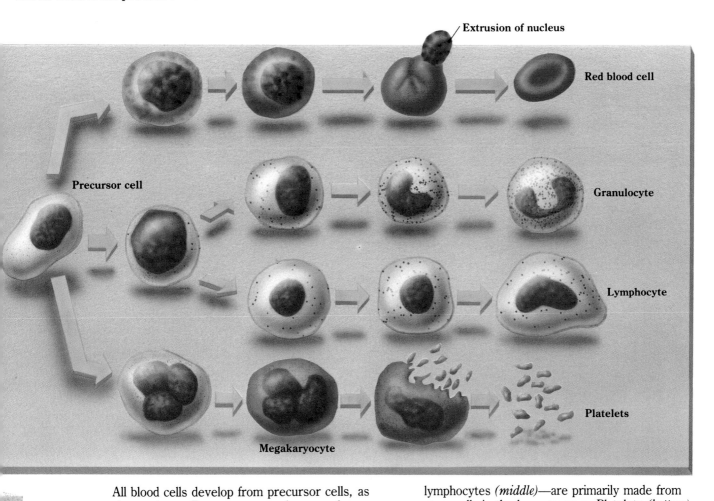

All blood cells develop from precursor cells, as shown above. Every precursor has a nucleus, which a developing red blood cell expels *(top)*. Two kinds of white blood cells—granulocytes and lymphocytes *(middle)*—are primarily made from stem cells in the bone marrow. Platelets *(bottom)* are fragments of megakaryocytes, which are cells with a giant nucleus.

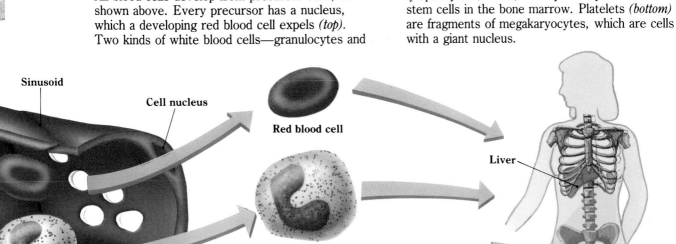

Red blood cells live for 100 to 125 days. Then they are filtered out of the bloodstream by the spleen *(right)* or liver, when the deteriorating cells can no longer slide through the narrow capillaries of these organs. White blood cells live from 6 to 9 days and are absorbed by the liver. Platelets live about 10 days and are then removed by the spleen.

What Is Blood Pressure?

With every heartbeat, blood pumped from the heart pushes and expands the artery walls from the inside. This pressure is called blood pressure. When the heart contracts *(below)* and pushes blood into the arteries, the pressure is highest and is called the systolic blood pressure. In the second half of the heartbeat, when the heart relaxes and fills with blood, the pressure is at its lowest and is called the diastolic blood pressure.

Blood pressure rises and falls as the body's activities change. It tends to rise with age and varies with race and gender. Above a certain standard value, blood pressure is called hypertension. When blood pressure falls below a certain value, it is called hypotension.

Heartbeat and blood pressure

These six drawings show the heart's action in one heartbeat. Blood pressure is lowest when the heart relaxes and fills with blood *(top right)* and highest when it contracts to force blood out *(bottom right)*.

Normal blood pressure

Blood pressure is measured with a sphygmomanometer *(below)*. Readings tell the height, in millimeters (mm), of the instrument's column of mercury (Hg). Blood pressure readings tell systolic pressure first, then diastolic; a typical reading is 120/80 mmHg. The normal systolic range is between 100 and 120.

Systolic pressure (mmHg)

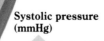

140			
139			
121			
120			
100			
99			
Low	Normal	Upper limit of normal	High
59	80	89	90

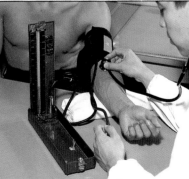

▲ **Taking blood pressure**

Diastolic pressure (mmHg)

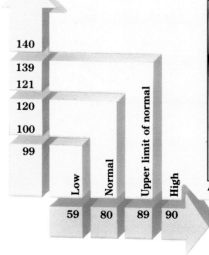

The pressure inside an artery

The pressure of blood, pushing against the artery from inside, is called the blood pressure. The artery wall *(above)*, strong and elastic, easily withstands the pressure.

Diastolic pressure

Systolic pressure

What raises blood pressure?

In response to vigorous exercise, surprise, or alarm *(below),* the heart speeds up, increasing the flow of oxygen-bearing blood and raising the blood pressure. In sudden cold, capillaries near the skin contract to conserve body heat, and blood pressure rises. The nervous system controls all these reactions.

When exercising

When suddenly cold

When frightened

Measuring blood pressure

To measure blood pressure, an inflated cuff around the patient's arm stops the pulse, as heard through a stethoscope. Air is let out of the cuff; when the heartbeat is heard again, the reading is the systolic pressure. The reading when the sound disappears is the diastolic pressure.

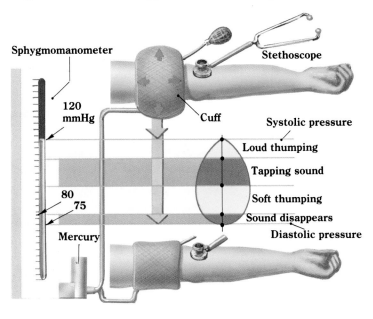

Sphygmomanometer

Stethoscope

120 mmHg

Cuff

Systolic pressure

Loud thumping

Tapping sound

80
75

Soft thumping

Sound disappears

Mercury

Diastolic pressure

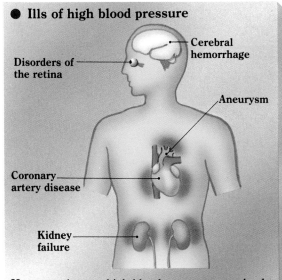

● **Ills of high blood pressure**

Disorders of the retina

Cerebral hemorrhage

Aneurysm

Coronary artery disease

Kidney failure

Hypertension, or high blood pressure, can lead to any of the serious conditions shown above. Since hypertension often has no symptoms, everyone should have regular medical checkups.

Why Are Blood Types Important?

When a patient receives a transfusion of another person's blood, the two people's blood must be carefully cross-matched. If the patient receives the wrong blood type, his or her own blood may react to the new blood so that the red cells clump together, or agglutinate. When this happens, the patient can die.

Two substances that distinguish one blood type from another are called agglutinogens and agglutinins. The way these substances react to each other determines a person's blood type—either A, B, AB, or O. Agglutination rarely occurs when patient and donor have blood of the same type. Type O blood can be transfused to any other person, and AB type blood can receive blood of any type.

Compatible blood transfusions

Blood is not interchangeable. Although all people can safely receive blood of their own type *(above)* or from a type O donor, a type A, for example, cannot receive blood from a type B or type AB donor.

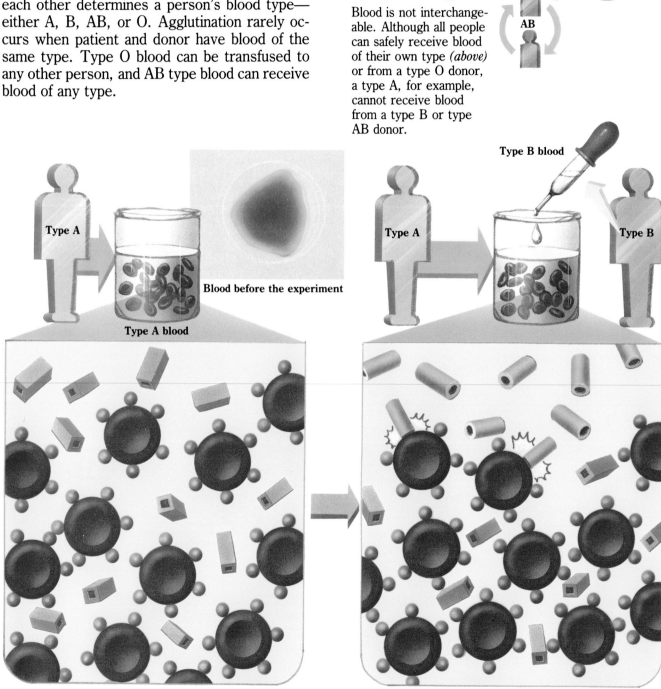

Blood before the experiment

Type A blood

Type B blood

In type A blood, the red cells have agglutinogen A *(orange spheres),* and the plasma has agglutinin anti-B *(blue hollow boxes).* There is no agglutination between agglutinogen A and agglutinin anti-B.

For a cross-match test, plasma from type B blood *(top)* is added to type A blood. Type B plasma has agglutinin anti-A *(hollow cylinders),* which attaches to the agglutinogen A of type A red cells.

The four major types

A test of any given sample of blood *(below)* will reveal the blood type—one of the four possible combinations of agglutinogens and agglutinins shown at right.

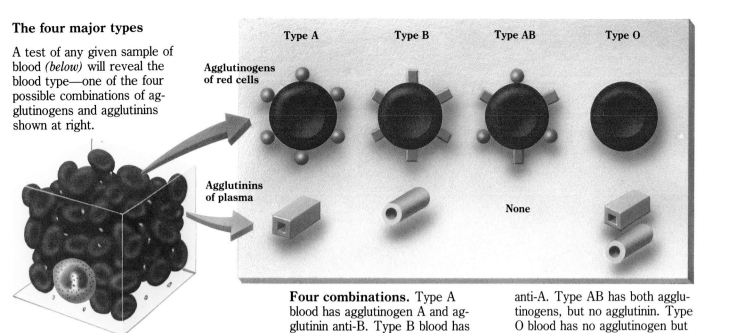

Four combinations. Type A blood has agglutinogen A and agglutinin anti-B. Type B blood has agglutinogen B and agglutinin anti-A. Type AB has both agglutinogens, but no agglutinin. Type O blood has no agglutinogen but both agglutinins.

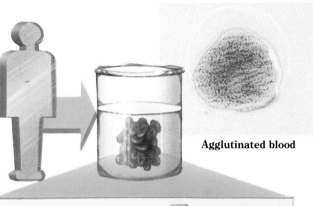

Agglutinated blood

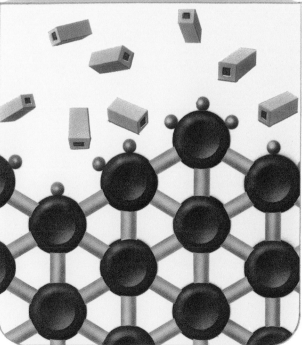

The agglutinin anti-A from the type B blood plasma attaches to agglutinogen A of the type A red cells. This mismatch makes the cells lock together, which can clog the kidneys, causing death.

Inheriting blood types

Every person inherits two blood-type genes, one from each parent. The chart below shows how these genes result in each of the four major blood types. The left column shows parents' blood types; the next column shows the combinations of genes their children can receive. The right half of the chart shows the probability of a child having a given blood type.

Parents' types	Genes	O	A		B		AB
		OO	AA	AO	BB	BO	AB
O × O	OO × OO	100					
O × A	OO × AA			100			
O × A	OO × AO	50		50			
O × B	OO × BB					100	
O × B	OO × BO	50				50	
O × AB	OO × AB			50		50	
A × A	AA × AA		100				
A × A	AA × AO		50	50			
A × A	AO × AO	25	25	50			
A × B	AA × BB						100
A × B	AA × BO			50			50
A × B	AO × BB					50	50
A × B	AO × BO	25		25		25	25
A × AB	AA × AB		50				50
A × AB	AO × AB		25	25		25	25
B × B	BB × BB				100		
B × B	BB × BO				50	50	
B × B	BO × BO	25			25	50	
B × AB	BB × AB				50		50
B × AB	BO × AB			25	25	25	25
AB × AB	AB × AB		25		25		50

What Is Carbon Monoxide Poisoning?

Carbon monoxide is a poisonous gas that interferes with the body's use of oxygen. Normally, oxygen inhaled into the body combines with the blood's hemoglobin in the lungs. Hemoglobin forms 95 percent of the substance of red blood cells; it consists of heme, an iron-bearing pigment, and globin, a protein. Heme picks up oxygen in the lungs; when the red cell is near tissues that need oxygen, heme releases it.

But carbon monoxide has a power to bind with heme *(opposite, top)* that is several hundred times

greater than that of oxygen. As a result, if the amount of carbon monoxide in the lungs is above a certain level, oxygen loses out to carbon monoxide in the race to bond with hemoglobin. Not only does carbon monoxide take oxygen's place on hemoglobin; it forms a very stable compound so the heme cannot release it. Carbon monoxide, not oxygen, is then carried to the tissues, and the body's organs are starved of the oxygen they need. This condition is known as carbon monoxide poisoning, and it can be fatal.

Sources of carbon monoxide

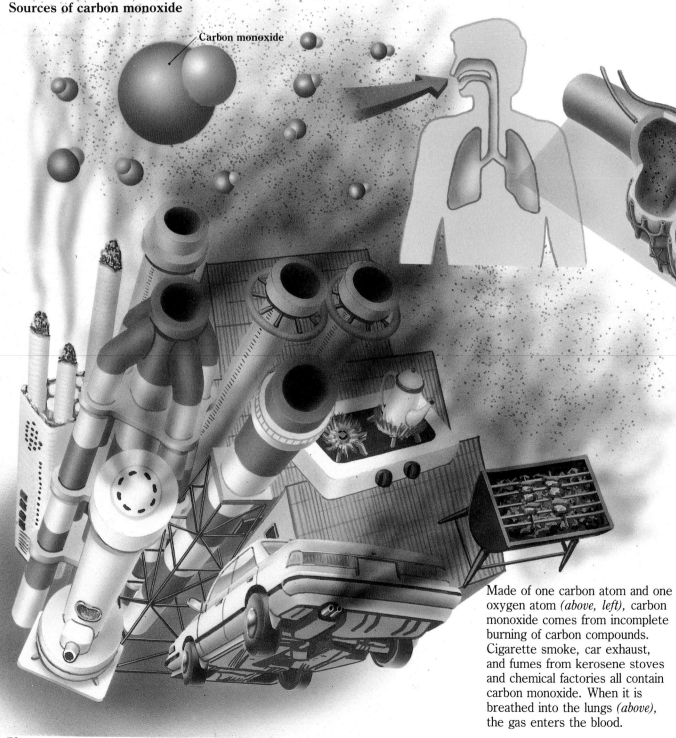

Carbon monoxide

Made of one carbon atom and one oxygen atom *(above, left)*, carbon monoxide comes from incomplete burning of carbon compounds. Cigarette smoke, car exhaust, and fumes from kerosene stoves and chemical factories all contain carbon monoxide. When it is breathed into the lungs *(above)*, the gas enters the blood.

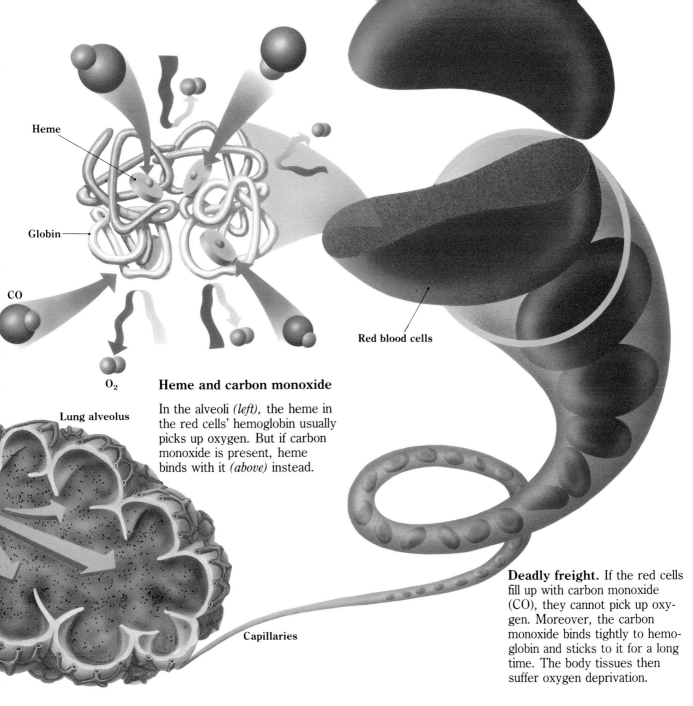

Heme

Globin

CO

O_2

Red blood cells

Heme and carbon monoxide

In the alveoli *(left)*, the heme in the red cells' hemoglobin usually picks up oxygen. But if carbon monoxide is present, heme binds with it *(above)* instead.

Lung alveolus

Deadly freight. If the red cells fill up with carbon monoxide (CO), they cannot pick up oxygen. Moreover, the carbon monoxide binds tightly to hemoglobin and sticks to it for a long time. The body tissues then suffer oxygen deprivation.

Capillaries

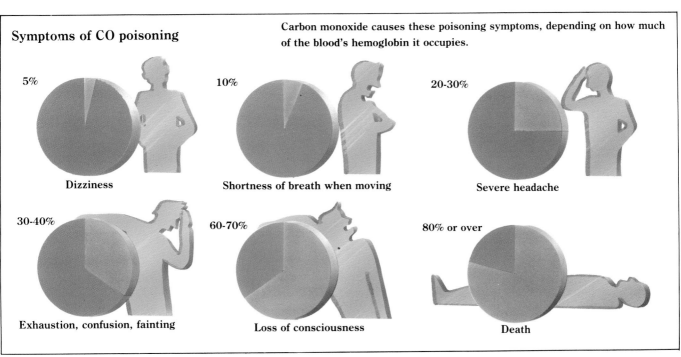

Symptoms of CO poisoning

Carbon monoxide causes these poisoning symptoms, depending on how much of the blood's hemoglobin it occupies.

5%
Dizziness

10%
Shortness of breath when moving

20-30%
Severe headache

30-40%
Exhaustion, confusion, fainting

60-70%
Loss of consciousness

80% or over
Death

What Are Hormones?

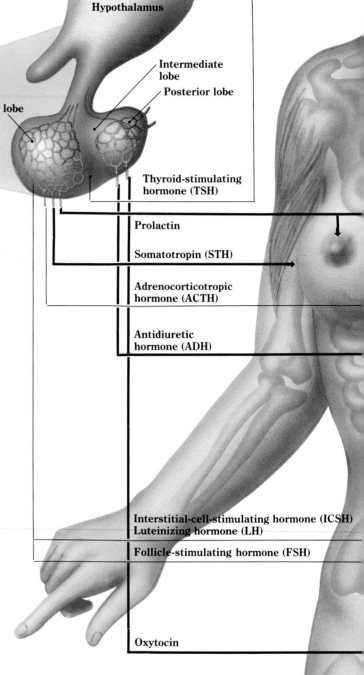

Pineal body

Hypothalamus

Pituitary gland

Intermediate lobe

Posterior lobe

Anterior lobe

Thyroid-stimulating hormone (TSH)

Prolactin

Somatotropin (STH)

Adrenocorticotropic hormone (ACTH)

Antidiuretic hormone (ADH)

Interstitial-cell-stimulating hormone (ICSH)
Luteinizing hormone (LH)

Follicle-stimulating hormone (FSH)

Oxytocin

Pituitary gland

Located in the brain *(above)*, the pea-size pituitary gland, enlarged at right, secretes hormones that control other endocrine glands. The pineal body affects sleep and gonad growth.

Hormones are chemical messengers that are produced by the ductless, or endocrine, glands. These chemicals are secreted directly into the blood to target cells and organs, where they regulate body processes and keep them in balance. In fact, the bloodstream carries hormones to all tissues, but only the target tissues respond.

The endocrine glands include the pituitary, pineal, thyroid, parathyroid, and adrenal glands, the pancreatic islets, and the gonads, or reproductive glands—ovaries or testes. The pituitary gland *(above)* is sometimes called the master gland, because its hormones affect the other endocrine glands.

Exocrine and endocrine glands

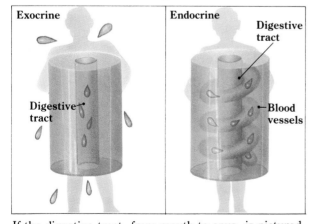

Exocrine

Endocrine

Digestive tract

Digestive tract

Blood vessels

If the digestive tract, from mouth to anus, is pictured as one tube, the body would form a cylinder around the tube *(above)*. Glands that secrete through ducts to the inner and outer walls of this cylinder, such as sweat, salivary, and gastric glands, are exocrine glands. Glands that secrete to blood vessels and tissues within the cylinder are endocrine glands.

Pituitary hormones may affect endocrine glands *(thin lines)* or target organs directly *(thick lines)*.
→ **Thyroid-stimulating hormone:** thyroid secretion and growth.
→ **Prolactin:** development of mammary glands.
→ **Somatotropin:** growth and skeletal development.
→ **Adrenocorticotropic hormone:** for growth of the adrenal cortex.
→ **Antidiuretic hormone:** absorption of water.
→ **Interstitial-cell-stimulating hormone:** stimulates males' testosterone secretion; **luteinizing hormone** stimulates ovulation in females.
→ **Follicle-stimulating hormone:** for growth of ovarian follicles in females and sperm in males.
→ **Oxytocin:** stimulates uterine contractions.

Endocrine glands and hormones

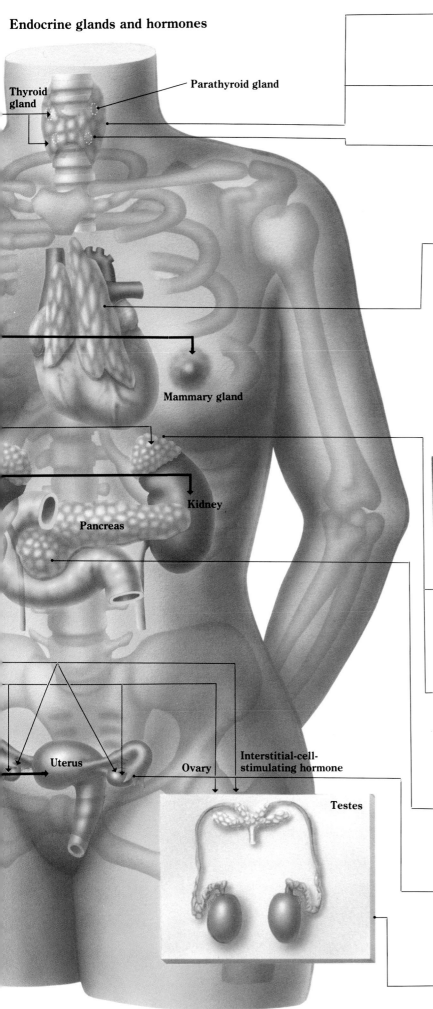

Parathyroid gland

Thyroid gland

Mammary gland

Kidney

Pancreas

Uterus

Ovary

Interstitial-cell-stimulating hormone

Testes

Thyroid gland. Situated astride the trachea, this gland secretes **thyroxine,** which raises the body's rate of metabolism and general activity level. Specialized **parafollicular cells** in the thyroid gland secrete **calcitonin,** which inhibits the release of calcium from the bones.

Parathyroid glands. Usually found in two pairs, on the back of the thyroid gland but not part of it, these glands secrete **parathyroid hormone,** which maintains a normal level of calcium in the bloodstream.

Thymus gland. An imperfectly understood gland, the thymus is believed to produce **thymosin,** which promotes the development of antibodies, especially T lymphocytes, or T cells. The thymus stops working after puberty.

The adrenal glands

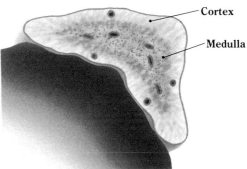

Cortex

Medulla

The adrenal medulla. This gland secretes two hormones that help the body react to stress. **Epinephrine** increases the heart rate and blood-sugar level. **Norepinephrine** raises blood pressure.

The adrenal cortex. Its three layers secrete **mineralocorticoids,** which keep body fluids in balance; **glucocorticoids,** which regulate metabolism of carbohydrates, protein, and fat; and **sex hormones,** which regulate development of sexual traits.

Islets of Langerhans. These cells in the pancreas secrete **insulin,** which helps the body use glucose, or sugar; and **glucagon,** which makes the liver release stored glucose for use as fuel.

Ovaries (in the female). The ovaries release **estrogen,** which makes hips widen and breasts enlarge; and **progesterone,** which prepares the body for pregnancy.

Testes (in the male). The male gonads secrete **testosterone,** which promotes male characteristics.

4

Digestion

Whether it's a carbohydrate-loaded bowl of spaghetti or a hamburger filled with proteins and fat, the food a person eats must be digested so the body can use the life-giving nutrients. To break food down to molecule size, the body grinds and churns it and attacks it with a host of strong chemicals before finally absorbing it.

Digestion begins in the mouth with the grinding of food and the addition of saliva, which contains chemicals that break down food starches. Swallowed food then moves down the esophagus and into the stomach, where gastric juices do their work. Next is the small intestine, where almost all the nutrients are absorbed. Those nutrients are the body's source of energy; some are used right away, while others are stored until needed. Finally, in the large intestine, the remaining water in the food waste is absorbed, and the waste is then excreted.

Along this digestive pathway are the salivary glands, the liver, and the pancreas, all of which secrete essential digestive juices. Kidneys come into play to filter waste from the blood and excrete it in urine; a small amount of waste is even excreted in sweat.

The varied surfaces of the digestive tract are shown here: Following the digestive process, the arrows from the upper left indicate the linings of the esophagus, stomach, duodenum, small intestine, appendix, and large intestine.

Where Does Saliva Come From?

Parotid glands ①
Submaxillary glands ②
Sublingual glands ③

Location of salivary glands

The three sets of major glands, working in pairs, are located around the mouth as shown above. Smaller salivary glands line the lips, cheeks, and tongue.

Digestion begins when food enters the mouth and mixes with saliva. A fluid that is 99 percent water, saliva contains a digestive enzyme called amylase, which breaks down starch in foods. The sight, smell, or even the thought of food can trigger the glands to release saliva.

Saliva flows into the mouth from three pairs of large salivary glands: the parotid glands, located just below the ears; the submaxillary glands in the lower jaw; and the sublingual glands under the tongue. Many smaller salivary glands are also located within the lips, cheeks, and tongue.

The parotid glands, largest of the three major pairs, secrete saliva into the mouth through tiny openings near the second molar on each side of the upper jaw. The submaxillary and sublingual glands also produce a mucous fluid that helps to make food slippery. Once the food is broken down by chewing and softened by saliva, it moves on to the rest of the digestive system.

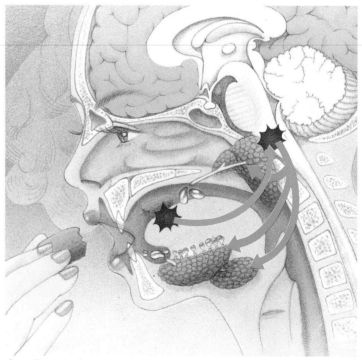

A reflex action

When food stimulates nerves in the tongue and the mucous membrane, signals travel to the salivary control center in the medulla of the brain. This reflex starts the secretion of saliva.

A parotid gland

Cells secreting serous fluid

Glands secreting serous fluid

Saliva containing serous fluid

A submaxillary gland

Gland containing mucous and serous fluids

Saliva with both mucous and serous fluids

Cell secreting serous fluid

Cell secreting mucous fluid

The action of saliva

The clear fluid secreted by the parotid glands and the thick fluid secreted by the submaxillary and sublingual glands give saliva several helpful properties. Beyond changing starch to sugar, saliva makes food easier to swallow. It also keeps the mouth sterile, enhances the sense of taste, and may contain substances that fight bacteria and help heal wounds.

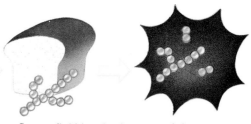

Serous fluid breaks down starch into sugar.

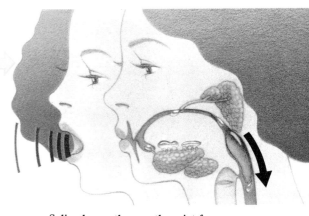

Saliva keeps the mouth moist for talking and swallowing.

Conditioned reflex

Food entering the mouth triggers the secretion of saliva, but this inborn, sensitive reflex also can be set off by the sight, smell, or thought of food. Even a memory can trigger the reflex, because experience with food conditions the nerve center that controls salivation.

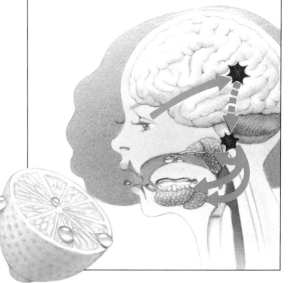

Why Doesn't Food Enter the Windpipe?

The structure of the throat

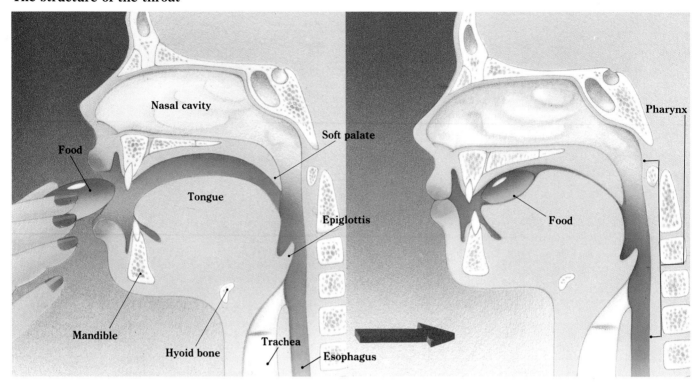

Nasal cavity

Soft palate

Food

Tongue

Epiglottis

Mandible

Hyoid bone

Trachea

Esophagus

Pharynx

Food

Before a person starts eating, the back of the mouth *(above)* is open to the nasal air passages. In the throat, the flaplike epiglottis is relaxed, thus allowing air into the lungs.

Swallowing begins after food is chewed. This action is voluntary until food reaches the back of the throat.

After food has been chewed and mixed with saliva, it is swallowed. As this happens, the passages into the nose and trachea, or windpipe, close up automatically to prevent choking.

First, as the tongue pushes food into the pharynx, the food pipe leading away from the mouth, a flap of tissue called the epiglottis closes like a tight lid over the top of the windpipe. At the same time, the soft palate at the back of the mouth lifts up, blocking the passages into the nose. Once food has entered the pharynx, muscles in the throat begin to contract automatically, moving food safely past the windpipe and into the esophagus. In the esophagus, wavelike muscle contractions known as peristalsis push the food to the stomach.

Choking

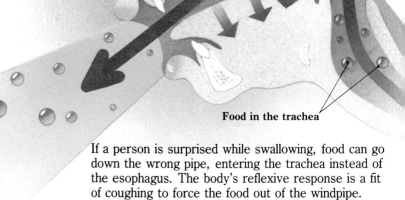

Food in the trachea

If a person is surprised while swallowing, food can go down the wrong pipe, entering the trachea instead of the esophagus. The body's reflexive response is a fit of coughing to force the food out of the windpipe.

As food moves toward the throat, the soft palate, including the dangling tissue at the back of the mouth called the uvula, lifts up and seals off the nasal passages.

The epiglottis closes as food moves toward it, preventing the food from entering the trachea and eventually the lungs. The food then moves into the esophagus.

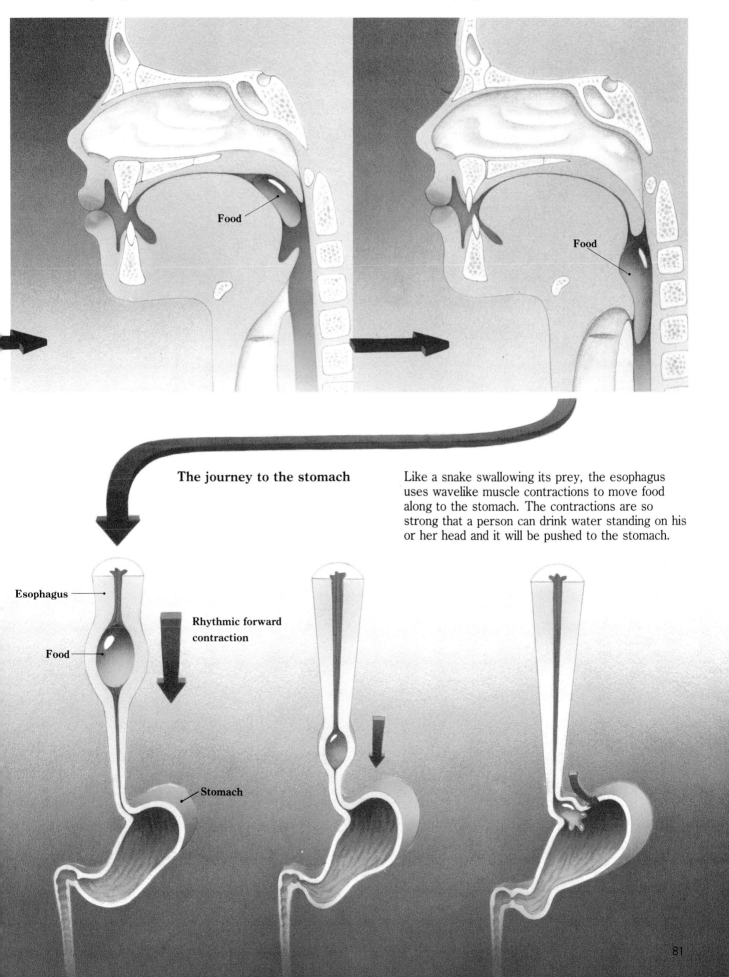

Food

Food

The journey to the stomach

Like a snake swallowing its prey, the esophagus uses wavelike muscle contractions to move food along to the stomach. The contractions are so strong that a person can drink water standing on his or her head and it will be pushed to the stomach.

Esophagus

Rhythmic forward contraction

Food

Stomach

Why Doesn't the Stomach Digest Itself?

Once through the esophagus, food reaches the stomach, a muscular, baglike organ that digests food with strong acids known as gastric juices. Produced by glands in the stomach lining, the gastric juices are made of hydrochloric acid and protein-digesting enzymes such as pepsin.

Because the stomach is itself made of protein, it has to keep from being digested along with the food. Therefore, the stomach lining is coated with a thick layer of mucus that protects against the acidic digestive juices. Furthermore, the enzyme pepsin enters the stomach in an inactive form called pepsinogen, which does not harm the stomach lining; it only becomes active when it combines with other juices. The stomach also sheds half a million cells a minute, so damaged cells are quickly replaced. Stress can cause the mucous membrane to thin out, however, allowing gastric juices to attack the stomach lining. The result can be a painful stomach ulcer.

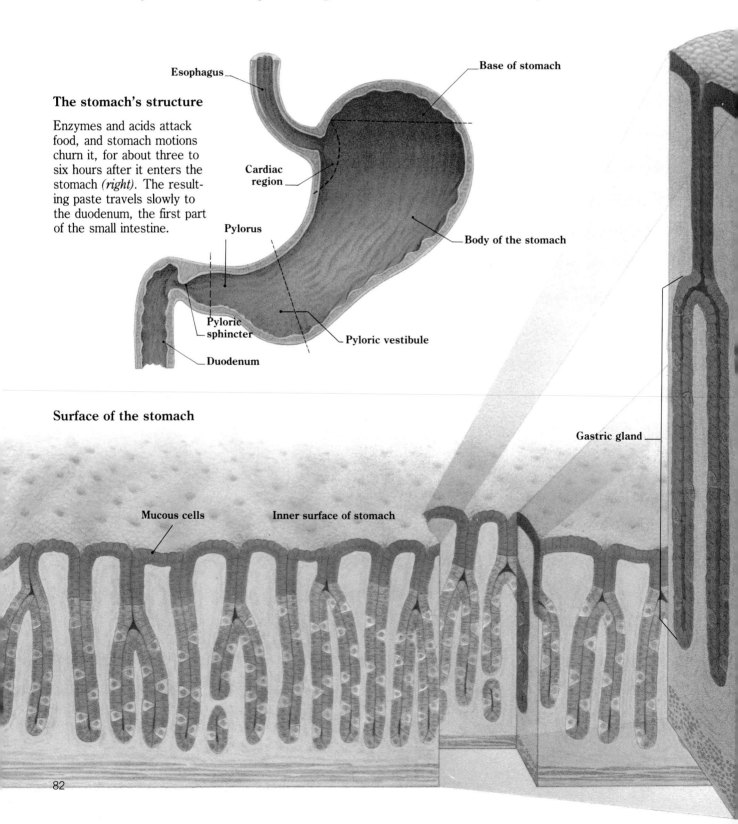

The stomach's structure

Enzymes and acids attack food, and stomach motions churn it, for about three to six hours after it enters the stomach *(right)*. The resulting paste travels slowly to the duodenum, the first part of the small intestine.

Esophagus

Base of stomach

Cardiac region

Pylorus

Body of the stomach

Pyloric sphincter

Duodenum

Pyloric vestibule

Surface of the stomach

Gastric gland

Mucous cells

Inner surface of stomach

Protecting stomach walls

Glands on the surface of the stomach walls contain both the cells that produce gastric juices and the cells that protect the stomach from those juices. For digestion, oxyntic cells secrete hydrochloric acid while chief cells produce pepsinogen. Mucous cells, meanwhile, secrete mucus to protect the stomach lining. Inactive pepsinogen becomes active protein-digesting pepsin only after mixing with hydrochloric acid in an area covered by a thick layer of mucus.

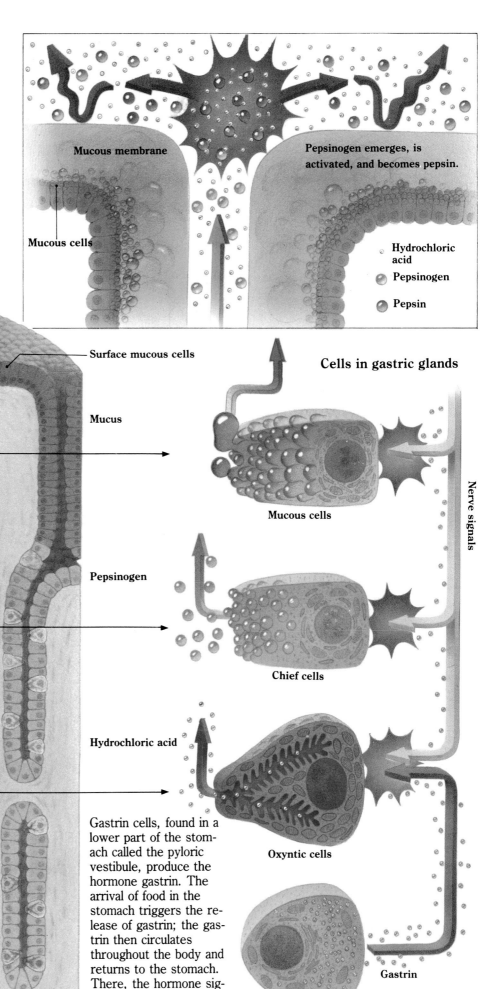

Mucous membrane

Mucous cells

Pepsinogen emerges, is activated, and becomes pepsin.

○ Hydrochloric acid

◉ Pepsinogen

◉ Pepsin

Surface mucous cells

Mucus

Pepsinogen

Hydrochloric acid

Cells in gastric glands

Nerve signals

Mucous cells

Chief cells

Oxyntic cells

Gastrin

Gastrin cells

Gastrin cells, found in a lower part of the stomach called the pyloric vestibule, produce the hormone gastrin. The arrival of food in the stomach triggers the release of gastrin; the gastrin then circulates throughout the body and returns to the stomach. There, the hormone signals to the glands to produce pepsinogen and other gastric juices.

What Does the Pancreas Do?

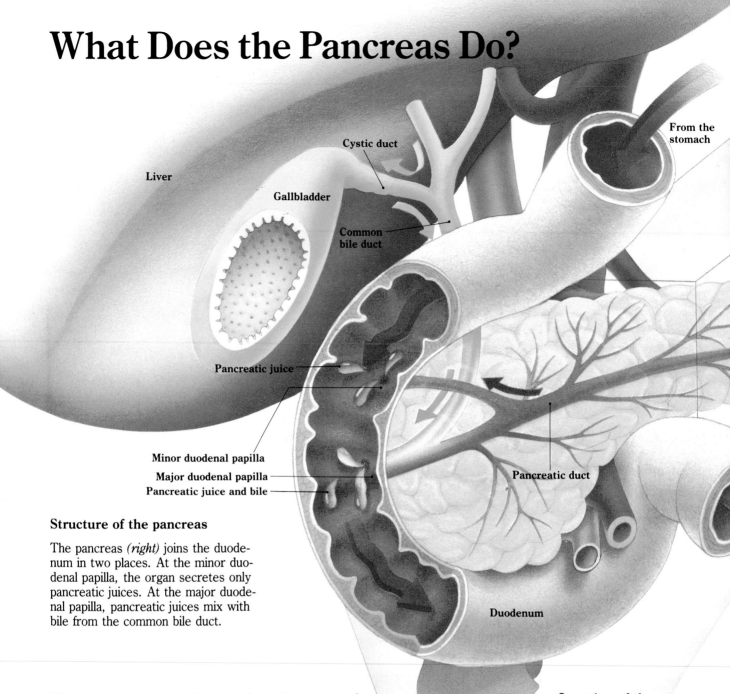

Cystic duct

Liver

Gallbladder

Common bile duct

From the stomach

Pancreatic juice

Minor duodenal papilla

Major duodenal papilla

Pancreatic juice and bile

Pancreatic duct

Duodenum

Structure of the pancreas

The pancreas *(right)* joins the duodenum in two places. At the minor duodenal papilla, the organ secretes only pancreatic juices. At the major duodenal papilla, pancreatic juices mix with bile from the common bile duct.

The pancreas—tucked neatly into the curve of the duodenum, the first part of the small intestine—behaves like two organs: One releases digestive enzymes to the duodenum, and the other releases important hormones to the blood. Because of this dual role—the result of two very different types of cells—the pancreas is known as both an exocrine gland and an endocrine gland.

The pancreas is about 6 inches long, 2 inches wide, and almost an inch thick. A group of lobes (rounded portions) in the organ, called acini, produce four important digestive enzymes. These travel through a series of small ducts to the main pancreatic duct. That duct carries the enzymes into the duodenum. Between the acini are groups of ductless cells known as islets of Langerhans, named after a nineteenth-century German doctor. These cells send hormones directly into the blood to control the level of glucose in the body.

Location of the pancreas

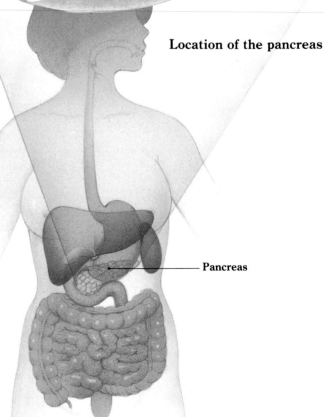

Pancreas

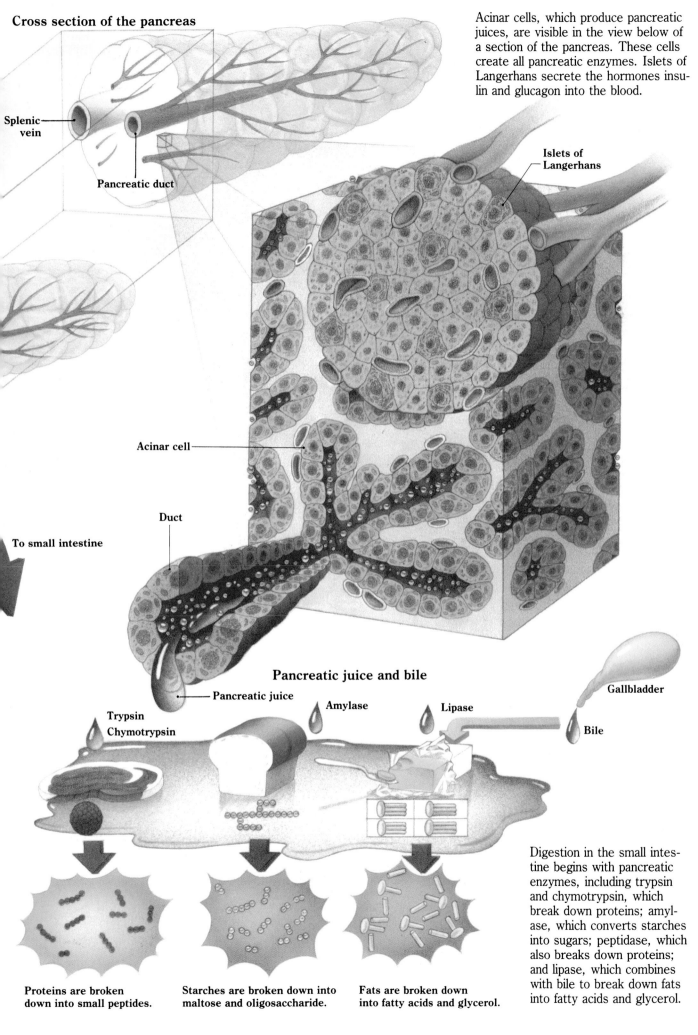

Cross section of the pancreas

Splenic vein

Pancreatic duct

Acinar cells, which produce pancreatic juices, are visible in the view below of a section of the pancreas. These cells create all pancreatic enzymes. Islets of Langerhans secrete the hormones insulin and glucagon into the blood.

Islets of Langerhans

Acinar cell

Duct

To small intestine

Pancreatic juice and bile

Pancreatic juice

Gallbladder

Trypsin
Chymotrypsin

Amylase

Lipase

Bile

Proteins are broken down into small peptides.

Starches are broken down into maltose and oligosaccharide.

Fats are broken down into fatty acids and glycerol.

Digestion in the small intestine begins with pancreatic enzymes, including trypsin and chymotrypsin, which break down proteins; amylase, which converts starches into sugars; peptidase, which also breaks down proteins; and lipase, which combines with bile to break down fats into fatty acids and glycerol.

What Does the Liver Do?

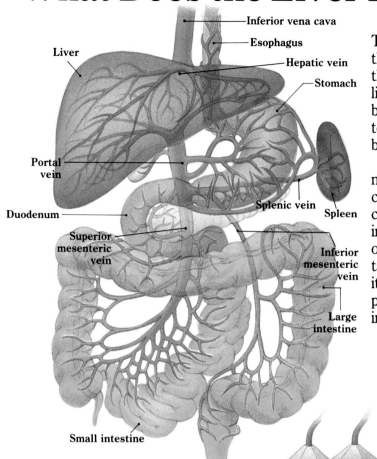

Inferior vena cava
Esophagus
Liver
Hepatic vein
Stomach
Portal vein
Duodenum
Splenic vein
Spleen
Superior mesenteric vein
Inferior mesenteric vein
Large intestine
Small intestine

The liver, the largest organ within the body, is the body's chemical factory. It carries out more than 500 separate tasks, many of them critical to life. The liver stores carbohydrates, controls blood sugar levels, changes harmful ammonia into harmless urea, and makes bile for later use in breaking down fats in the duodenum.

The liver is located in the upper right abdomen, just below the diaphragm. It is made of closely packed units of cells and blood vessels, called hepatic lobules. Bathing the organ, bringing it nutrition as well as poisons to be filtered out, is blood from the hepatic artery and the portal vein. Because the liver has so many functions, its cells must be replaced frequently. Even if 90 percent of the liver were removed, the remaining 10 percent could regenerate the entire organ.

The liver and blood vessels

The portal vein, formed by the union of three other veins, brings nutrient-laden blood from the digestive tract *(above)* to the liver. The hepatic artery carries oxygen-rich blood from the heart.

The hepatic lobules

The surface of the liver looks like smooth, reddish rubber, but close examination shows it to be a remarkable collection of 50,000 to 100,000 tiny units of tissue, called lobules. A cross section of the lobules *(right)* reveals orderly systems of cells interwoven with bile ducts and blood vessels. At the core of each lobule is a central vein. Blood from branches of both the portal vein and the hepatic artery passes through spaces between the cells called sinusoids.

The cells take nutrients from the blood and change toxic substances into harmless ones. Old blood cells and bacteria are disposed of by Kupffer cells and carried to the central vein. Bile created by liver cells flows from the bile canaliculi to the bile ducts, which lead to the gallbladder.

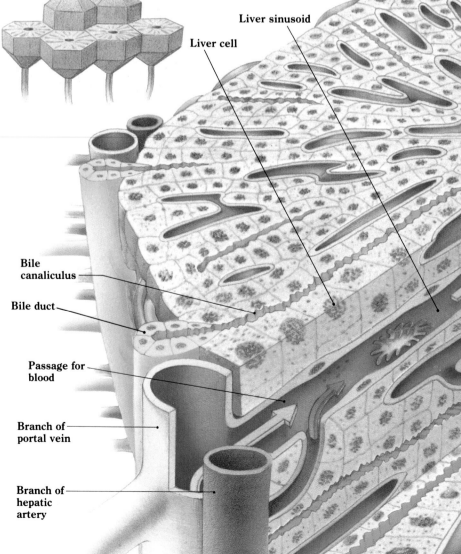

Liver sinusoid
Liver cell
Bile canaliculus
Bile duct
Passage for blood
Branch of portal vein
Branch of hepatic artery

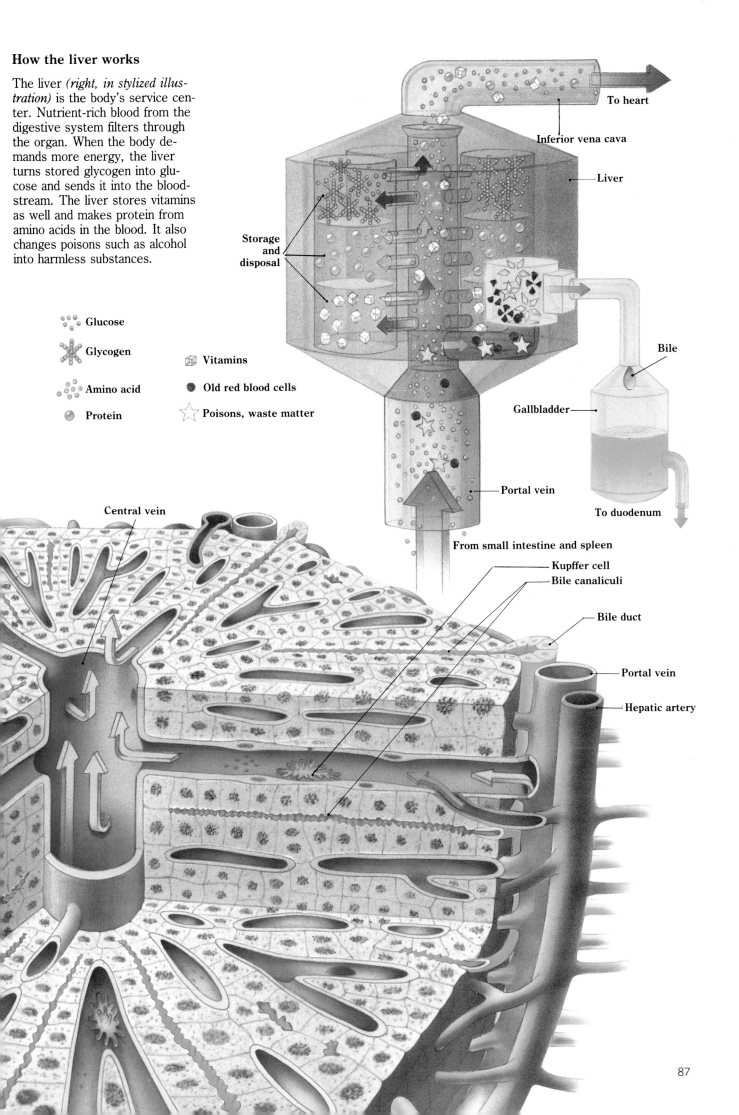

How the liver works

The liver *(right, in stylized illustration)* is the body's service center. Nutrient-rich blood from the digestive system filters through the organ. When the body demands more energy, the liver turns stored glycogen into glucose and sends it into the bloodstream. The liver stores vitamins as well and makes protein from amino acids in the blood. It also changes poisons such as alcohol into harmless substances.

Glucose

Glycogen

Amino acid

Protein

Vitamins

Old red blood cells

Poisons, waste matter

To heart

Inferior vena cava

Liver

Storage and disposal

Bile

Gallbladder

Portal vein

To duodenum

From small intestine and spleen

Central vein

Kupffer cell

Bile canaliculi

Bile duct

Portal vein

Hepatic artery

87

What Does the Small Intestine Do?

Lining of the small intestine

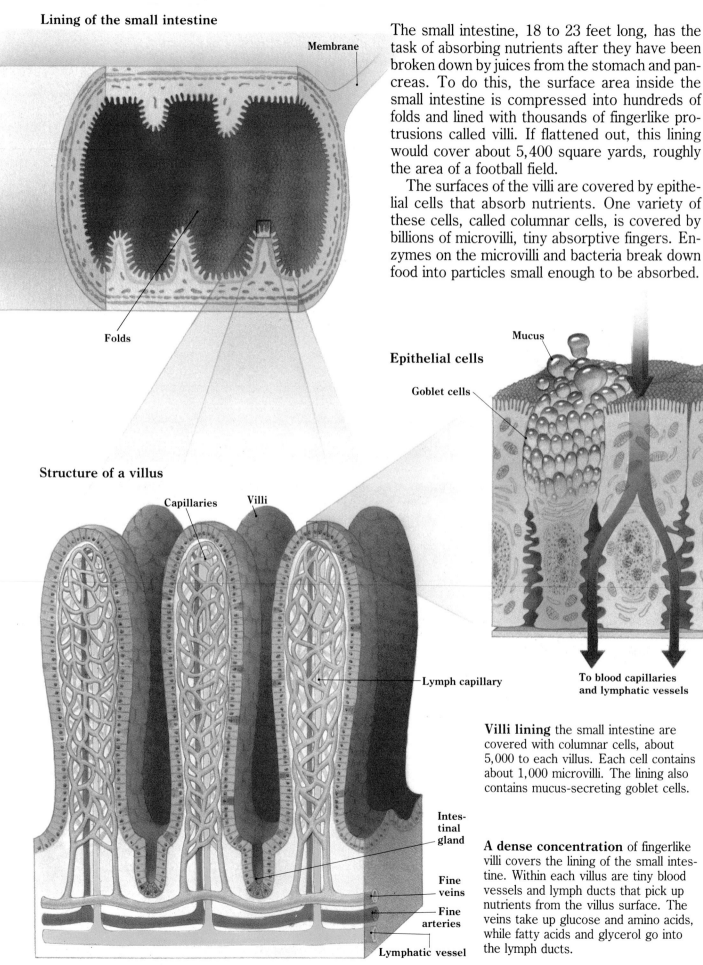

Membrane

Folds

The small intestine, 18 to 23 feet long, has the task of absorbing nutrients after they have been broken down by juices from the stomach and pancreas. To do this, the surface area inside the small intestine is compressed into hundreds of folds and lined with thousands of fingerlike protrusions called villi. If flattened out, this lining would cover about 5,400 square yards, roughly the area of a football field.

The surfaces of the villi are covered by epithelial cells that absorb nutrients. One variety of these cells, called columnar cells, is covered by billions of microvilli, tiny absorptive fingers. Enzymes on the microvilli and bacteria break down food into particles small enough to be absorbed.

Epithelial cells

Mucus

Goblet cells

To blood capillaries
and lymphatic vessels

Structure of a villus

Capillaries

Villi

Lymph capillary

Intestinal gland

Fine veins

Fine arteries

Lymphatic vessel

Villi lining the small intestine are covered with columnar cells, about 5,000 to each villus. Each cell contains about 1,000 microvilli. The lining also contains mucus-secreting goblet cells.

A dense concentration of fingerlike villi covers the lining of the small intestine. Within each villus are tiny blood vessels and lymph ducts that pick up nutrients from the villus surface. The veins take up glucose and amino acids, while fatty acids and glycerol go into the lymph ducts.

The surface of microvilli

The space between the microvilli in the small intestines is so tiny that nutrients arrive there in a form too big to be absorbed. To deal with this, the microvilli have chemicals called end digestive enzymes on their surfaces, and these enzymes break down the nutrients to a digestible size. This prevents the nutrients from being stolen by the many bacteria in the small intestine. The nutrient-eating bacteria are too big to fit between the microvilli, so when a nutrient is broken down by the end digestive enzyme, the bacteria can't get to it.

Nutrients

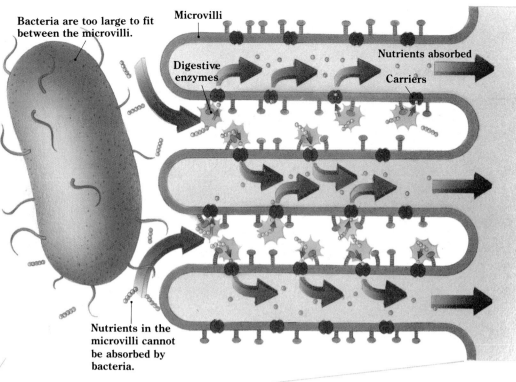

Bacteria are too large to fit between the microvilli.

Microvilli

Digestive enzymes

Nutrients absorbed

Carriers

Nutrients in the microvilli cannot be absorbed by bacteria.

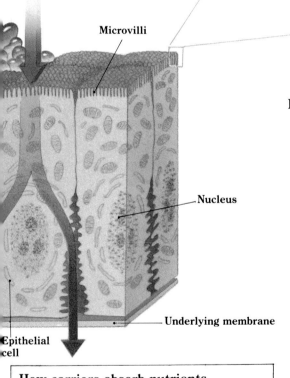

Microvilli

Nucleus

Underlying membrane

Epithelial cell

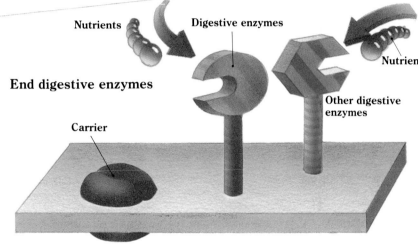

Nutrients

Digestive enzymes

Nutrients

End digestive enzymes

Carrier

Other digestive enzymes

Nutrients are broken down when they meet matching enzymes.

Carriers absorb the nutrients.

Enzyme does not match.

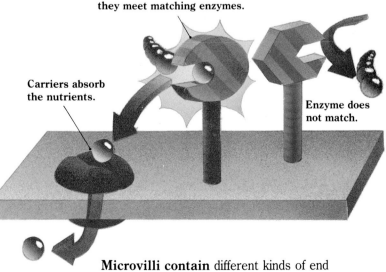

How carriers absorb nutrients

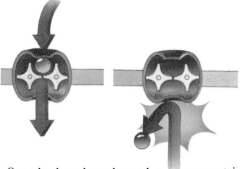

Once broken down by end enzymes, nutrients are quickly absorbed by nearby protein enzyme carriers. Nutrients can only pass through the carriers in one direction.

Microvilli contain different kinds of end enzymes, each one matched to only one type of nutrient. When an enzyme comes in contact with the wrong kind of nutrient, nothing happens. When it meets its matching nutrient, the enzyme quickly breaks it down for absorption.

89

What Is the Large Intestine's Job?

The large intestine is the last section of the digestive tract. It has two tasks: removing water from remaining food waste, thereby creating semisolid feces; and storing the feces until they are expelled through the anus.

About 5 feet long and 2 to 3 inches thick, the large intestine is divided into three sections: the cecum, the colon, and the rectum. Matter from the small intestine enters the large intestine at the pouchlike cecum. At one end of the cecum is the appendix, a tube, several inches long, with no known role in digestion, although it contains lymph nodes and may play a part in the immune system. As waste moves from the cecum through the ascending colon, transverse colon, and descending colon, water is absorbed and feces are created. The feces are excreted through the anus. The entire digestive process, from eating to excreting, usually takes between 12 and 24 hours.

Duodenum

Moving food

6-18 hours

Transverse colon

Fluid state

Peristaltic motion

Ascending colon

Fluid state

4-15 hours

Cecum

Appendix

External muscle band

Large intestine section

Intestinal glands

Blood vessels

Lymph nodes

Smooth muscle

A flat mucous membrane, supporting intestinal glands, lines the large intestine. Below it is a layer of tissue containing lymph nodes as well as blood vessels to carry water to the liver. A thin layer of muscle surrounding the intestine helps to move the feces.

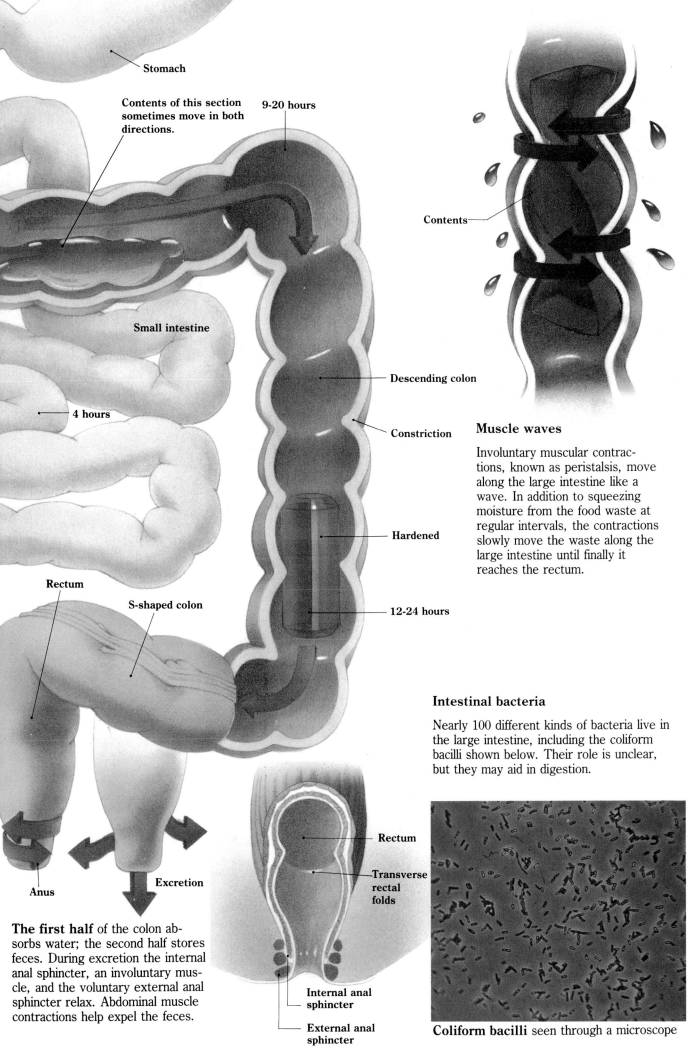

Stomach

Contents of this section sometimes move in both directions.

9-20 hours

Small intestine

4 hours

Descending colon

Constriction

Hardened

12-24 hours

Rectum

S-shaped colon

Anus

Excretion

The first half of the colon absorbs water; the second half stores feces. During excretion the internal anal sphincter, an involuntary muscle, and the voluntary external anal sphincter relax. Abdominal muscle contractions help expel the feces.

Rectum

Transverse rectal folds

Internal anal sphincter

External anal sphincter

Contents

Muscle waves

Involuntary muscular contractions, known as peristalsis, move along the large intestine like a wave. In addition to squeezing moisture from the food waste at regular intervals, the contractions slowly move the waste along the large intestine until finally it reaches the rectum.

Intestinal bacteria

Nearly 100 different kinds of bacteria live in the large intestine, including the coliform bacilli shown below. Their role is unclear, but they may aid in digestion.

Coliform bacilli seen through a microscope

How Does Digestion Work?

A girl bites into an apple and the process of digestion begins.

When food enters the mouth, it begins a journey through the body's digestive system during which nearly everything of nutritional value is absorbed. By the time digestion is complete, only fiber, fats, and other waste matter are left to be excreted.

Digestion begins in the mouth. Teeth grind the food, while chemicals in saliva, primarily one called amylase, turn starches into sugars. Once food is swallowed, the stomach takes over, using muscle contractions to mix the food with gastric juices containing enzymes such as pepsin, which breaks down proteins. Food then moves to the first section of the small intestine, called the duodenum, where some juices from the pancreas continue the breakdown of proteins and carbohydrates, while others work with bile from the liver to break down fats.

The small intestine takes in almost all of the nutrients the body needs. The large intestine absorbs moisture from the matter that is left, then excretes the waste from the anus. The portal vein carries most of the nutrients and moisture absorbed during digestion to the liver.

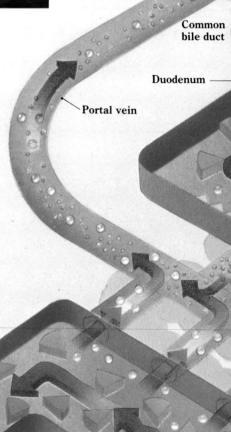

Liver

Common bile duct

Duodenum

Portal vein

Anus

Waste is excreted as feces.

Large intestine

Transverse colon

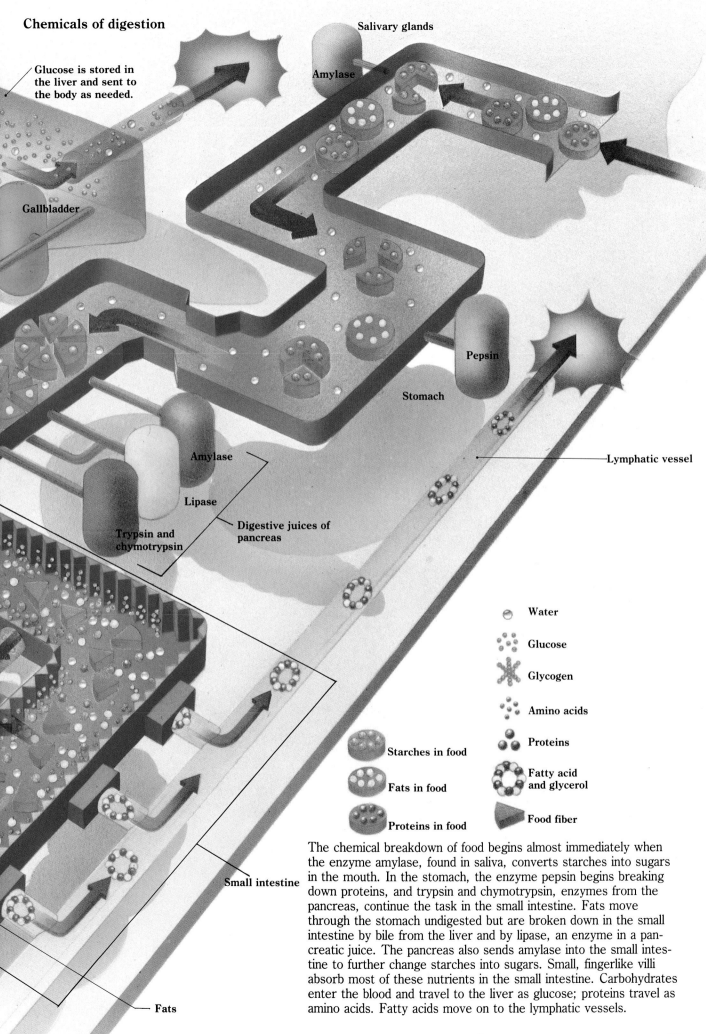

Chemicals of digestion

Glucose is stored in the liver and sent to the body as needed.

Salivary glands

Amylase

Gallbladder

Pepsin

Stomach

Amylase

Lipase

Trypsin and chymotrypsin

Digestive juices of pancreas

Lymphatic vessel

Small intestine

Fats

Water

Glucose

Glycogen

Amino acids

Proteins

Fatty acid and glycerol

Starches in food

Fats in food

Proteins in food

Food fiber

The chemical breakdown of food begins almost immediately when the enzyme amylase, found in saliva, converts starches into sugars in the mouth. In the stomach, the enzyme pepsin begins breaking down proteins, and trypsin and chymotrypsin, enzymes from the pancreas, continue the task in the small intestine. Fats move through the stomach undigested but are broken down in the small intestine by bile from the liver and by lipase, an enzyme in a pancreatic juice. The pancreas also sends amylase into the small intestine to further change starches into sugars. Small, fingerlike villi absorb most of these nutrients in the small intestine. Carbohydrates enter the blood and travel to the liver as glucose; proteins travel as amino acids. Fatty acids move on to the lymphatic vessels.

93

What Do the Kidneys Do?

Kidneys, two organs about the size of fists, are located on each side of the spine behind the stomach. The right kidney sits below the liver and, as a result, is slightly lower than the left kidney. The bean-shaped organs work hard, filtering wastes out of the body's blood about 240 times a day, cleaning a total of about 475 gallons. This helps to balance the body's chemistry.

As the blood enters the kidney through the renal artery, it is filtered through tiny structures called nephrons—about one million in each kidney. Much of the liquid is reabsorbed into the bloodstream after passing through a cuplike structure known as Bowman's capsule and reaching tubes called uriniferous tubules. About 1 percent of the liquid reaching the tubules is not useful for the body, however, and is sent to the bladder as urine.

The structure of the kidneys

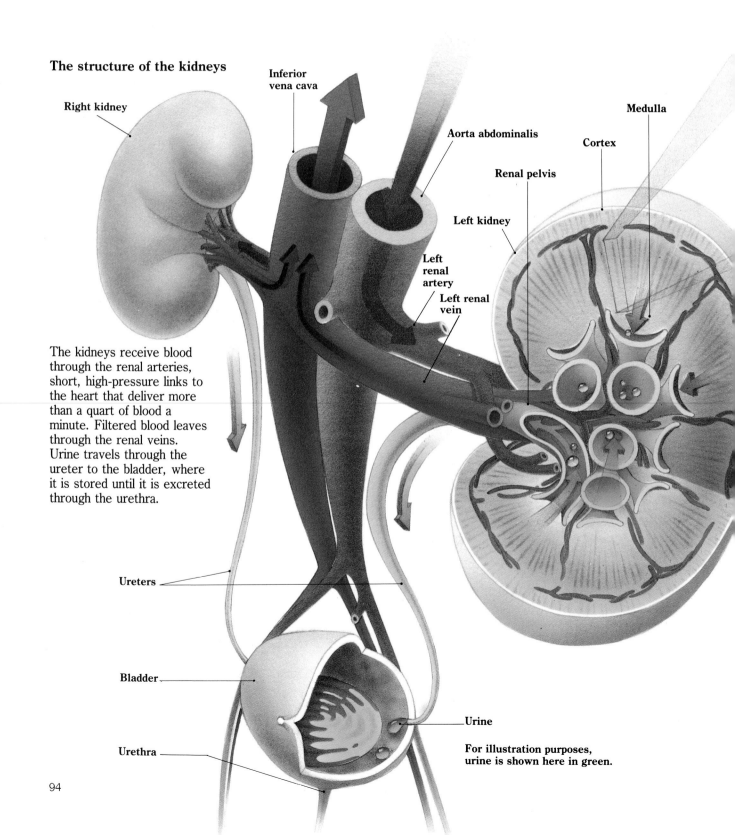

Right kidney

Inferior vena cava

Aorta abdominalis

Renal pelvis

Left kidney

Left renal artery

Left renal vein

Medulla

Cortex

The kidneys receive blood through the renal arteries, short, high-pressure links to the heart that deliver more than a quart of blood a minute. Filtered blood leaves through the renal veins. Urine travels through the ureter to the bladder, where it is stored until it is excreted through the urethra.

Ureters

Bladder

Urethra

Urine

For illustration purposes, urine is shown here in green.

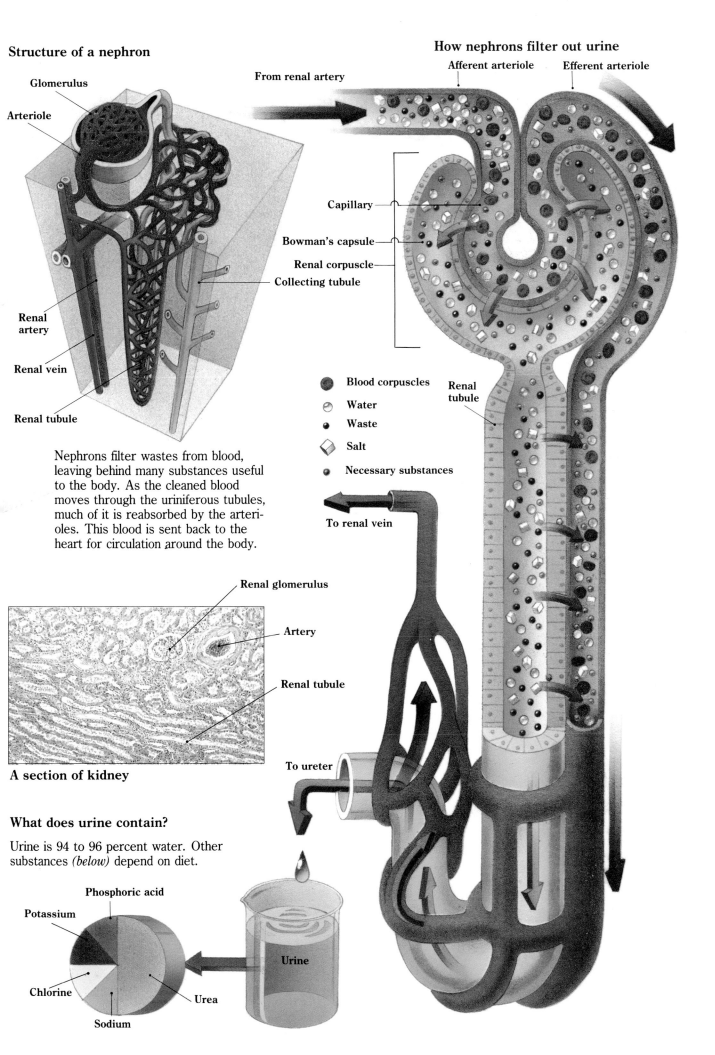

Structure of a nephron

Glomerulus

Arteriole

Renal artery

Renal vein

Renal tubule

Nephrons filter wastes from blood, leaving behind many substances useful to the body. As the cleaned blood moves through the uriniferous tubules, much of it is reabsorbed by the arterioles. This blood is sent back to the heart for circulation around the body.

A section of kidney

Renal glomerulus

Artery

Renal tubule

What does urine contain?

Urine is 94 to 96 percent water. Other substances *(below)* depend on diet.

Phosphoric acid

Potassium

Chlorine

Sodium

Urea

Urine

How nephrons filter out urine

From renal artery

Afferent arteriole

Efferent arteriole

Capillary

Bowman's capsule

Renal corpuscle

Collecting tubule

Renal tubule

- ● Blood corpuscles
- ◉ Water
- • Waste
- ◇ Salt
- ◉ Necessary substances

To renal vein

To ureter

5
The Amazing Nervous System

The human nervous system—made up of the brain, the spinal cord, and the peripheral nerves—is an engineering and communications marvel. The tiniest movement of the body owes its completion to the workings of this system. The nervous system will protect the body from harm, notify it when fuel is needed, maintain balance in practically any situation, shut itself down for rest and recuperation, and adapt to the abuses and injuries the body receives in a lifetime.

The basic functional unit of the nervous system is the nerve cell, or neuron. Each neuron consists of a cell body with long nerve fibers projecting from it. These cells, 97 percent of them located in the brain and spinal cord, are present at birth and do not reproduce. Instead of increasing the number of its neurons, the nervous system grows by developing additional nerve fibers and creating complex networks.

The sensory organs—the eyes, ears, nose, tongue, and skin—receive information from the outside world and pass it via the nerves to the brain, which responds by sending commands to the body over another set of neural pathways. Thanks to this flow of data, the human body can adapt to darkness and bright light, sip a drink without spilling a drop, calculate mathematical equations, and perform a wide range of other physical and mental feats.

The brain, a complex organ that weighs only about 3 pounds, serves as the body's command center. It is shown at right in four different views: from above *(top left)*, from below *(top right)*, from the left side *(bottom right)*, and in cross section.

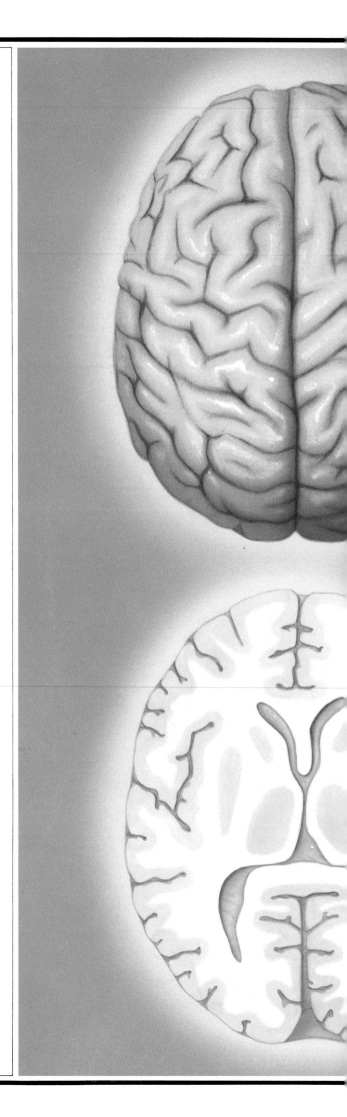

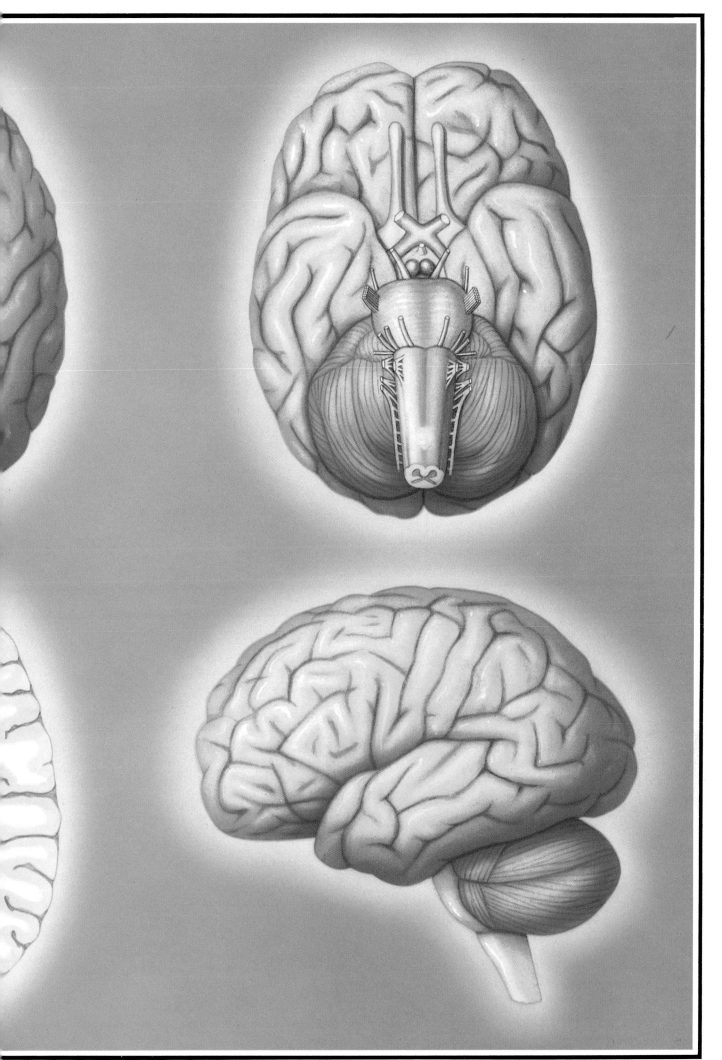

How Does Skin Feel Pain and Heat?

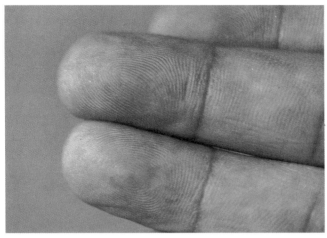

Fingertips are among the most sensitive skin surfaces.

To protect the body, the skin must register a number of sensations—pain, heat and cold, touch and pressure—and relay them to the brain. The parts of the nervous system that detect these feelings are called receptors, located at nerve endings buried in the skin. Most receptors are in the middle layer of the skin. Others appear in the outer layer, while the inner layer has the fewest.

Different receptors pick up different sensations, and receptors are distributed unevenly over the skin. Some areas of the skin are therefore more sensitive than others to certain stimuli. The lips and tongue, for example, are more sensitive to heat than the elbows or the thighs.

1 Near the surface, free nerve endings sense pain and heat.
2 The onion-shaped Pacinian corpuscles sense pressure. They are the largest and deepest receptors.
3 Ruffini endings detect touch and pressure.
4 Krause end bulbs sense coldness.
5 Meissner's corpuscles are sensitive to touch.

For every feeling, a receptor

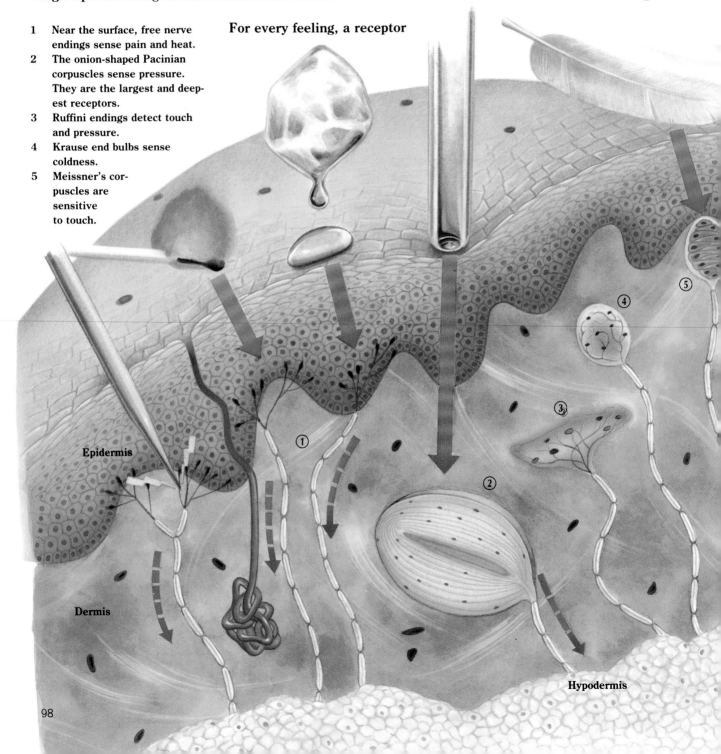

Epidermis

Dermis

Hypodermis

Two points or one?

The chart at right shows the results of a "two-point discrimination test," which measures the sensitivity of various areas of the skin. Two points on the skin are pricked at the same time. Then two more points— slightly closer to each other— are pricked. The test continues until the person feels the two points as one. The closer the points get, the more sensitivity it requires to tell them apart. The most sensitive skin is on the fingertips, the tongue, and the lips.

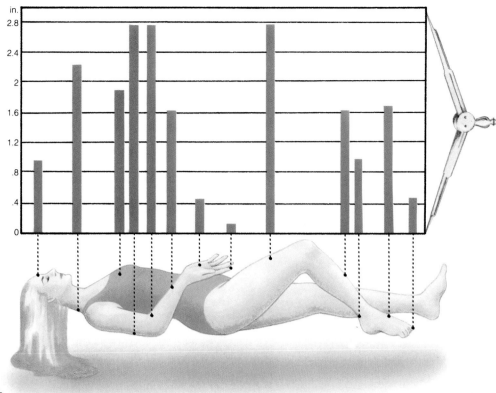

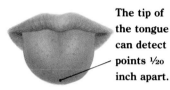

The tip of the tongue can detect points ½₀ inch apart.

Detecting the slightest touch

When a hair tip is gently touched, free nerve endings woven around its follicle instantly send a message to the brain.

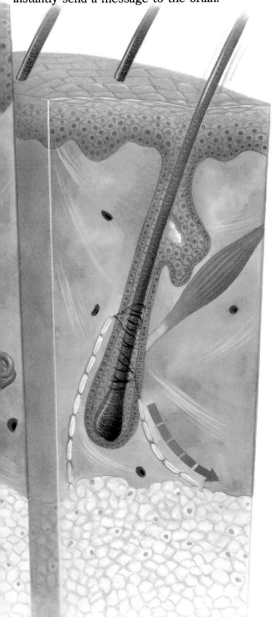

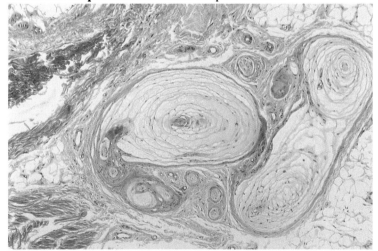

Pacinian corpuscles are buried deep in the skin.

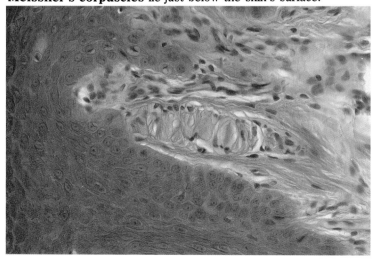

Meissner's corpuscles lie just below the skin's surface.

The tip of the tongue can detect points 1/20 inch apart.

How Do Feelings Reach the Brain?

When a body part comes in contact with another object—when, for example, the finger touches a glass of cold water—receptors in the skin detect the contact and fire off a minute electrical current called a nerve impulse. The nerve impulse travels immediately through billions of nerve fibers to the spinal cord, where it is relayed to the brain. Nerves that send an impulse from a receptor to the brain are called sensory nerves. Those that send a message from the brain to a muscle are motor nerves.

A nerve cell, or neuron, is a three-part conduit designed for speed. At one end of the neuron are several dendrites, or networks of branching fibers. The dendrites receive nerve impulses and conduct them to the cell body, a tiny gob of sticky fluid, called cytoplasm, that surrounds a central nucleus. The cell body forwards the impulses to the axon, a vinelike transmitter that carries the signals to the dendrites of other neurons. An axon can measure from $\frac{1}{100}$ of an inch to more than 3 feet in length.

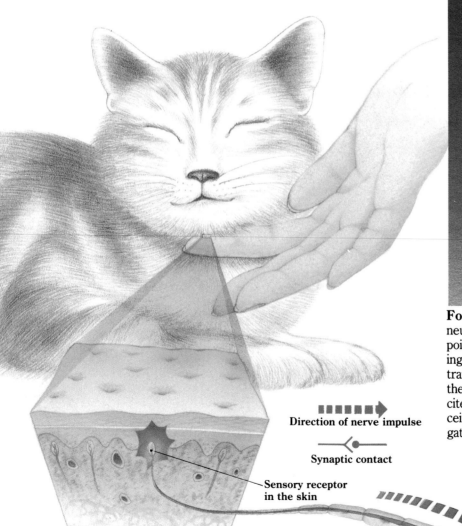

■ **A synapse in action**

Nerve impulse

Postsynaptic membrane

Presynaptic membrane

Mitochondria

Neurotransmitters—molecules of acetylcholine—excite receptors in the receiving cell, then return to the axon terminal *(steps 1-7)*.

For a nerve impulse to pass from one neuron to the next, it must cross a contact point known as a synapse *(above)*. The sending neuron releases chemicals called neurotransmitters into the synaptic cleft between the two neurons. The neurotransmitters excite receptors on the membrane of the receiving neuron, causing an impulse to propagate along the second neuron.

■■■■■■➤
Direction of nerve impulse

——●◀——
Synaptic contact

Sensory receptor in the skin

Node of Ranvier

Sensory receptors in the finger stroking this cat's chin communicate the feeling to the brain through a series of nerve impulses, or chemically produced electrical bursts. Sensory nerves are not consciously controlled.

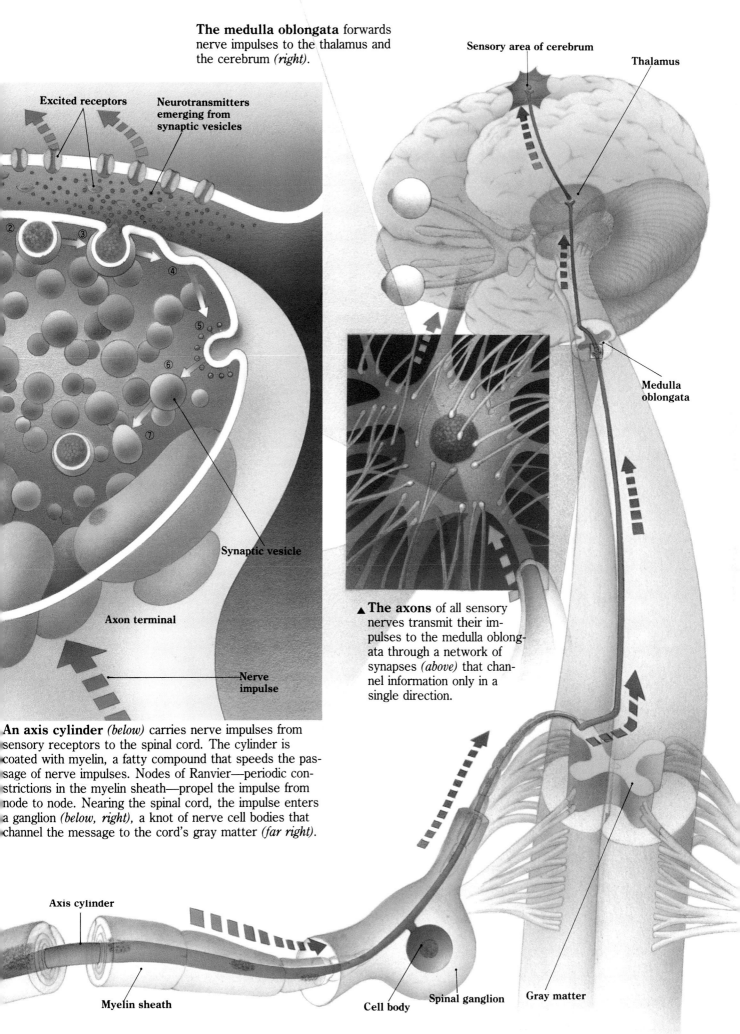

The medulla oblongata forwards nerve impulses to the thalamus and the cerebrum *(right)*.

Excited receptors

Neurotransmitters emerging from synaptic vesicles

② ③ ④ ⑤ ⑥ ⑦

Synaptic vesicle

Axon terminal

Nerve impulse

An axis cylinder *(below)* carries nerve impulses from sensory receptors to the spinal cord. The cylinder is coated with myelin, a fatty compound that speeds the passage of nerve impulses. Nodes of Ranvier—periodic constrictions in the myelin sheath—propel the impulse from node to node. Nearing the spinal cord, the impulse enters a ganglion *(below, right)*, a knot of nerve cell bodies that channel the message to the cord's gray matter *(far right)*.

Axis cylinder

Myelin sheath

Sensory area of cerebrum

Thalamus

Medulla oblongata

▲ **The axons** of all sensory nerves transmit their impulses to the medulla oblongata through a network of synapses *(above)* that channel information only in a single direction.

Cell body

Spinal ganglion

Gray matter

What Is a Reflex Action?

A reflex action is one of the many ways the body protects itself from harm. Designed to occur at maximum speed, the action takes place involuntarily—that is, without any immediate instructions from the brain. When a finger comes in contact with something very hot, for example, the hand pulls away instantly and automatically. The stimulus is felt and the response is carried out before the brain even realizes the danger.

Because this reaction bypasses the nerve pathway to the brain, it is often called a spinal reflex. Heat receptors in the fingertip produce a nerve impulse that is flashed to a reflex center in the spinal cord. The reflex center immediately orders the appropriate arm muscles to contract, removing the finger from danger.

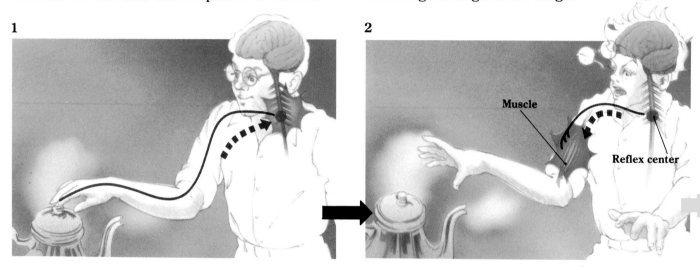

A system built for speed

A simple matter of distance explains why a reflex action, diagramed at right, is so much faster than a reaction controlled by the brain. From the point of sensory contact—in this case, a burned fingertip—the nerve impulses need travel only as far as the spinal cord to elicit a response. The brain will not register the pain until a few thousandths of a second after the finger has been drawn back.

Neurons that carry impulses to the spinal cord and brain are called afferent neurons. Efferent neurons carry impulses from the nervous system to a muscle.

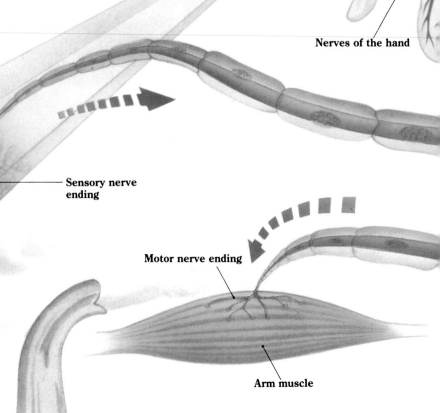

Finger surface

Sensory nerve ending

Nerves of the hand

Motor nerve ending

Arm muscle

How a reflex action works

When a finger touches a hot object like the teapot shown below, afferent neurons transmit impulses signifying "Pain!" to the spinal cord. There an intermediate neuron shunts the impulses to the appropriate efferent neurons, which order muscles in the arm to contract and withdraw the finger. Milliseconds later, the sensation of pain reaches the cerebrum, so that heat is felt only after the body has remedied the situation. This unconscious reflex action minimizes the risk of a bad burn.

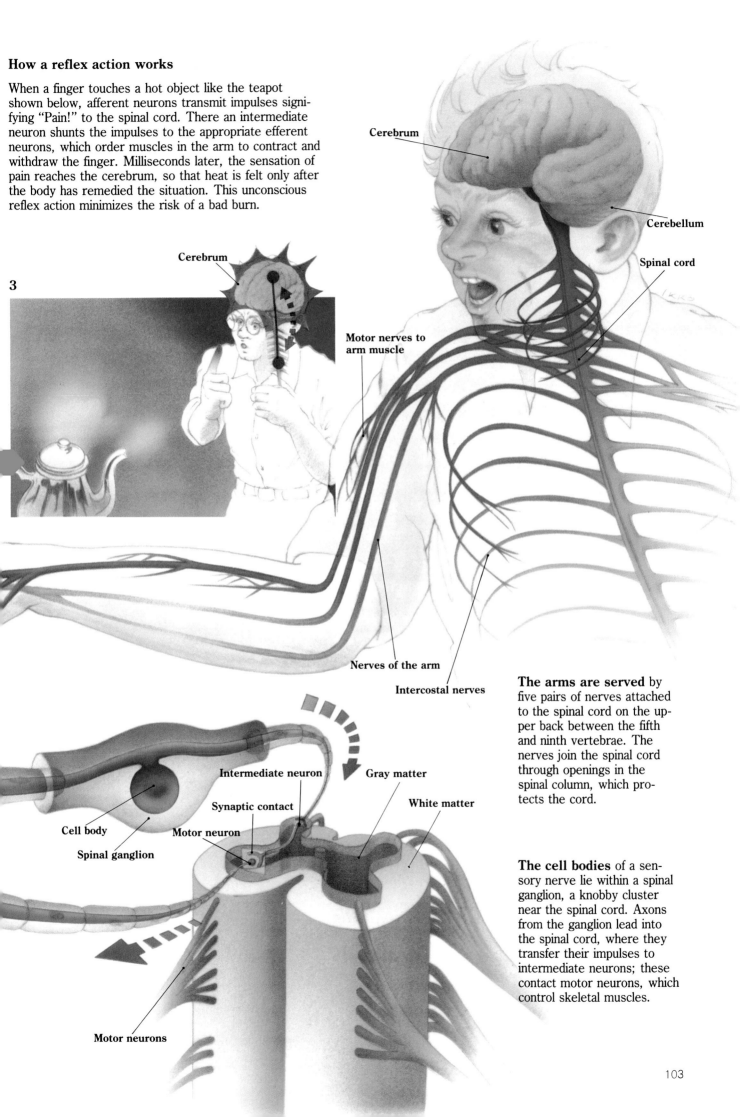

3

Cerebrum

Cerebrum

Cerebellum

Spinal cord

Motor nerves to arm muscle

Nerves of the arm

Intercostal nerves

Intermediate neuron

Gray matter

Synaptic contact

White matter

Cell body

Motor neuron

Spinal ganglion

Motor neurons

The arms are served by five pairs of nerves attached to the spinal cord on the upper back between the fifth and ninth vertebrae. The nerves join the spinal cord through openings in the spinal column, which protects the cord.

The cell bodies of a sensory nerve lie within a spinal ganglion, a knobby cluster near the spinal cord. Axons from the ganglion lead into the spinal cord, where they transfer their impulses to intermediate neurons; these contact motor neurons, which control skeletal muscles.

103

Why Does the Brain Have Ridges?

The surface of the brain is covered with ridges and grooves, called convolutions, that triple the surface area of the brain's outer layer, or cerebral cortex. The larger surface area makes for a superior brain, because the surface layer is the site where nerve impulses are received and analyzed; it is the place, in short, where thinking occurs and knowledge accumulates.

Beneath the cerebral cortex is the core of the cerebrum, consisting of neuron masses bound up in bundles of nerve fibers *(below)*. The cerebrum is divided front to back by the longitudinal fissure. Each half, or hemisphere, comprises four sections, called lobes. Every lobe is dedicated to one or more specific tasks. The frontal lobe, for example, governs the body's voluntary muscle movements; the temporal lobe interprets impulses from the ears and nose, while the occipital lobe analyzes input from the eye.

Inside the cerebral cortex

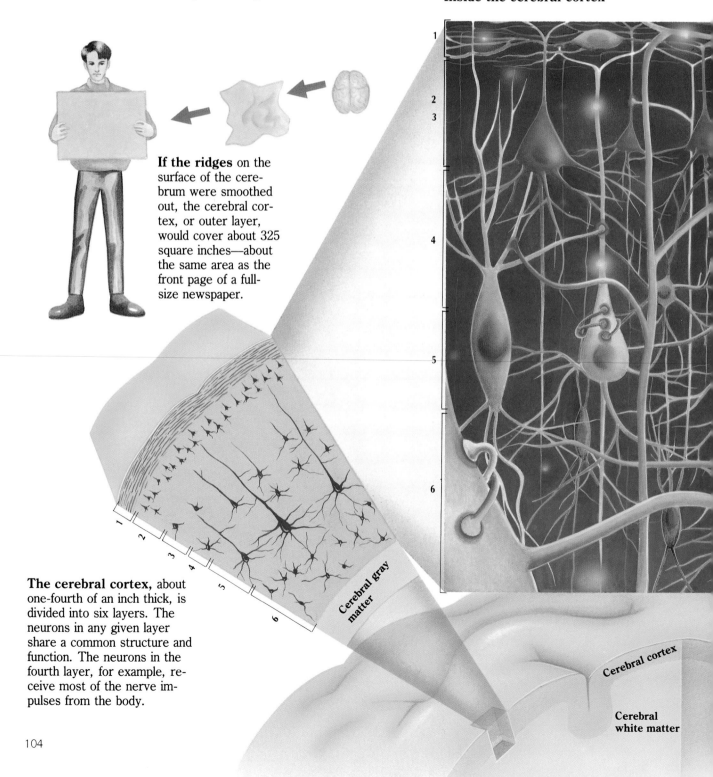

If the ridges on the surface of the cerebrum were smoothed out, the cerebral cortex, or outer layer, would cover about 325 square inches—about the same area as the front page of a full-size newspaper.

The cerebral cortex, about one-fourth of an inch thick, is divided into six layers. The neurons in any given layer share a common structure and function. The neurons in the fourth layer, for example, receive most of the nerve impulses from the body.

Cerebral gray matter

Cerebral cortex

Cerebral white matter

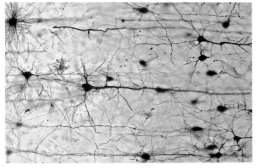

Side view of neurons in the cerebral cortex

As shown below, the cerebral cortex is a labyrinth of neurons—some 14 billion in all—that form a multitude of connections with one another. Impulses leave the cortex through the cells of each of the six layers.

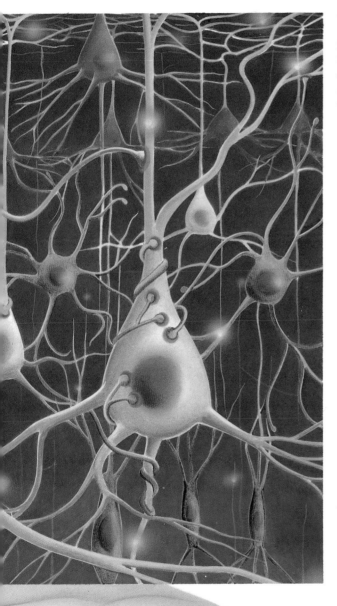

A center for motion and senses

The neurons that govern the body's movements occupy the motor cortex, a narrow strip in front of the central sulcus, or fissure, of the cerebral cortex *(bottom illustration).* The sensory cortex, which controls the senses, lies behind the motor cortex, on the other side of the central sulcus. Listed below are the 11 areas influenced by the motor cortex and the 14 areas commanded by the sensory cortex.

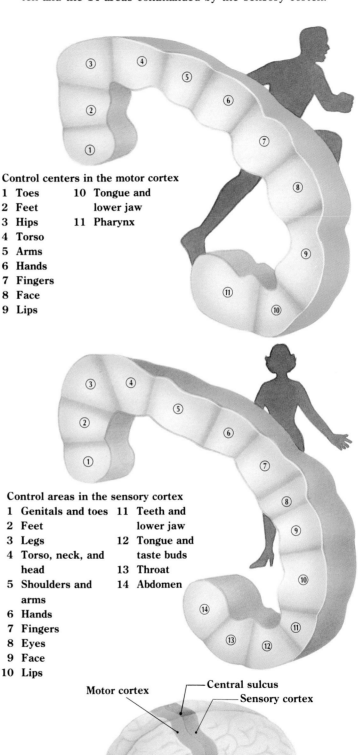

Control centers in the motor cortex

1 Toes	10 Tongue and
2 Feet	lower jaw
3 Hips	11 Pharynx
4 Torso	
5 Arms	
6 Hands	
7 Fingers	
8 Face	
9 Lips	

Control areas in the sensory cortex

1 Genitals and toes	11 Teeth and
2 Feet	lower jaw
3 Legs	12 Tongue and
4 Torso, neck, and	taste buds
head	13 Throat
5 Shoulders and	14 Abdomen
arms	
6 Hands	
7 Fingers	
8 Eyes	
9 Face	
10 Lips	

Motor cortex

Central sulcus

Sensory cortex

Why Do Humans Need Two Eyes?

Two eyes, working together, provide the brain with a remarkable amount of essential information. Because the eyes view an object from approximately the same height but from two separate positions, they see the item from slightly different angles. When these two separate images are relayed to the brain and assembled into a single image, the brain is able to perceive the object in three dimensions. This system is called stereoscopic vision.

The angle at which the eyes see an object changes at various distances, so stereoscopic vision also allows the brain to judge how far away the object is. The position of the eyes is important: Animals with wide-set eyes have poor stereoscopic vision. And though the ability of humans to judge distance through stereoscopic vision requires experience, one thing is certain: Two eyes working together enable a person to see more accurately than one eye working alone.

How stereoscopic vision works

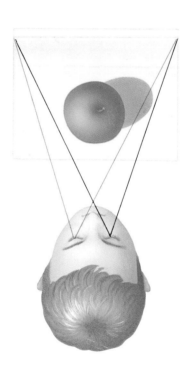

The left eye, working by itself, views this apple from a little to the left of the center of the face. This makes the apple appear to be sitting just to the right of the background's center. This slight distortion is crucial to stereoscopic vision.

The right eye views the apple from a little to the right of center on the face, so the apple seems left of the background's center.

Working together, the two eyes produce a stereoscopic view of the apple in its proper position—centered on the background.

Do you see what I see?

A human's field of vision

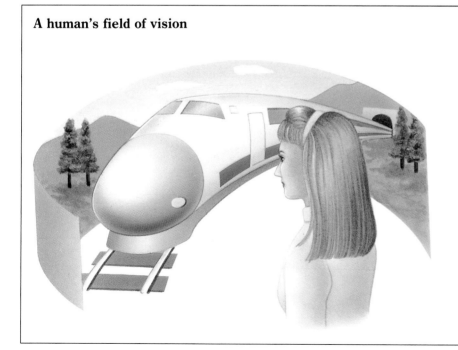

Human eyes—and those of most other animals that hunt—are set roughly in the front of the face. This eye placement limits our field of vision to about 180 degrees *(below)* but allows for stereoscopic vision, which is the key to determining an object's shape and distance. For predators, this information is essential for success.

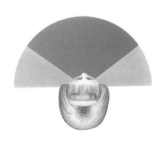

How two eyes produce one image

When a person looks at something *(left),* the retina of each eye produces an image of the object that is reversed and upside down *(below).* The portion of the image that lay in the left visual field is sent via the optic nerve and the optic tract to the right occipital lobe. The portion in the right visual field is sent to the left occipital lobe. The cerebral cortex then combines the two portions to form a single image and reverses and inverts the image, restoring its correct orientation.

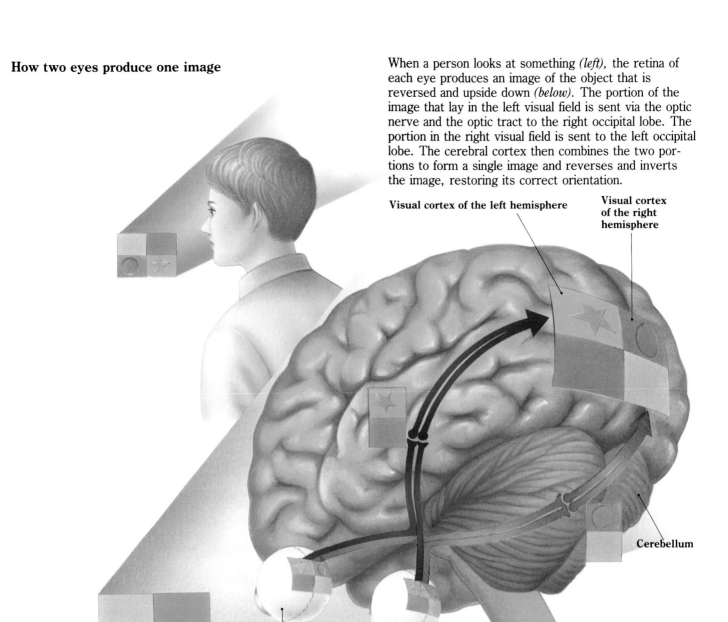

Visual cortex of the left hemisphere

Visual cortex of the right hemisphere

Cerebellum

Left eye　　**Right eye**　　**Brainstem**

A horse's field of vision

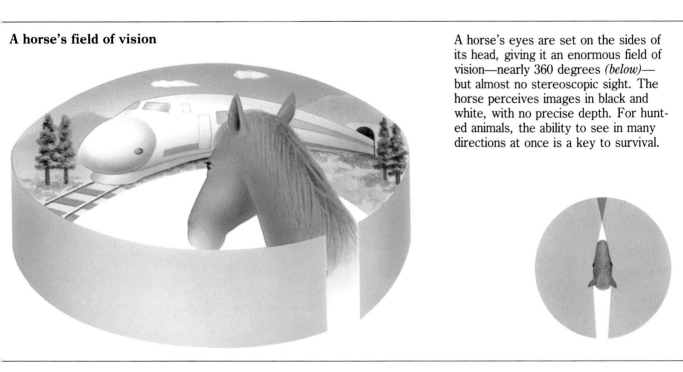

A horse's eyes are set on the sides of its head, giving it an enormous field of vision—nearly 360 degrees *(below)*—but almost no stereoscopic sight. The horse perceives images in black and white, with no precise depth. For hunted animals, the ability to see in many directions at once is a key to survival.

How Do Eyes Adapt to Darkness?

Two special kinds of cells in the eye's retina, or inner lining, help it adjust to darkness and light. Called rods and cones for their distinctive shapes *(right)*, each type of cell plays a specific role. Cones, which are more sensitive to bright light, are responsible for sharp vision and can differentiate colors. Rods, by contrast, are excellent detectors of dim light but cannot distinguish colors; they are used for night vision.

When a person goes outdoors on a sunny day, the cones do the job of transmitting images to the brain because the rods are too saturated in light to work. If the person moves suddenly into a dark room, the rods take over the task.

The process of switching from cones to rods, called darkness adaptation, takes place gradually; this is why a person cannot see clearly the instant he or she enters a darkened room. Similarly, lightness adaptation—the process of switching from rods to cones—requires an adjustment period of several seconds.

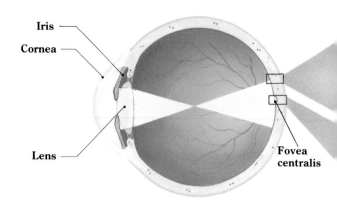

This curve shows how the eyes adjust to total darkness, point A. After 10 minutes, the cones are 100 times more sensitive to light. At point B, the rods take over; at 40 minutes, they are 1,000 times more sensitive than cones.

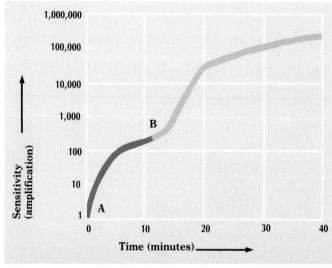

Inside an eyeball looking out

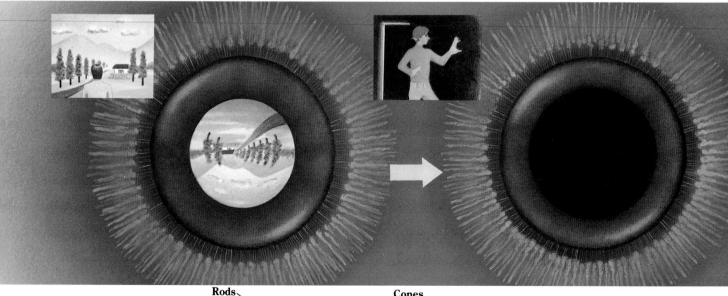

When the eye views something bright in a well-lit place *(above)*, the cones *(right)* send an image of the scene to the brain.

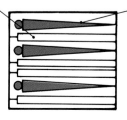

Plunged into darkness, the cones grow more photosensitive, but the rods are not yet activated. The eye therefore registers only darkness.

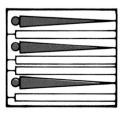

108

How the retina works

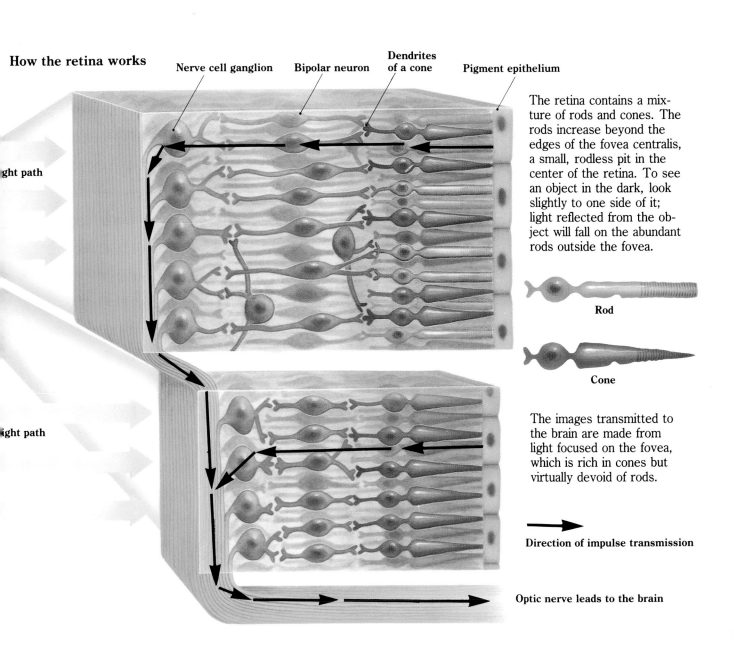

Nerve cell ganglion   Bipolar neuron   Dendrites of a cone   Pigment epithelium

ight path

ight path

The retina contains a mixture of rods and cones. The rods increase beyond the edges of the fovea centralis, a small, rodless pit in the center of the retina. To see an object in the dark, look slightly to one side of it; light reflected from the object will fall on the abundant rods outside the fovea.

Rod

Cone

The images transmitted to the brain are made from light focused on the fovea, which is rich in cones but virtually devoid of rods.

Direction of impulse transmission

Optic nerve leads to the brain

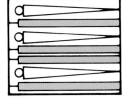

Within a few moments, the rods become sufficiently light-sensitive to transmit a clear image to the brain.

Exposed to bright light again, the rods become saturated and cease to work. Until the cones begin to function, the eye will see only brightness.

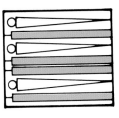

What Causes Vision Defects?

A slight misshaping of one or both eyeballs can cause myopia (nearsightedness), hyperopia (far-sightedness), or astigmatism (uneven focusing in different planes). In a normal eye, the lens at the front of the eye focuses images on the retina at the back of the eye. If the eyeball is too long from front to back, the images of faraway objects will focus slightly in front of the retina, and the viewer will see them as blurred. This condition is called nearsightedness. If the eyeball is too short from front to back, the images of nearby objects will focus beyond the retina, causing farsightedness. Like other vision defects, both conditions appear to be hereditary.

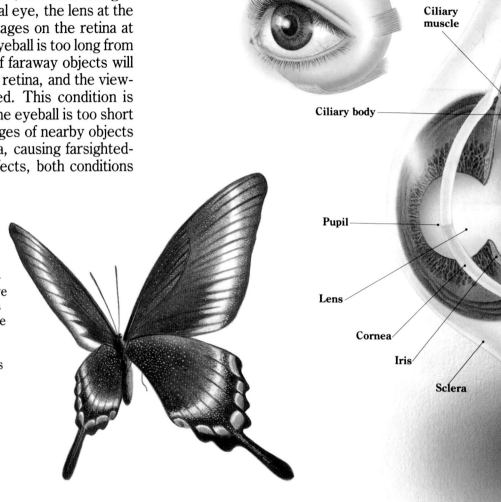

Ciliary muscle

Ciliary body

Pupil

Lens

Cornea

Iris

Sclera

Capturing a butterfly

Light reflected from an object—here, a butterfly—enters the eye through the lens. It then travels through the vitreous humor—the jelly that fills the eyeball—and focuses the image upside down and reversed on the retina. This image passes over the optic nerves to the brain, which restores its proper orientation.

● The nearsighted eye

The eyeball shown in a side view at right is too long from front to back; only the images of nearby objects focus properly on the retina.

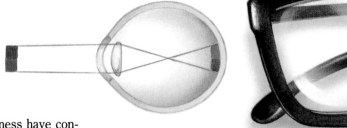

Eyeglasses used to correct nearsightedness have concave lenses; their rear surfaces curve toward the wearer. The lenses diffuse light rays about to enter the eye.

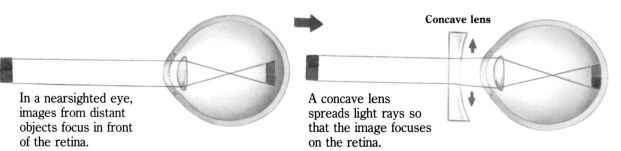

Concave lens

In a nearsighted eye, images from distant objects focus in front of the retina.

A concave lens spreads light rays so that the image focuses on the retina.

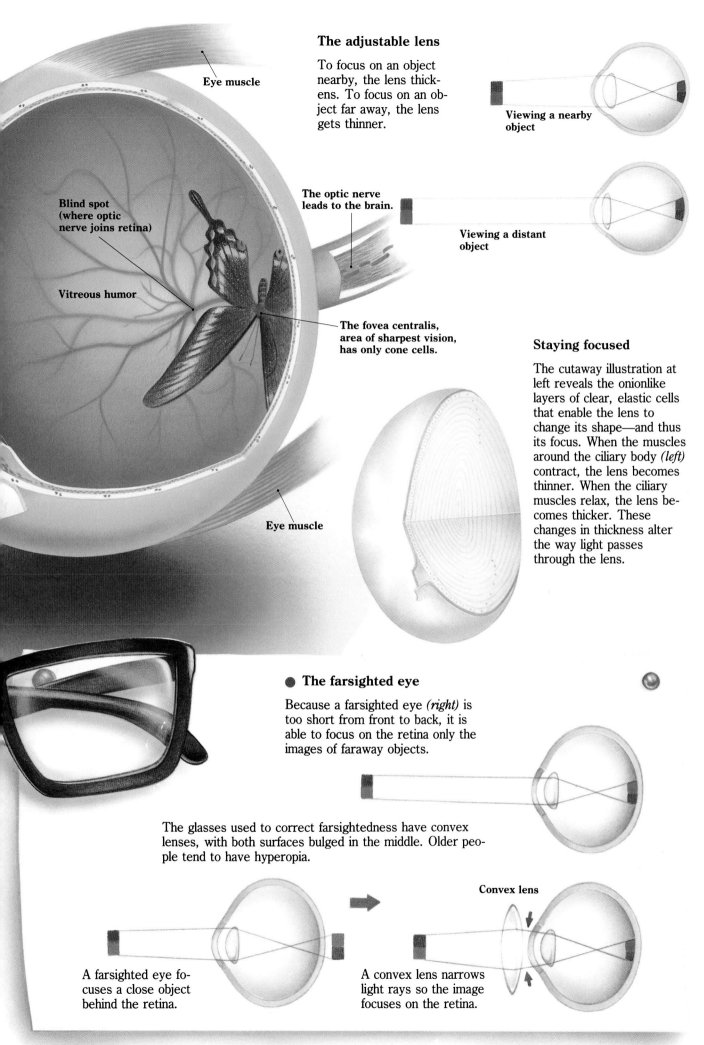

The adjustable lens

To focus on an object nearby, the lens thickens. To focus on an object far away, the lens gets thinner.

Viewing a nearby object

Viewing a distant object

Eye muscle

Blind spot (where optic nerve joins retina)

Vitreous humor

The optic nerve leads to the brain.

The fovea centralis, area of sharpest vision, has only cone cells.

Eye muscle

Staying focused

The cutaway illustration at left reveals the onionlike layers of clear, elastic cells that enable the lens to change its shape—and thus its focus. When the muscles around the ciliary body *(left)* contract, the lens becomes thinner. When the ciliary muscles relax, the lens becomes thicker. These changes in thickness alter the way light passes through the lens.

● The farsighted eye

Because a farsighted eye *(right)* is too short from front to back, it is able to focus on the retina only the images of faraway objects.

The glasses used to correct farsightedness have convex lenses, with both surfaces bulged in the middle. Older people tend to have hyperopia.

Convex lens

A farsighted eye focuses a close object behind the retina.

A convex lens narrows light rays so the image focuses on the retina.

How Does the Ear Identify Sounds?

The ear is an extremely sensitive and specialized organ. It has three main sections: the outer ear, the middle ear, and the inner ear. Each area plays a crucial role in identifying sounds.

Like a funnel channeling liquids into a bottle, the cartilage flap of the outer ear directs sound waves into the ear canal. When the sound waves hit the eardrum—the boundary of the middle ear—they make it vibrate. Inside the middle ear, three tiny bones amplify the vibrations and pass them through a bony plate, the oval window, which forms the entry to the inner ear.

Whereas the middle ear is filled with air, the inner ear is filled with fluid. For example, the cochlea—a bony coil whose name means "snail shell"—contains a watery fluid known as perilymph. The perilymph conducts the vibrations of the oval window to the cochlear duct, one of three coiled tubes that follow the inner contours of the cochlea. Along one side of the duct is the basilar membrane, a film lined with sensory cells collectively known as the organ of Corti. High tones are sensed by the organ of Corti at the base of the cochlea, low tones at the top.

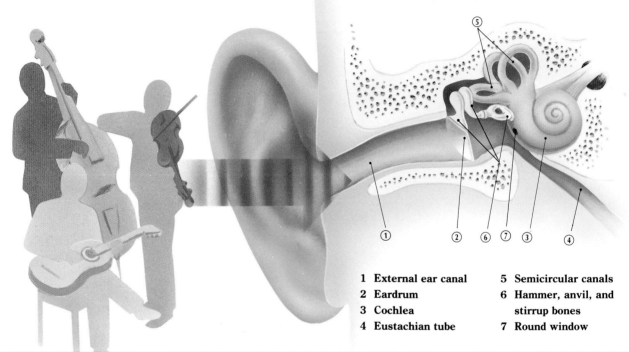

1	External ear canal	5	Semicircular canals
2	Eardrum	6	Hammer, anvil, and
3	Cochlea		stirrup bones
4	Eustachian tube	7	Round window

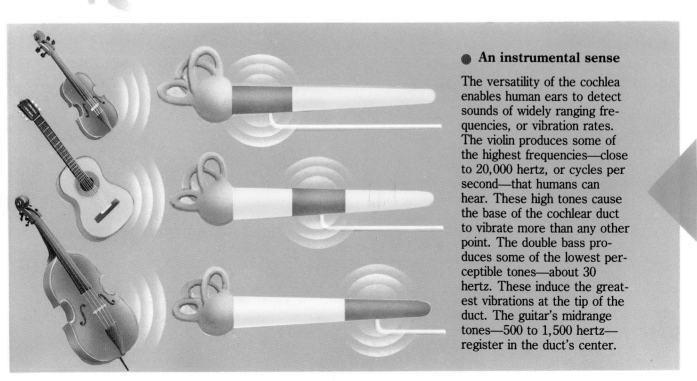

● An instrumental sense

The versatility of the cochlea enables human ears to detect sounds of widely ranging frequencies, or vibration rates. The violin produces some of the highest frequencies—close to 20,000 hertz, or cycles per second—that humans can hear. These high tones cause the base of the cochlear duct to vibrate more than any other point. The double bass produces some of the lowest perceptible tones—about 30 hertz. These induce the greatest vibrations at the tip of the duct. The guitar's midrange tones—500 to 1,500 hertz—register in the duct's center.

A sinuous trip for sound waves

Seen in cross section *(below)*, the cochlea reveals its fluid-filled inner passages. Vibrations enter the cochlea via the bony oval window and spiral in toward the center through the vestibular canal; they exit via the tympanic canal and the round window. On the way, the vibrations are relayed to the cochlear duct, where they become nerve impulses and are sent to the brain.

Vibrations from the perilymph (1) are picked up by the basilar membrane (2) of the cochlear duct. Auditory receptor cells (3), which make up the organ of Corti, have hairlike tips (4) buried in the tectorial membrane (5). The receptors send impulses to the brain via the cochlear nerve (6).

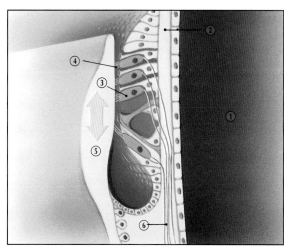

← Sounds moving through vestibular canal

→ Sounds moving through tympanic canal

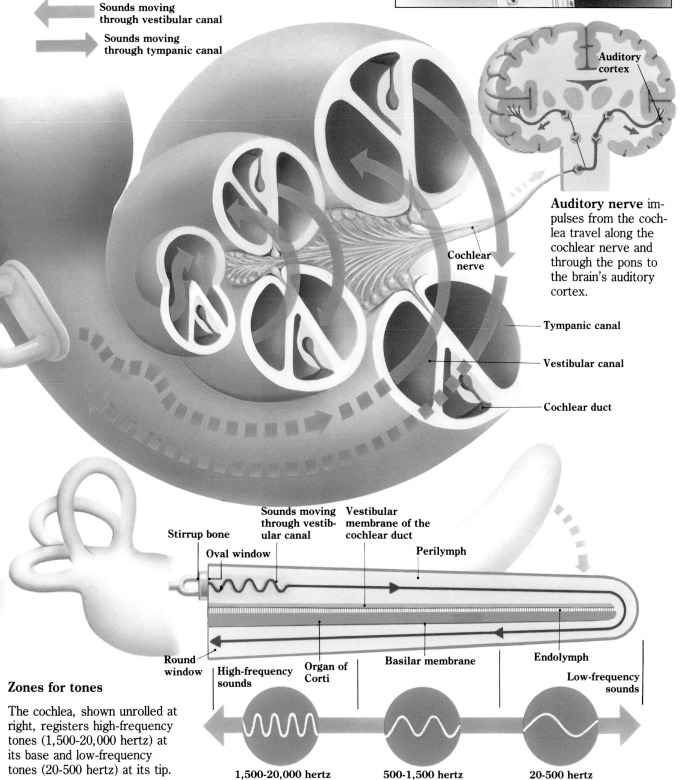

Auditory cortex

Auditory nerve impulses from the cochlea travel along the cochlear nerve and through the pons to the brain's auditory cortex.

Cochlear nerve

Tympanic canal

Vestibular canal

Cochlear duct

Stirrup bone

Oval window

Sounds moving through vestibular canal

Vestibular membrane of the cochlear duct

Perilymph

Round window

High-frequency sounds

Organ of Corti

Basilar membrane

Endolymph

Low-frequency sounds

Zones for tones

The cochlea, shown unrolled at right, registers high-frequency tones (1,500-20,000 hertz) at its base and low-frequency tones (20-500 hertz) at its tip.

1,500-20,000 hertz

500-1,500 hertz

20-500 hertz

Why Does Spinning Cause Dizziness?

Dizziness stems from a loss of equilibrium—the ability to detect motion and rotation. The sense of equilibrium is provided by the semicircular canals, three bony loops that branch out from the base of the cochlea. Each canal is lined with hair cells surrounded by a fluid called lymph. When the head tilts, the lymph causes the bristles to sway in the opposite direction, generating nerve impulses that inform the brain of the body's orientation. If a person spins around and then stops suddenly, the lymph briefly continues to flow, and the hair cells continue to send impulses signifying motion. This conflict between what the body is doing and what it is being told causes temporary dizziness.

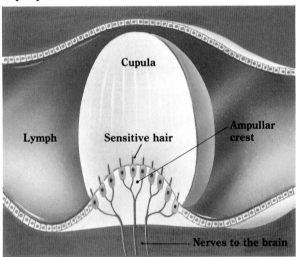

A jelly-covered detective

Cupula

Lymph

Sensitive hair

Ampullar crest

Nerves to the brain

When the head swivels, turns, or nods, lymph flows against the jellylike cupula, bending it and moving the sensitive hairs of the ampullar crest. Hair cells detect the movement and send impulses to the brain.

Keeping an even keel

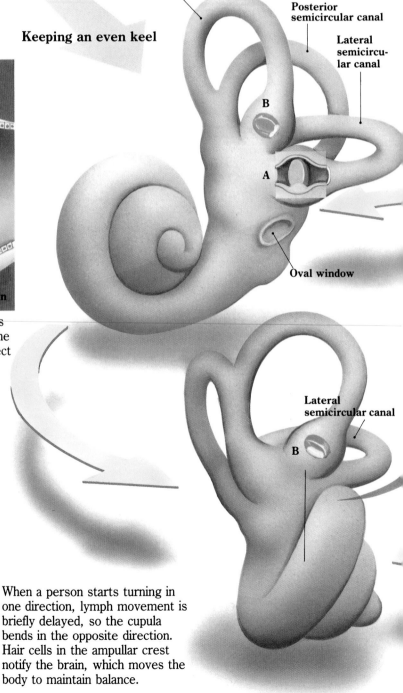

Anterior semicircular canal

Posterior semicircular canal

Lateral semicircular canal

B

A

Oval window

Lateral semicircular canal

B

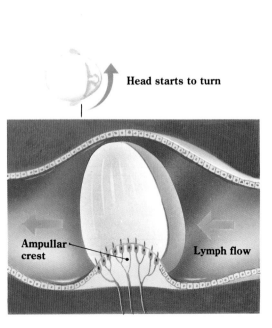

Head starts to turn

Ampullar crest

Lymph flow

When a person starts turning in one direction, lymph movement is briefly delayed, so the cupula bends in the opposite direction. Hair cells in the ampullar crest notify the brain, which moves the body to maintain balance.

● A tubular system

The cochlea and the semicircular canals are membranous tubes, filled with endolymph, that nestle inside a larger tube, the bony labyrinth. Between the outer walls of the membranous labyrinth and the inner walls of the bony labyrinth is a fluid called perilymph. The receptors that help maintain equilibrium line both sets of tubes.

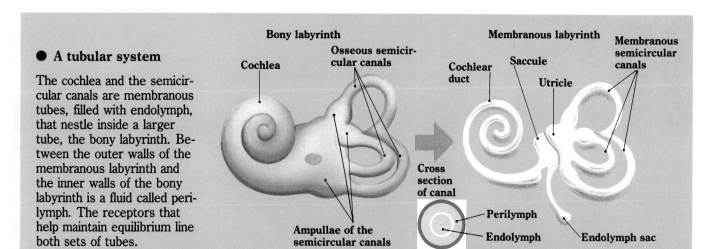

Bony labyrinth
Cochlea
Osseous semicircular canals
Ampullae of the semicircular canals
Cross section of canal
Perilymph
Endolymph

Membranous labyrinth
Cochlear duct
Saccule
Utricle
Membranous semicircular canals
Endolymph sac

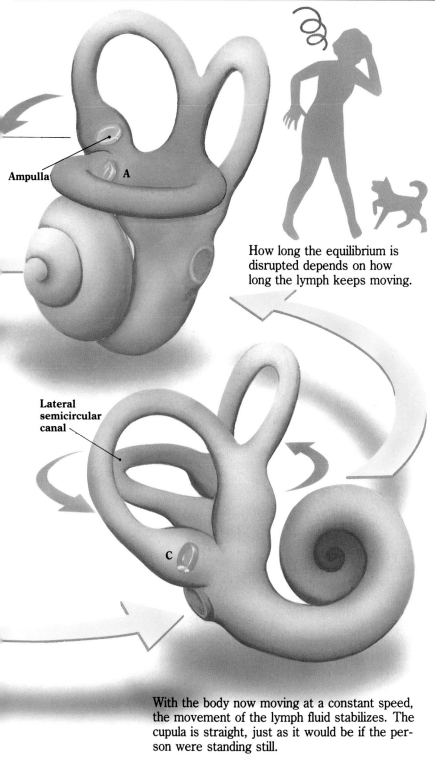

Ampulla
A
Lateral semicircular canal
C

How long the equilibrium is disrupted depends on how long the lymph keeps moving.

With the body now moving at a constant speed, the movement of the lymph fluid stabilizes. The cupula is straight, just as it would be if the person were standing still.

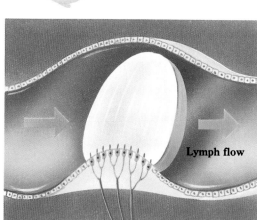

Turn ends in sudden stop

Lymph flow

When the person suddenly stops spinning, inertia (here, an object's tendency to retain its velocity along a straight line) keeps the lymph flowing, so the cupula remains bent in the direction of movement. The body has stopped, yet the hair cells still detect movement and so inform the brain. This disrupts the body's equilibrium, producing brief dizziness.

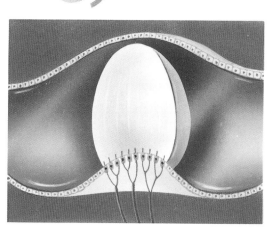

Head continues turning

115

How Are Odors Detected?

Odors are molecules of evaporated chemicals floating in the air. When these airborne particles are drawn in through a nostril, they rise upward until they come in contact with a small patch of skin—only about half a square inch—called the olfactory epithelium.

Mucus, the thin layer of watery material that covers the olfactory epithelium, is essential to the sense of smell. It dissolves the odor molecules and makes them accessible to the hairlike cilia that project into the mucus from receptor cells in the membrane.

Scientists have yet to determine precisely how the receptor cells identify various odors. They do know, however, that the receptors are versatile enough to distinguish about 10,000 different odors and sensitive enough to detect one part mercaptan (a sulfur compound) in 460 million parts air.

Impulses from the olfactory epithelium are channeled to the olfactory bulb, which integrates the signals sent by groups of similar receptors and relays them to the brain. The impulses travel along the olfactory nerve, passing through the thalamus and hypothalamus, to reach the olfactory areas near the cerebral cortex.

Airborne odor molecules enter the nose.

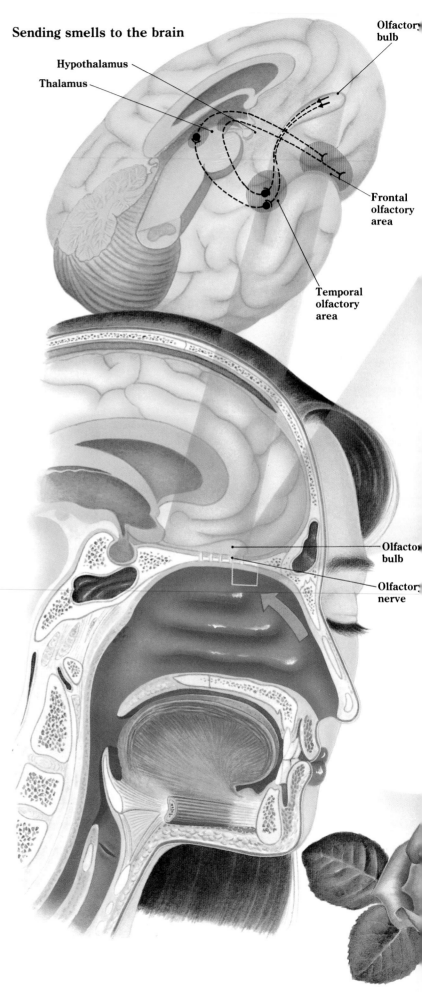

Sending smells to the brain

Olfactory bulb

Hypothalamus

Thalamus

Frontal olfactory area

Temporal olfactory area

Olfactory bulb

Olfactory nerve

A membrane designed for smell

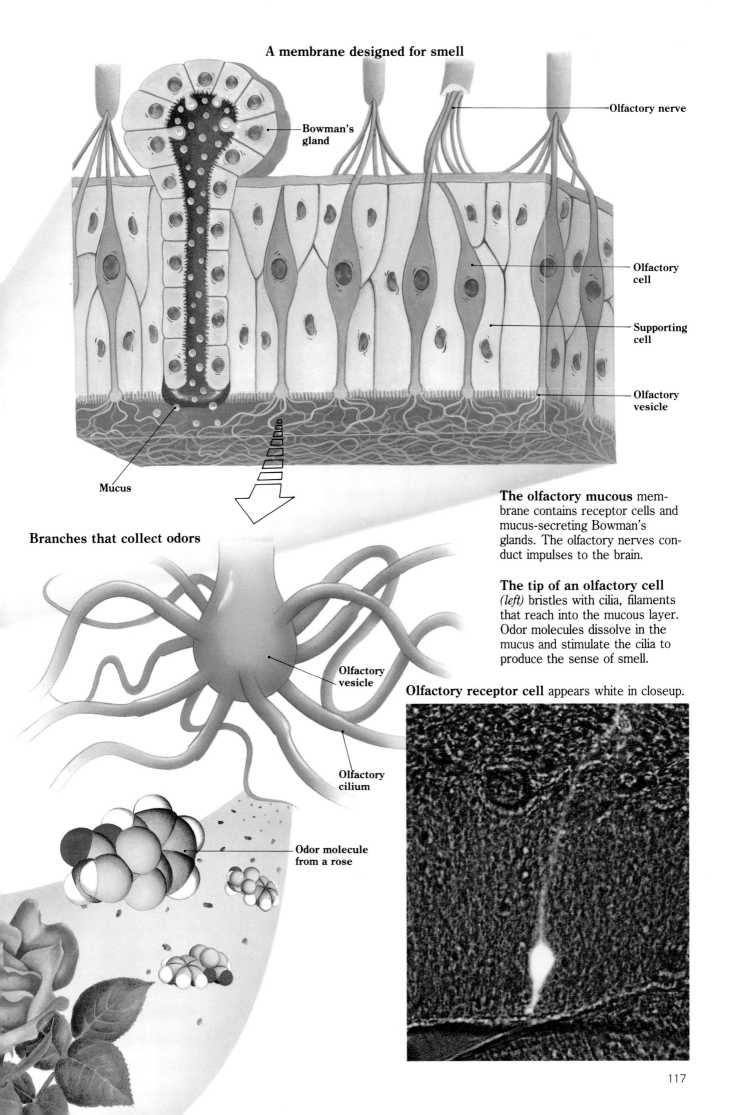

Bowman's gland

Olfactory nerve

Olfactory cell

Supporting cell

Olfactory vesicle

Mucus

Branches that collect odors

Olfactory vesicle

Olfactory cilium

Odor molecule from a rose

The olfactory mucous membrane contains receptor cells and mucus-secreting Bowman's glands. The olfactory nerves conduct impulses to the brain.

The tip of an olfactory cell *(left)* bristles with cilia, filaments that reach into the mucous layer. Odor molecules dissolve in the mucus and stimulate the cilia to produce the sense of smell.

Olfactory receptor cell appears white in closeup.

117

How Does the Tongue Taste Food?

■ **The inside story**

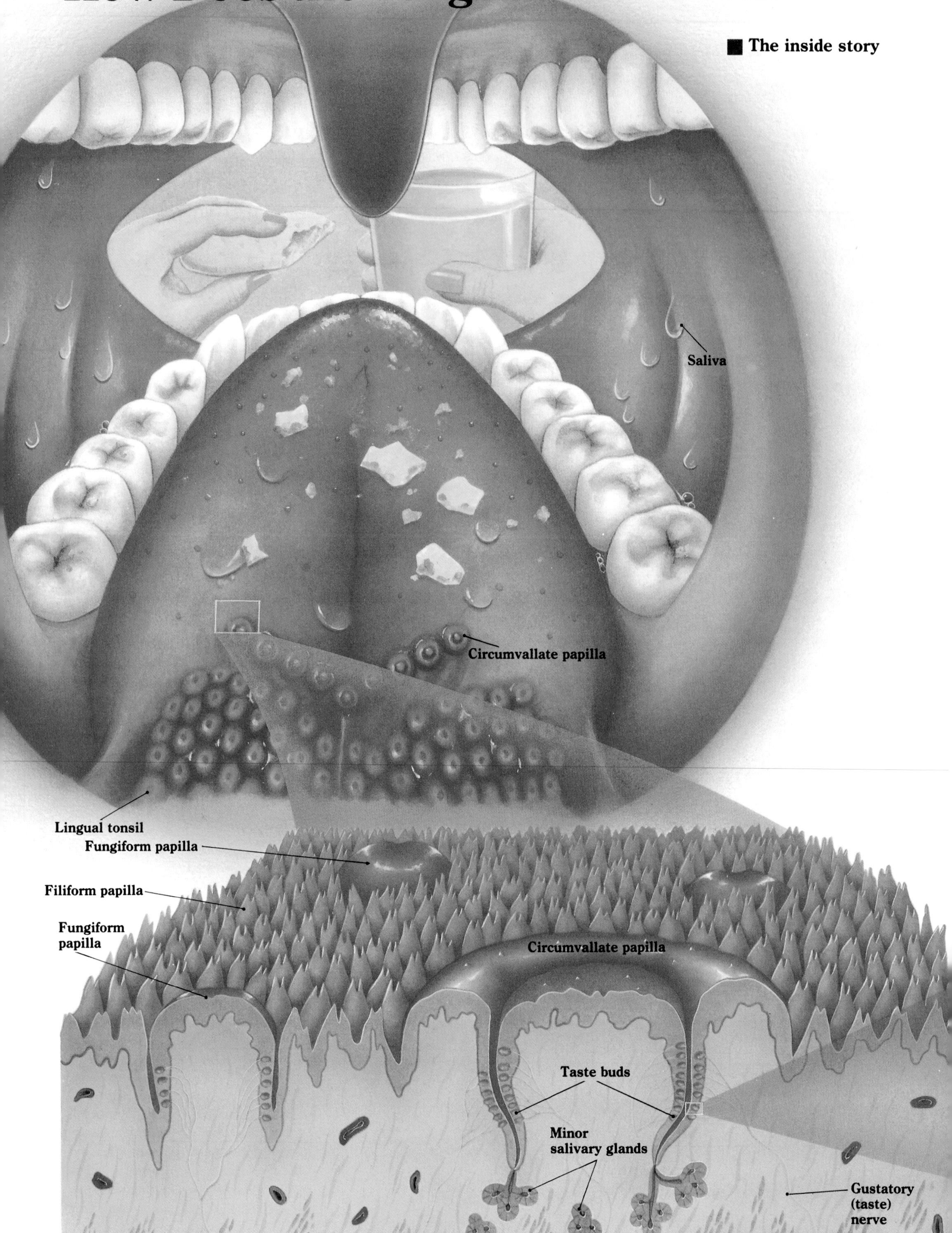

Saliva

Circumvallate papilla

Lingual tonsil

Fungiform papilla

Filiform papilla

Fungiform papilla

Circumvallate papilla

Taste buds

Minor salivary glands

Gustatory (taste) nerve

The surface of the tongue is covered with thousands of minuscule bumps, known as papillae. Buried near the base of each papilla are sensory cells in clusters called taste buds, which can distinguish four basic types of taste: sweet, sour, salty, and bitter. All other tastes—including those considered pleasant or delicious—are simply combinations or various intensities of the original four.

Babies have many more taste buds than most adults. They also have taste buds in nearly every part of their mouths, whereas the taste buds of an adult are confined mainly to the tongue. These differences explain why babies favor bland foods and dislike bitter tastes. A baby's keen sensitivity to taste decreases with age, so children are able to appreciate a wider range of foods as they grow older.

A map of the taste buds

Sweet and salty tastes are detected at the tip of the tongue, sour at the center of the sides, and bitter at the base. Researchers have yet to discover how the taste buds are able to specialize.

Sweet tastes

Sour tastes

Salty tastes

Bitter tastes

As shown at left, the tongue is studded with different kinds of papillae, the tiny projections that house taste buds. Largest are the circumvallate (literally, "surrounded by a rampart") papillae, which form a V at the back of the tongue. Centered on each side of the tongue are the broad, flat papillae called fungiform, meaning "shaped like a mushroom." The slender filiform ("threadlike") papillae gather at the tip of the tongue. The saliva dissolves chemicals in food so they can reach the taste buds.

A tasteful process

Taste sensations travel along gustatory nerves to the medulla oblongata, which forwards them to the thalamus. From there, the impulses go to the taste center of the cerebral cortex.

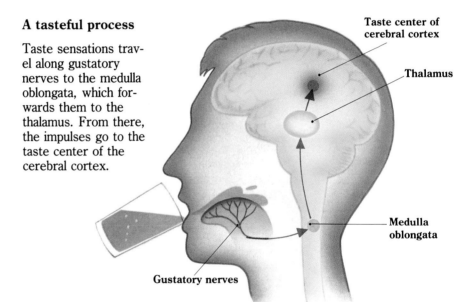

Taste center of cerebral cortex

Thalamus

Medulla oblongata

Gustatory nerves

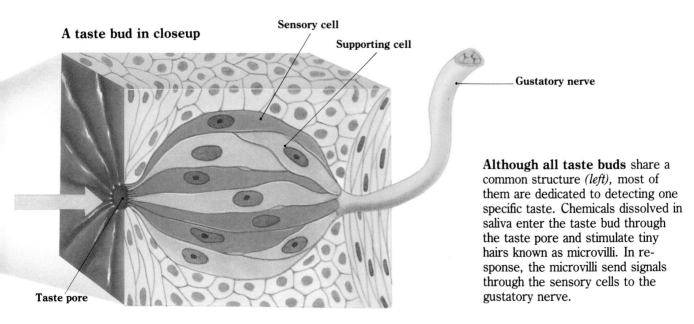

A taste bud in closeup

Sensory cell

Supporting cell

Gustatory nerve

Taste pore

Although all taste buds share a common structure *(left)*, most of them are dedicated to detecting one specific taste. Chemicals dissolved in saliva enter the taste bud through the taste pore and stimulate tiny hairs known as microvilli. In response, the microvilli send signals through the sensory cells to the gustatory nerve.

What Does Each Half of the Brain Do?

Though both halves of the brain seem to be nearly identical, scientists have discovered some interesting differences in the tasks performed by the two. The brain's right hemisphere controls the sensory functions and movement of the left side of the body, while the left hemisphere controls the same processes in the body's right side.

In addition to governing certain areas, each half of the brain specializes in doing certain jobs. The dominant hemisphere—usually the left—handles language and speech. The other hemisphere performs spatial integration and adjusts a person's temperament.

The division of cerebral labor is not total, however. In vision, for example, objects seen in the right visual field are channeled to the left hemisphere, and vice versa. And, through nerve fibers called the corpus callosum, the two hemispheres constantly trade information.

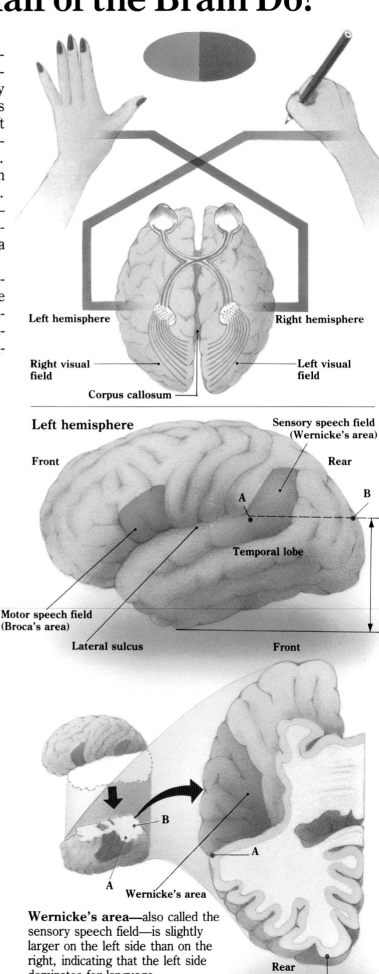

Left hemisphere

Right hemisphere

Right visual field

Left visual field

Corpus callosum

Left hemisphere

Sensory speech field (Wernicke's area)

Front

Rear

A

B

Temporal lobe

Motor speech field (Broca's area)

Lateral sulcus

Front

Images of the brain at work

Parts of the brain that are at rest emit alpha waves—electrical waves that can be monitored by an electroencephalograph, commonly called an EEG. The alpha waves can be made into computer images known as electroencephalograms.

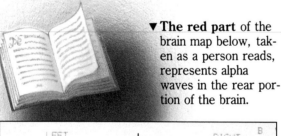

▼ **The red part** of the brain map below, taken as a person reads, represents alpha waves in the rear portion of the brain.

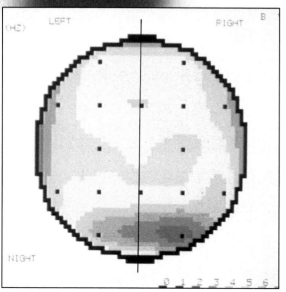

Wernicke's area—also called the sensory speech field—is slightly larger on the left side than on the right, indicating that the left side dominates for language.

Wernicke's area

● The split-brain experiment

In the experiment at right, reported by psychologist Roger Sperry in 1961, a man whose brain had been surgically split (by severance of the corpus callosum) to prevent epileptic seizures was positioned in front of a projector screen. When the word "spoon" was shown on the left half of the screen, the patient was able to pick out the spoon from a choice of four objects, but he was unable to articulate the word "spoon." From these and other results, Sperry concluded that the right hemisphere—which receives information presented in the left visual field—specializes in visual discrimination, whereas the left hemisphere specializes in verbal and analytical skills.

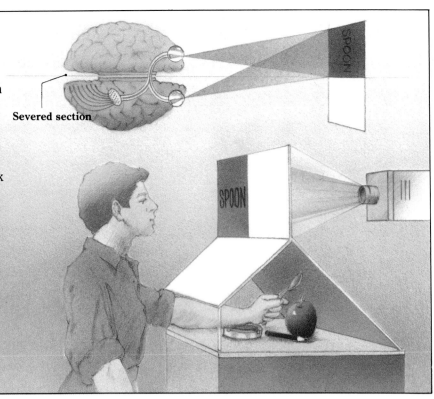

Severed section

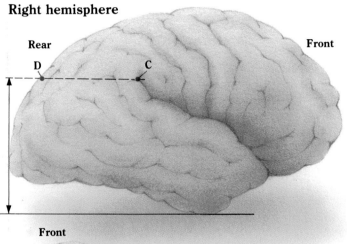

Right hemisphere

Rear

Front

D   C

Front

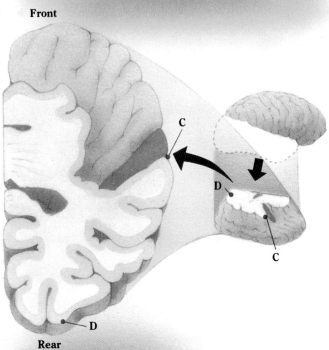

C

D

C

D

Rear

The brain is not totally symmetrical. When both sides are cut along the dotted lines shown at left, the rear part of the left half's temporal lobe is revealed to be larger than the same area on the right half. This section, called Wernicke's area, is crucial to language comprehension. A separate section in the left hemisphere known as Broca's area controls articulation.

The waves in this graph show that both halves of the brain are involved in listening to music.

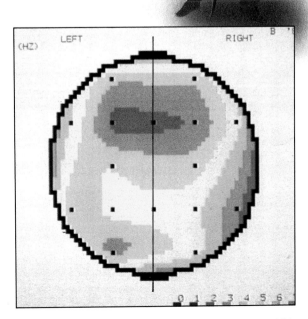

Why Do People Get Sleepy?

Over the tens of thousands of years that they have inhabited the earth, humans and many other types of animals have developed a rhythm of being active in the day and resting in the dark. This circadian rhythm, as it is known, follows a 24-hour cycle; a person gets sleepy at night whether the lights are burning or not.

So regular is the circadian rhythm that its disruption can disorient the body. Jet lag—a condition resulting from high-speed air travel across several time zones—can cause disorientation, fatigue, and slower thought processes.

Scientists have classified sleep into rapid eye movement (REM) sleep and non-REM sleep. Normally, a person shifts from REM to non-REM sleep at 80- to 90-minute intervals during the night. Because brain waves monitored during REM sleep resemble those emitted by alert humans and animals, non-REM sleep is thought to be the deeper of the two kinds.

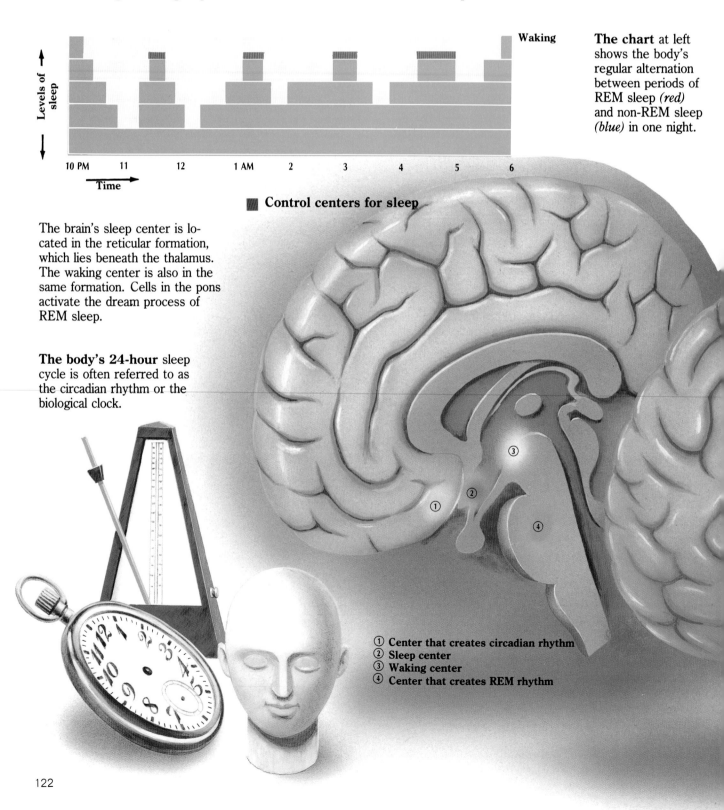

The chart at left shows the body's regular alternation between periods of REM sleep *(red)* and non-REM sleep *(blue)* in one night.

The brain's sleep center is located in the reticular formation, which lies beneath the thalamus. The waking center is also in the same formation. Cells in the pons activate the dream process of REM sleep.

The body's 24-hour sleep cycle is often referred to as the circadian rhythm or the biological clock.

① Center that creates circadian rhythm
② Sleep center
③ Waking center
④ Center that creates REM rhythm

Chemical lullabies and alarms

Studies of sleeping cats have enabled researchers to identify several neurotransmitters believed to induce sleep. Two of them, serotonin and norepinephrine, are released by the brain at regular intervals during the sleeping-and-waking cycle.

Certain neurons in the raphe nuclei, a cluster of cells in the cat's brainstem, contain large amounts of serotonin. When the serotonin is artificially depleted, severe insomnia disrupts both REM and non-REM sleep. Neurons in a part of the brain called the locus coeruleus contain norepinephrine, which is released after the serotonin. If the locus coeruleus is destroyed, non-REM sleep is unaffected, but REM sleep is eliminated. Scientists know that both substances are intimately involved in sleep but have yet to discover precisely what triggers their release.

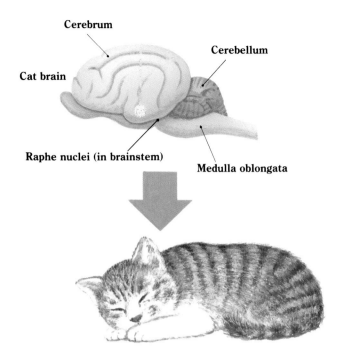

Excess serotonin from the raphe nuclei resulted in this cat's nap.

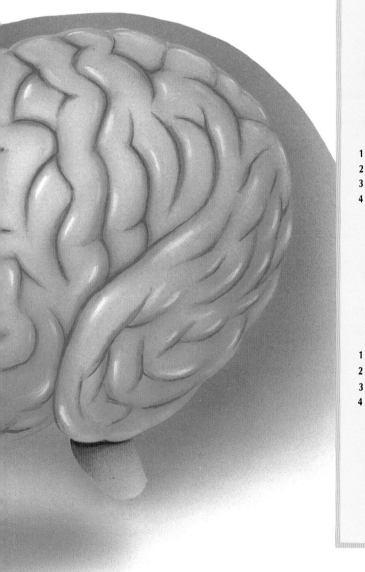

● The consequences of sleep loss

When the subject in this sleep deprivation experiment was kept constantly awake, the level of the sleep-inducing neurotransmitter known as serotonin did not increase as it usually would. When the subject was allowed to sleep even a short time, however, the amount of serotonin increased normally.

Blocking REM sleep is an invitation to irritability.

When only REM sleep was blocked, the subject became sensitive, irritable, and confused.

Blocking non-REM sleep has milder results.

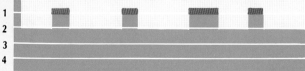

When non-REM sleep was blocked, the subject became listless but displayed few other specific changes.

When Do Dreams Occur?

Nearly all dreams take place during the shallow state of sleep referred to as REM, for "rapid eye movement." Only limited and fragmentary dreaming occurs during the deeper, non-REM sleep. Dream-filled REM sleep occurs at intervals between longer periods of non-REM sleep.

In non-REM sleep, the mind is resting and quite inactive. In REM sleep, by contrast, the mind is highly active. This is evidenced by EEG tracings and rapid movements of the sleeper's eyes, which dart from side to side almost as quickly and as often as during waking hours.

A number of other changes have been noted during REM sleep. The pupil of each eye constricts, allowing less light to enter the eyeballs. And certain muscles inside the ear relax, permitting less sound to reach the brain.

Scientists contend that everyone dreams, including those who cannot remember a single dream upon waking. Periods of especially intense brain activity during REM sleep, they speculate, stem from dreams of danger and pursuit. And according to psychologists, dreaming may even be an important way to preserve mental health.

The cycles of normal sleep

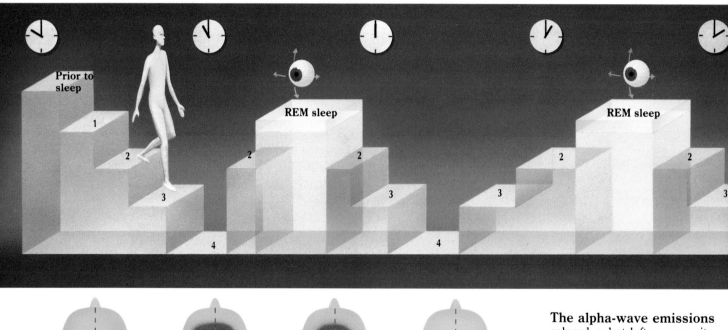

 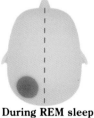

Awake

During stage 1 non-REM sleep

During stages 3 and 4 non-REM sleep

During REM sleep

The alpha-wave emissions colored red at left were emitted by the brain as the subject was falling asleep.

The image at right shows alpha waves *(red)* in a test patient's head during REM sleep. When the subject is awake, the left brain—responsible for language—tends to predominate.

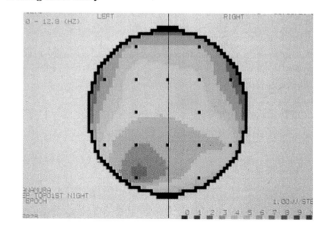

Electrodes measure a sleeping test subject's brain waves and eye movements. Researchers have identified waves of four frequencies—beta, alpha, theta, and delta—but the significance of each is not yet understood.

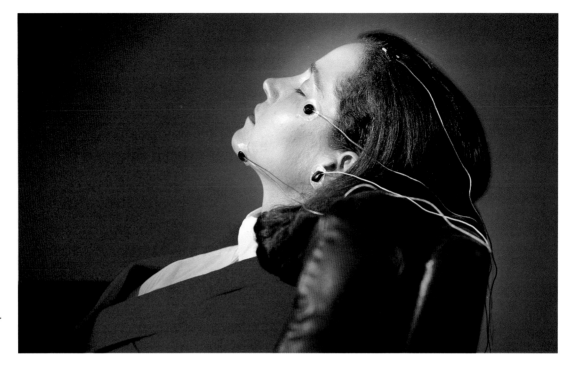

REM and non-REM sleep alternate in a typical night *(below)*.

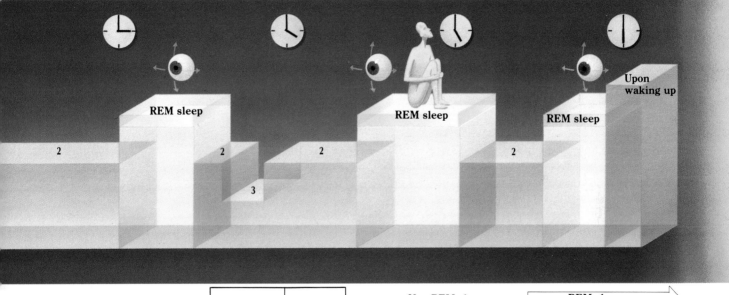

REM sleep

2

REM sleep

2

2

3

2

REM sleep

2

Upon waking up

A map of dreams

Electrodes used to monitor a sleeping brain produce a graph showing that limited muscle activity and eye movement occur during non-REM sleep. During REM sleep, however, strong eye movement continues after other muscles have stopped moving. The point at which eye-muscle movement subsides is considered the start of the non-REM stage.

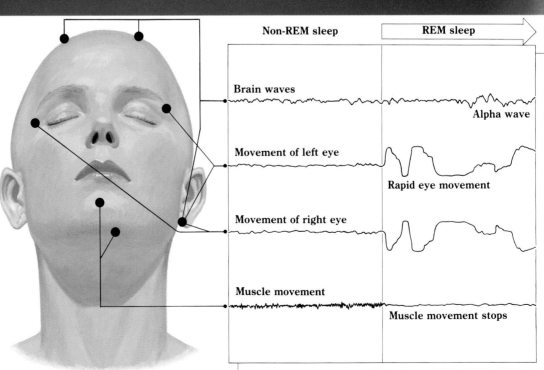

Non-REM sleep

REM sleep

Brain waves

Alpha wave

Movement of left eye

Rapid eye movement

Movement of right eye

Muscle movement

Muscle movement stops

6

Disease and Immunity

Because human beings are among the most complex organisms on earth, they are vulnerable to more breakdowns—commonly called illnesses—than any other living thing. The delicate life-sustaining balance that is maintained by the body's systems can be disturbed in millions of different ways. But for all the disorders that can befall it, the body is strong enough to either fight off or live with most of them.

The diseases that affect the human body may be infectious or noninfectious. The infectious diseases are caused by pathogens—tiny organisms such as viruses, bacteria, and fungi—which can enter the body in many different ways. Pathogens range in severity from the viruses that cause colds, which are usually harmless, to those that cause AIDS, which is virtually always fatal. To protect the body from these pathogens, human beings have evolved an array of defenses known as the immune system *(pages 128-129)*. The immune system operates by analyzing pathogen proteins and using this information to make its own proteins, called antibodies, to attack the invaders.

Noninfectious diseases, such as diabetes and atherosclerosis, have many different causes. Often, they are hereditary, occurring more often in some families than in others. The immune system can rarely help with these kinds of diseases. Medical treatment is necessary.

Swarming to the body's defense, B cells *(yellow)* produce Y-shaped antibodies to combat cylindrical bacteria and invading viruses *(lower left corner)*.

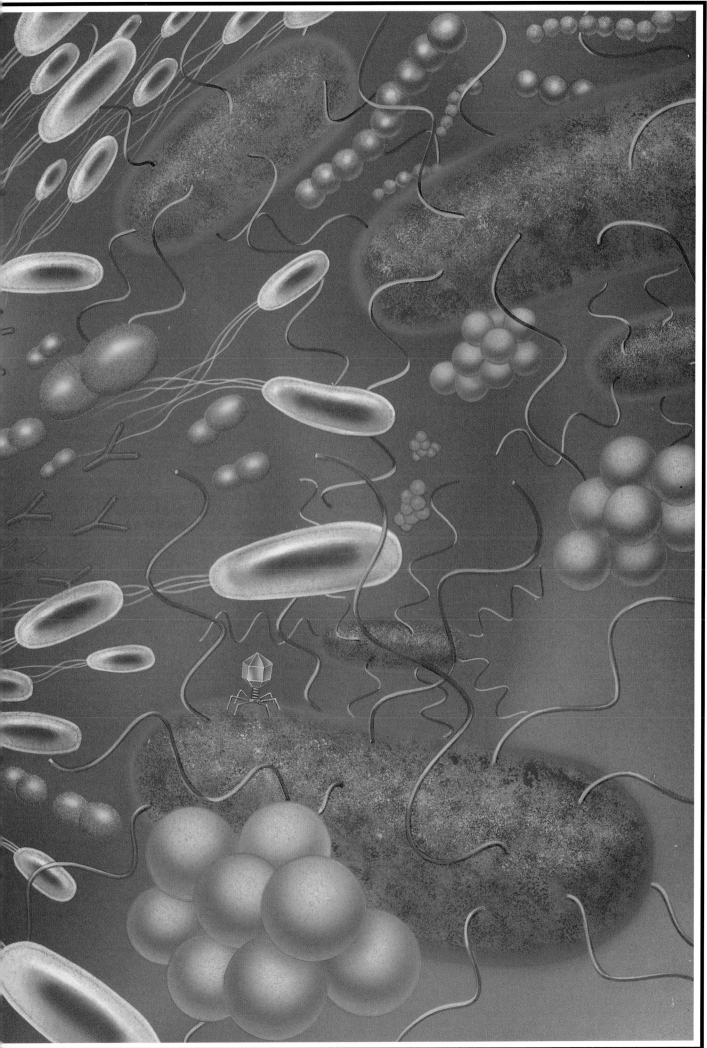

What Is Immunity?

When pathogens invade the human body, a complex defense network of cells springs into action. At the core of this immune system are white blood cells *(below)*, produced primarily in the bone marrow and spleen.

Lymphocytes, one kind of white blood cell, turn into two distinct types shortly after they are formed. T lymphocytes, or T cells, coordinate the immune system's attack, signaling other types of white blood cells to join the fight, while B lymphocytes, or B cells, produce proteins called antibodies, which attach themselves to the pathogens and disable them.

While the immune system does an excellent job of protecting the body, it cannot fight off every infection. Many pathogens can defeat the immune system. Some, such as the AIDS virus *(pages 136-137)*, kill anyone who contracts the disease they carry. Furthermore, since the immune system usually takes a few days to reach full strength, even weak pathogens can make a person sick before they are destroyed.

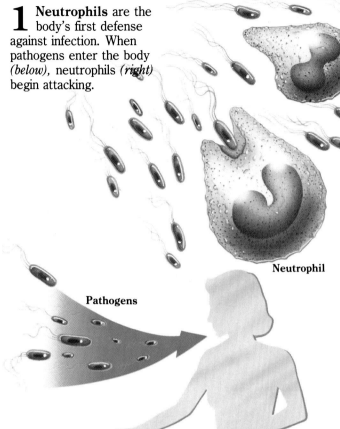

1 **Neutrophils** are the body's first defense against infection. When pathogens enter the body *(below)*, neutrophils *(right)* begin attacking.

Neutrophil

Pathogens

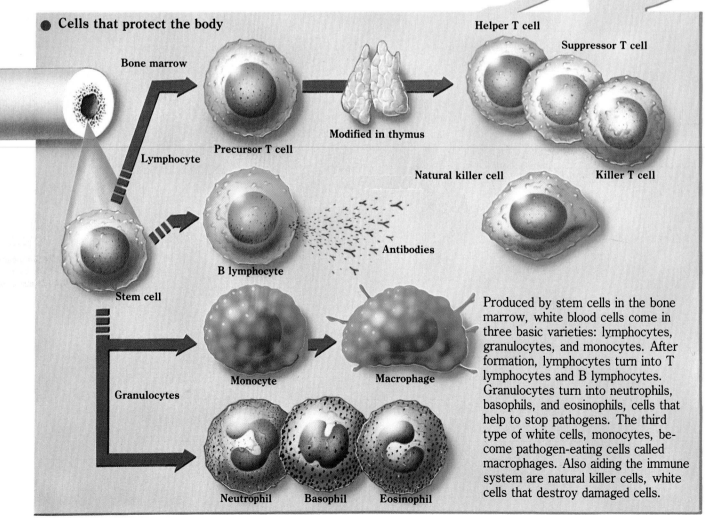

● **Cells that protect the body**

Bone marrow

Lymphocyte

Precursor T cell

Modified in thymus

Helper T cell

Suppressor T cell

Killer T cell

Natural killer cell

Antibodies

B lymphocyte

Stem cell

Monocyte

Macrophage

Granulocytes

Neutrophil   Basophil   Eosinophil

Produced by stem cells in the bone marrow, white blood cells come in three basic varieties: lymphocytes, granulocytes, and monocytes. After formation, lymphocytes turn into T lymphocytes and B lymphocytes. Granulocytes turn into neutrophils, basophils, and eosinophils, cells that help to stop pathogens. The third type of white cells, monocytes, become pathogen-eating cells called macrophages. Also aiding the immune system are natural killer cells, white cells that destroy damaged cells.

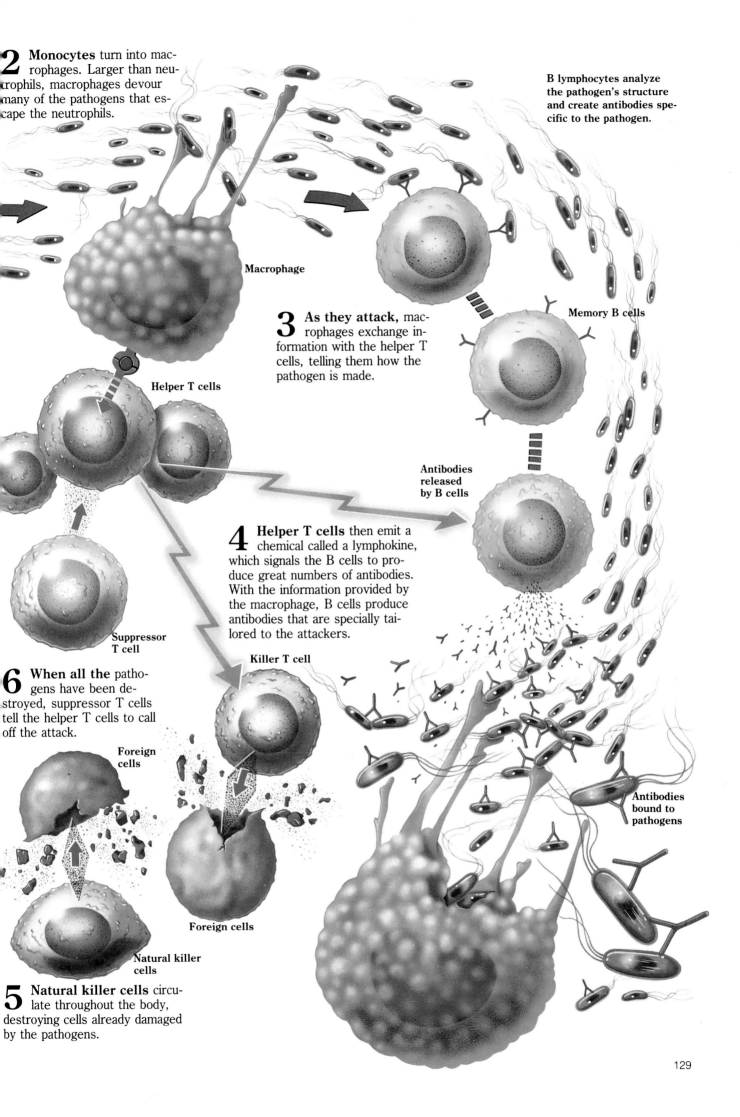

2 **Monocytes** turn into macrophages. Larger than neutrophils, macrophages devour many of the pathogens that escape the neutrophils.

B lymphocytes analyze the pathogen's structure and create antibodies specific to the pathogen.

Macrophage

3 **As they attack,** macrophages exchange information with the helper T cells, telling them how the pathogen is made.

Memory B cells

Helper T cells

Antibodies released by B cells

4 **Helper T cells** then emit a chemical called a lymphokine, which signals the B cells to produce great numbers of antibodies. With the information provided by the macrophage, B cells produce antibodies that are specially tailored to the attackers.

Suppressor T cell

Killer T cell

6 **When all the** pathogens have been destroyed, suppressor T cells tell the helper T cells to call off the attack.

Foreign cells

Antibodies bound to pathogens

Foreign cells

Natural killer cells

5 **Natural killer cells** circulate throughout the body, destroying cells already damaged by the pathogens.

What Is the Lymphatic System?

The lymphatic system consists of hundreds of pinhead-size to bean-size glands called lymph nodes, connected by a network of artery-like vessels. It plays an essential role in fighting illness, for it is within the lymph nodes that white blood cells take on most pathogens. When pathogens enter the body, they eventually make their way into the lymphatic system, where they travel through the lymphatic vessels to lymph nodes. There, white blood cells that live and multiply within the node attack most kinds of invaders. In addition to serving as the infection-fighting battleground, the lymph nodes also filter out other impurities that have entered the body.

Circulating throughout the lymphatic system is a clear, colorless fluid called lymph, similar to blood plasma. Lymph is forced through lymph vessels by outside pressures, such as those that are created by breathing and muscle movements. Valves within the lymphatic vessels keep the lymph from flowing backward.

When a person becomes sick, a common symptom is swollen lymph nodes. This swelling means that the lymphatic system is working especially hard, producing far more lymphocytes than usual and filtering many pathogens from the lymph. Upon recovery, lymphocyte production slows, and the nodes return to their normal size.

A cutaway view of a lymph node *(below)* shows afferent vessels leading into the node and efferent vessels leading away. Lymphocytes multiply in structures known as follicles; the germs they fight enter the nodes through lymphatic capillary walls.

The lymphatic system

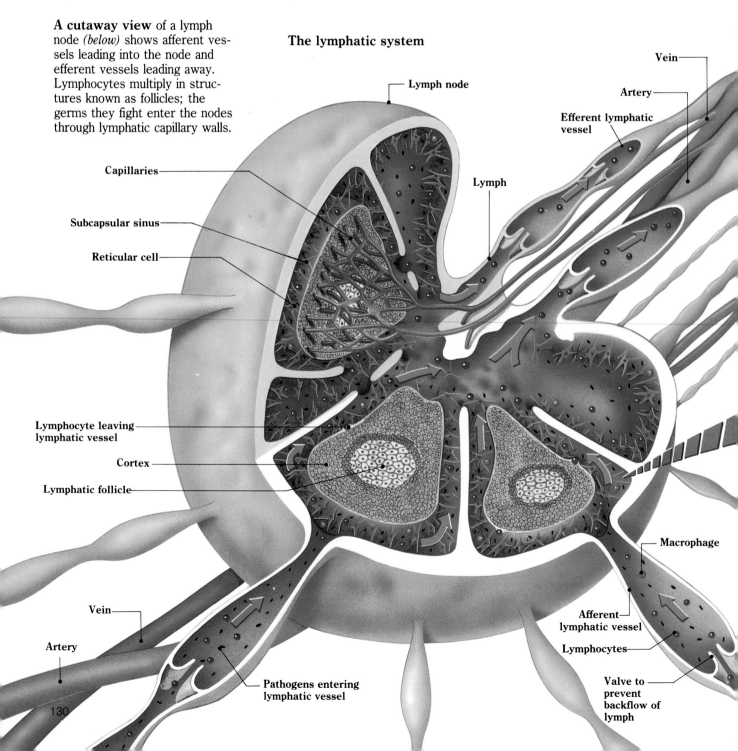

- Vein
- Artery
- Efferent lymphatic vessel
- Lymph node
- Lymph
- Capillaries
- Subcapsular sinus
- Reticular cell
- Lymphocyte leaving lymphatic vessel
- Cortex
- Lymphatic follicle
- Macrophage
- Vein
- Afferent lymphatic vessel
- Artery
- Lymphocytes
- Pathogens entering lymphatic vessel
- Valve to prevent backflow of lymph

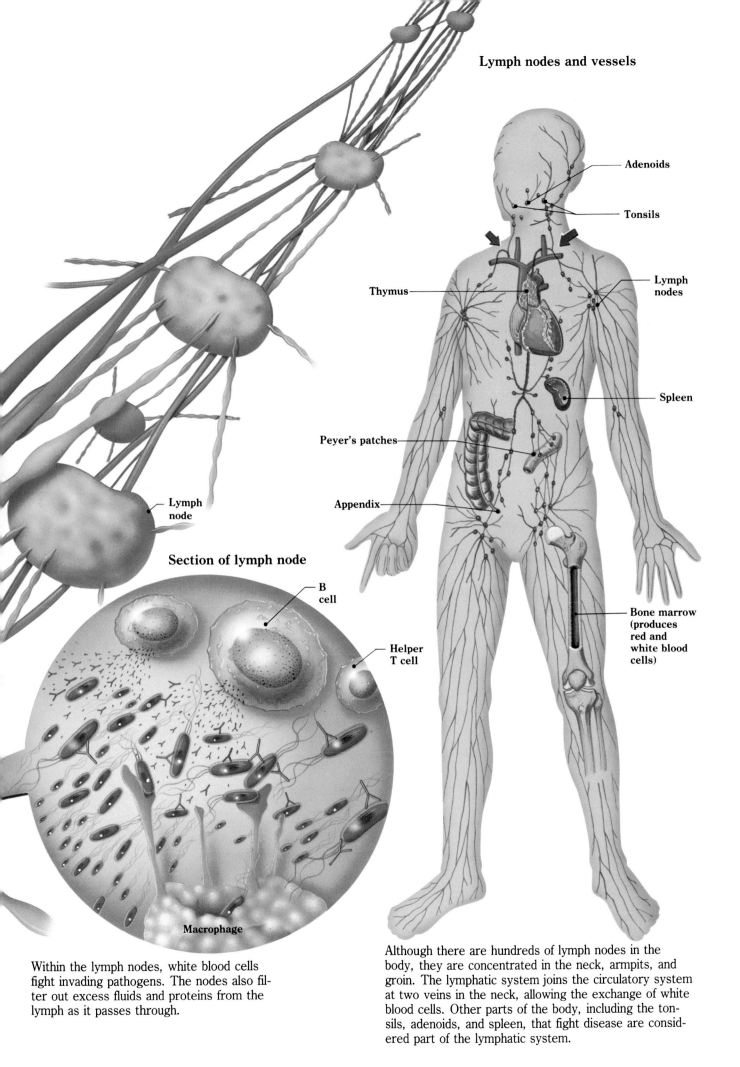

Lymph nodes and vessels

Adenoids

Tonsils

Thymus

Lymph nodes

Spleen

Peyer's patches

Appendix

Bone marrow (produces red and white blood cells)

Lymph node

Section of lymph node

B cell

Helper T cell

Macrophage

Within the lymph nodes, white blood cells fight invading pathogens. The nodes also filter out excess fluids and proteins from the lymph as it passes through.

Although there are hundreds of lymph nodes in the body, they are concentrated in the neck, armpits, and groin. The lymphatic system joins the circulatory system at two veins in the neck, allowing the exchange of white blood cells. Other parts of the body, including the tonsils, adenoids, and spleen, that fight disease are considered part of the lymphatic system.

131

Why Do People Catch Measles Only Once?

Mainly affecting children between the ages of 5 and 12, measles is a highly contagious viral disease that creates a reddish rash all over the patient's body. Along with mumps and chickenpox —two other kinds of childhood diseases—it is a kind of illness that usually makes people sick only once in their lives, no matter how many times they are exposed to it.

When the measles virus first enters the body, it takes a few days—during which the person becomes sick—for white blood cells called B lym-phocytes to produce enough measles antibodies to combat the disease *(pages 128-129)*. But even after the antibodies have destroyed the virus and the patient recovers, B cells "remember" the virus's structure. If the virus returns, the B cells can produce so many antibodies so quickly that the disease never gains a foothold. As a result, a person who has had measles almost never gets the disease a second time. This phenomenon is called natural immunity and gives the patient a lifelong resistance to the illness.

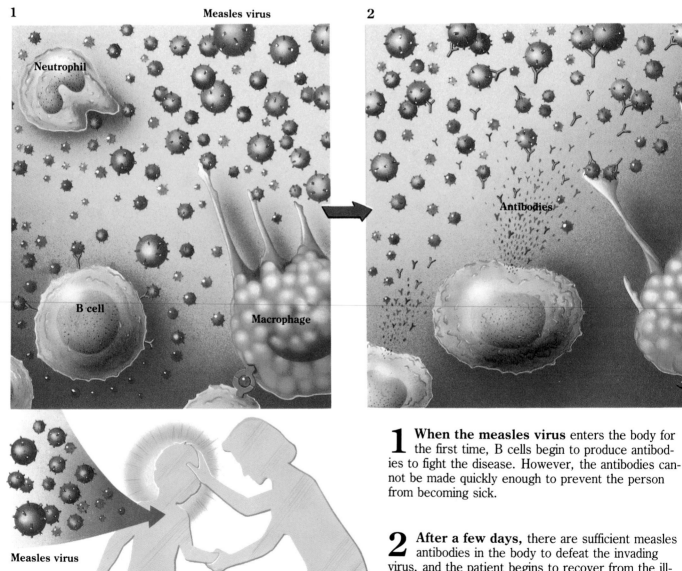

1 Measles virus

Neutrophil

B cell

Macrophage

2 Antibodies

Measles virus

Since symptoms of the disease do not appear for 7 to 14 days, a person with measles can infect others unknowingly. The most common way to transmit the virus is to cough or to sneeze, releasing it into the air.

1 **When the measles virus** enters the body for the first time, B cells begin to produce antibodies to fight the disease. However, the antibodies cannot be made quickly enough to prevent the person from becoming sick.

2 **After a few days,** there are sufficient measles antibodies in the body to defeat the invading virus, and the patient begins to recover from the illness in 4 to 7 days.

3 **Although the virus** has been destroyed, B lymphocytes remember its structure and are capable of producing antibodies very quickly should the virus reappear.

Structure of an antibody

Changeable section

Section that attaches to antigens on pathogen surface

Section that connects to white blood cells

How antibodies work

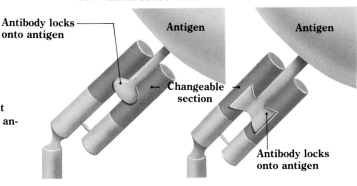

Antibody locks onto antigen

Antigen

Changeable section

Antigen

Antibody locks onto antigen

Produced by B cells, antibodies *(left)* are Y-shaped structures built from two long protein chains called heavy chains and two short ones called light chains. While antibodies share a similar structure *(pink)*, each has a changeable segment *(orange)*, making it specific to one pathogen.

An antibody attaches its changeable section to proteins called antigens on the surface of a pathogen *(above)*, allowing macrophages to find and destroy the pathogen.

4

3

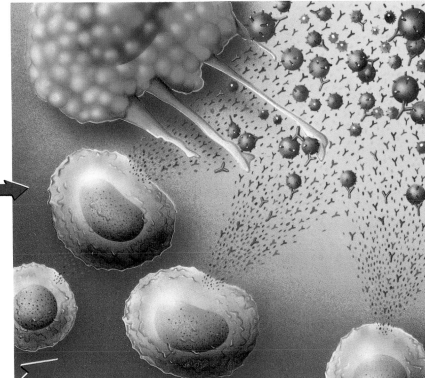

B cell "remembers" the virus

4 **If the virus** invades the body a second time, the B cells release great numbers of antibodies right away. The antibodies spring into action, preventing the virus from spreading through the body and making the person sick a second time.

● Immunization

To prevent children from catching measles, doctors usually inject them at a very early age with a version of the virus that has been made harmless. B cells then produce measles antibodies, and the body becomes able to fight off the active version of the virus when it strikes. Immunization also works for many other diseases and has saved millions of lives.

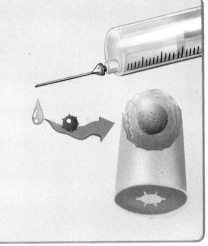

What Causes Hay Fever?

■ The immune reaction to pollen

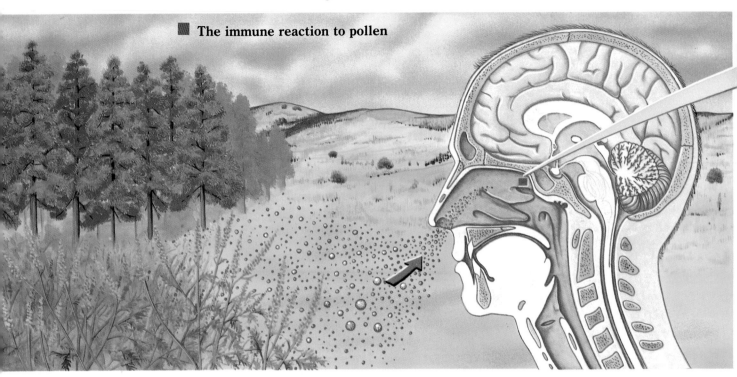

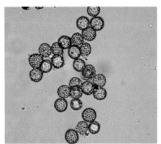

Ragweed pollen

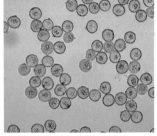

Japanese cedar pollen

The causes of hay fever. Hay fever begins when a person breathes in pollen from a plant to which he or she is allergic *(above)*, triggering the sequence illustrated at right. A common culprit in the United States is pollen from ragweed *(far left)*. In Japan, a likely cause of hay fever is cryptomeria pollen *(left)*, which comes from a cedar tree.

Hay fever, an uncomfortable condition that brings on sneezing, a runny nose, and watery eyes, is an allergy—an immune reaction to a substance that doesn't actually harm the body. In the case of hay fever, the immune system is responding to pollen, dustlike spores that are released by plants.

When a person breathes in pollen spores, antigens attached to the spores trigger the release of an antibody called immune globulin E. While this response occurs in all people, in hay fever sufferers B cells produce—for unknown reasons—too much of this antibody. Excess immune globulin E binds to special receptors on the surfaces of mast cells, which live in the body's connective tissues. When this happens, the cells are said to be sensitized. Sensitized mast cells release a molecule called histamine, which causes the symptoms of hay fever *(right)*. Although medications known as antihistamines provide some relief from the symptoms, a true cure has yet to be discovered.

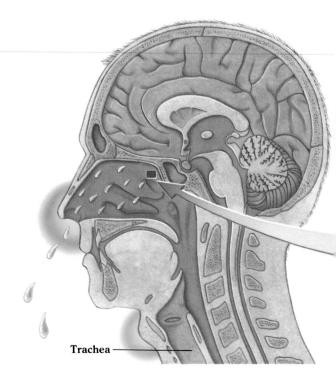

Trachea

6 **Plasma leaving capillaries** in the head irritates mucous glands, causing a runny nose.

134

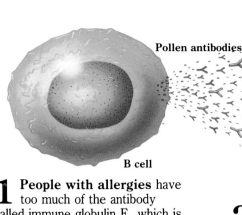

Pollen antibodies

Mast cell

Receptor that unites with immune globulin E

B cell

1 **People with allergies** have too much of the antibody called immune globulin E, which is produced by B cells.

2 **Receptors on** the surfaces of mast cells bind to the immune globulin E.

Immune globulin E antibody united with receptor

Sensitized mast cell

3 **Once antibodies** have attached themselves to the mast cell receptors, the cells become sensitized to pollen.

Causes of allergies

In addition to pollen from plants such as ragweed or cedar trees, other common substances can cause sneezing, itchy eyes, and a runny nose. Cat hair, molds, and dust, among other things, can trigger the same immune response.

Pollen

Pollen antigens

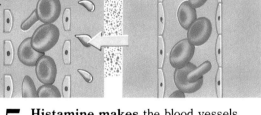

Histamine released

5 **Histamine makes** the blood vessels dilate and become more porous, which then allows some of the plasma that is in the blood to seep out.

4 **The arrival** of pollen spores, which bind to the immune globulin E, signals the sensitized mast cells to release histamine.

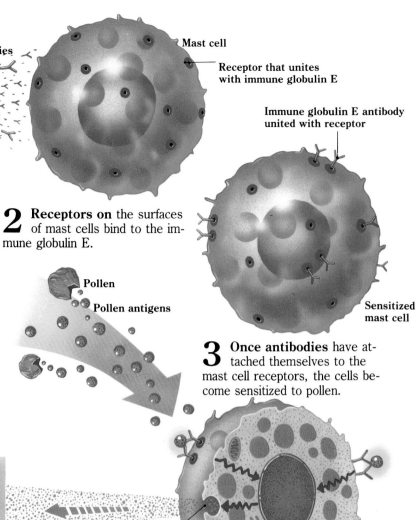

Nasal mucus

Epithelial cells

Blood plasma passes through gaps in blood vessels

Mast cell releases histamine

What Is AIDS?

The HIV consists of genetic material surrounded by a coating of proteins and lipids. Unlike most viruses, the AIDS virus contains no DNA, only RNA. Such viruses are called retroviruses. As the HIV invades helper T cells *(below)*, it uses an enzyme called reverse transcriptase to convert its RNA into DNA. The new DNA then instructs the T cell to duplicate the virus.

The AIDS virus

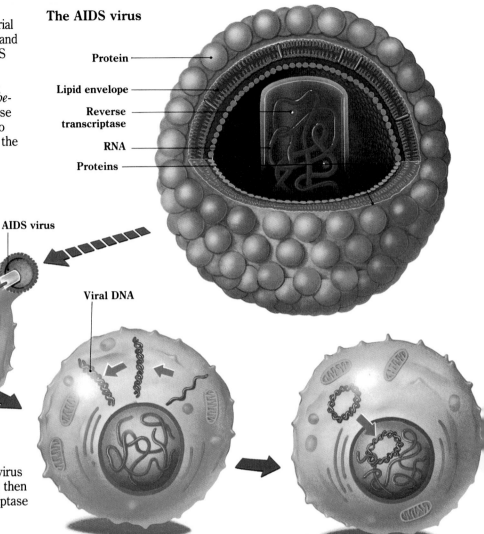

Protein

Lipid envelope

Reverse transcriptase

RNA

Proteins

How the AIDS virus works

AIDS virus

Viral DNA

Upon entering the body, the AIDS virus attaches itself to a helper T cell and then injects its RNA and reverse transcriptase into the T cell.

With the help of the reverse transcriptase, the cell then produces viral DNA, using the RNA as a blueprint.

The newly produced viral DNA forms a ring and proceeds to penetrate the nucleus of the helper T cell.

Acquired immune deficiency syndrome, commonly referred to as AIDS, is a disease that destroys the body's immune system. It does this by attacking helper T cells *(pages 128-129)*, which play an essential role in fighting illness. With the immune system disabled, an AIDS patient will usually die from an illness, called a secondary disease, that the body could have fought off successfully if its immune system were intact. AIDS was first identified in the 1980s, and scientists still do not understand many things about how the disease works.

While AIDS is almost always fatal, the virus that causes it—known as HIV, for human immunodeficiency virus—is only transmitted under specific circumstances. Unlike the viruses that cause the common cold, for example *(pages 140-141)*, the AIDS virus cannot be contracted through the air. Furthermore, since its life span outside the human body is very short, the virus cannot be left on a surface by an infected person and picked up later by someone else. The only known ways for the AIDS virus to be transmitted are through direct exchanges of bodily fluids, which occur through transfusions of infected blood, the sharing of needles with infected drug abusers, and sexual intercourse with people who are infected.

Crippling the immune system

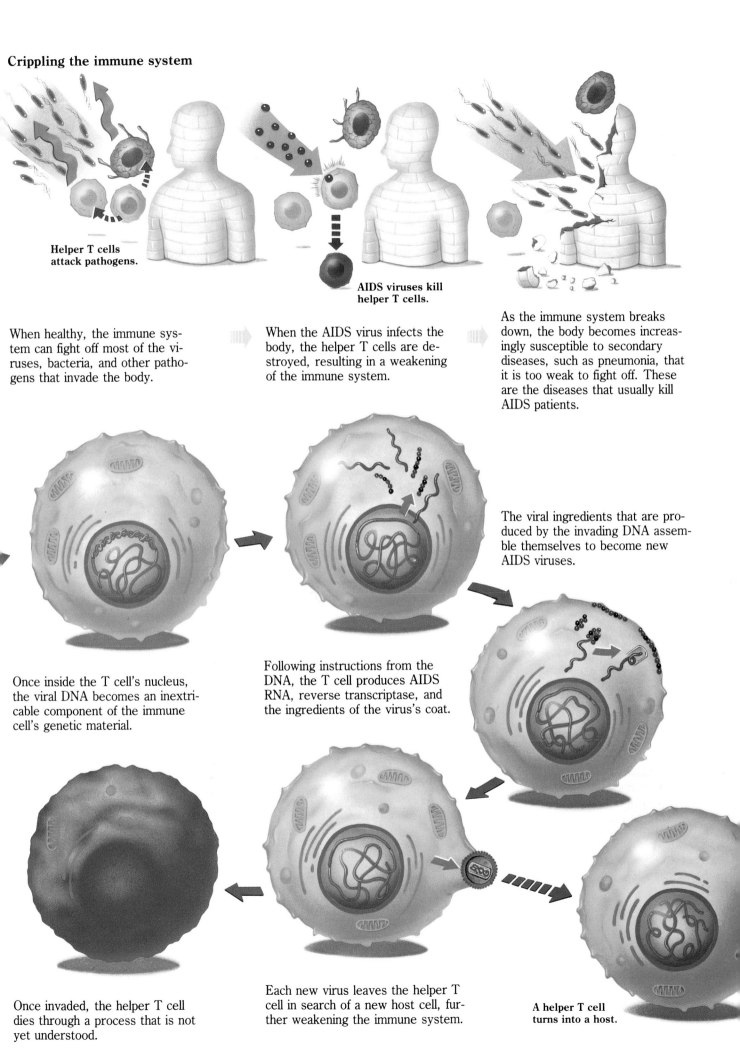

Helper T cells attack pathogens.

AIDS viruses kill helper T cells.

When healthy, the immune system can fight off most of the viruses, bacteria, and other pathogens that invade the body.

When the AIDS virus infects the body, the helper T cells are destroyed, resulting in a weakening of the immune system.

As the immune system breaks down, the body becomes increasingly susceptible to secondary diseases, such as pneumonia, that it is too weak to fight off. These are the diseases that usually kill AIDS patients.

The viral ingredients that are produced by the invading DNA assemble themselves to become new AIDS viruses.

Once inside the T cell's nucleus, the viral DNA becomes an inextricable component of the immune cell's genetic material.

Following instructions from the DNA, the T cell produces AIDS RNA, reverse transcriptase, and the ingredients of the virus's coat.

Once invaded, the helper T cell dies through a process that is not yet understood.

Each new virus leaves the helper T cell in search of a new host cell, further weakening the immune system.

A helper T cell turns into a host.

What Is Cancer?

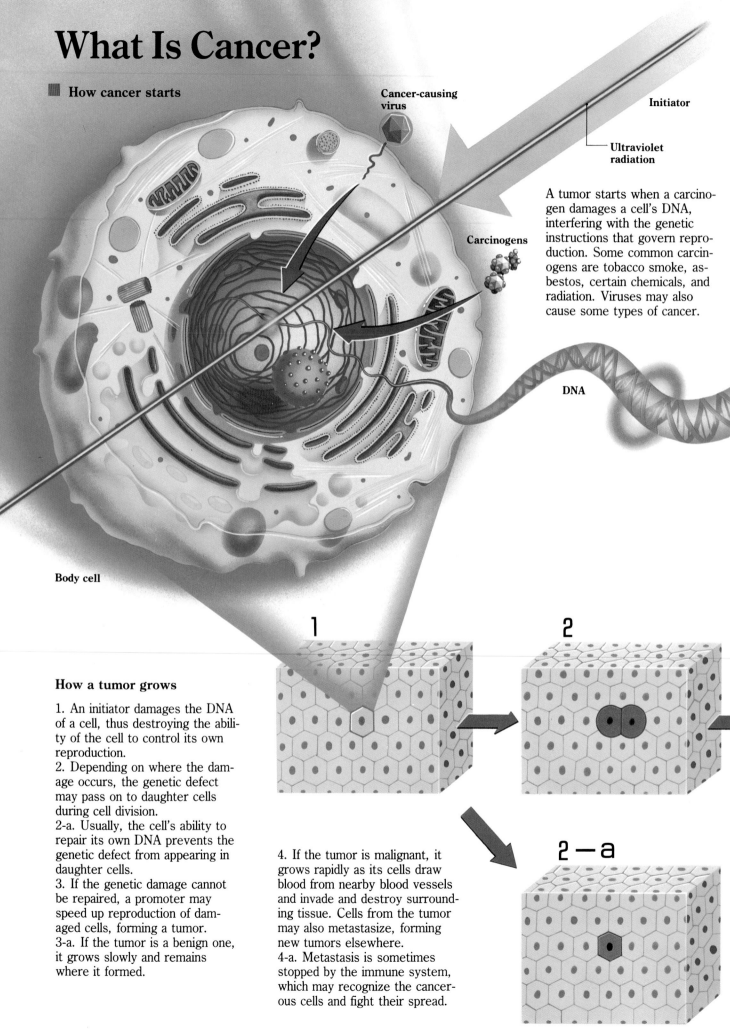

■ **How cancer starts**

Cancer-causing virus

Initiator

└ Ultraviolet radiation

Carcinogens

A tumor starts when a carcinogen damages a cell's DNA, interfering with the genetic instructions that govern reproduction. Some common carcinogens are tobacco smoke, asbestos, certain chemicals, and radiation. Viruses may also cause some types of cancer.

DNA

Body cell

1

2

2 — a

How a tumor grows

1. An initiator damages the DNA of a cell, thus destroying the ability of the cell to control its own reproduction.
2. Depending on where the damage occurs, the genetic defect may pass on to daughter cells during cell division.
2-a. Usually, the cell's ability to repair its own DNA prevents the genetic defect from appearing in daughter cells.
3. If the genetic damage cannot be repaired, a promoter may speed up reproduction of damaged cells, forming a tumor.
3-a. If the tumor is a benign one, it grows slowly and remains where it formed.

4. If the tumor is malignant, it grows rapidly as its cells draw blood from nearby blood vessels and invade and destroy surrounding tissue. Cells from the tumor may also metastasize, forming new tumors elsewhere.
4-a. Metastasis is sometimes stopped by the immune system, which may recognize the cancerous cells and fight their spread.

Cancer is a disease in which cells begin reproducing too quickly, usually forming a growth called a tumor. Nearly every part of the body, including the skin, most organs, and the lymphatic system, can develop a tumor. No one knows exactly how cancer works, but scientists believe that it begins when a substance from outside the body, called a carcinogen, changes a cell so that it will multiply too rapidly *(left)*. Some families are predisposed to the disease.

Not all tumors are defined as cancer, and the distinction between cancerous and noncancerous lies in the tumor's behavior. Noncancerous tumors, commonly called benign tumors, stay in the spot where they begin and grow very slowly. Cancerous, or malignant, tumors, are much more serious because they invade and destroy the surrounding healthy cells. Moreover, in a process called metastasis, cells from malignant tumors can break away and travel to other parts of the body, where they form new tumors and destroy still more tissue. Left untreated, malignant tumors eventually destroy enough tissue to kill the victim.

While cancer is a leading cause of death in adults, it is often curable if it is discovered in its early stages. Doctors usually treat the disease either by removing the tumor or by destroying it with drugs or radiation.

Many carcinogens can also act as promoters—substances that stimulate growth in damaged cells. Promoters usually stimulate a specific kind of cancer—tobacco smoke, for instance, promotes lung cancer.

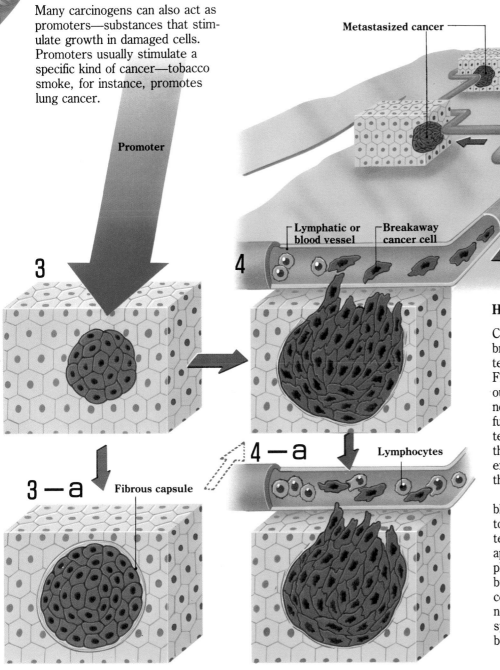

Promoter

3

3 — a Fibrous capsule

4

Lymphatic or blood vessel ⌐Breakaway cancer cell

4 — a Lymphocytes

Metastasized cancer ⌐

Metastasized cancer cell

How cancer spreads

Cancer spreads as malignant cells break free from a tumor and enter a blood or lymphatic vessel. From there, they travel throughout the body, ultimately finding a new home where they multiply further. Certain types of cancer tend to spread to specific parts of the body—stomach cancer, for example, tends to metastasize to the lungs and liver.

What makes metastasis possible is the ability of malignant cells to evade the body's immune system. Normally, any foreign cell appearing in the blood or lymphatic system will be destroyed by white blood cells. However, cells from malignant tumors do not trigger the body's immune system even though cells from benign tumors do.

What Is the Common Cold?

The term "common cold" actually refers to a group of similar illnesses caused by over 100 different pathogens, mostly viruses. The invaders infect the airways and mucous membranes of the respiratory system, causing the classic cold symptoms of sneezing, coughing, and a runny nose. The most widespread illness known to humankind, common colds afflict most of the population of the world each year, frequently in rainy seasons and in the winter.

The sheer number of cold-causing agents has made it hard for doctors to find a good treatment. Fortunately, colds are rarely serious. Furthermore, as a person grows up, he or she will develop milder, shorter colds, because the body builds up a partial immunity to cold viruses.

What causes colds

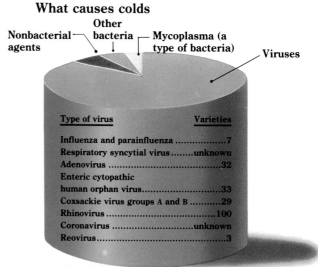

Type of virus	Varieties
Influenza and parainfluenza	7
Respiratory syncytial virus	unknown
Adenovirus	32
Enteric cytopathic human orphan virus	33
Coxsackie virus groups A and B	29
Rhinovirus	100
Coronavirus	unknown
Reovirus	3

The pathogens that cause colds vary, but most are viruses. The largest group are rhinoviruses, a name taken from the Greek word for "nose," indicating that these viruses affect the nose and respiratory tract.

Colds and the respiratory system

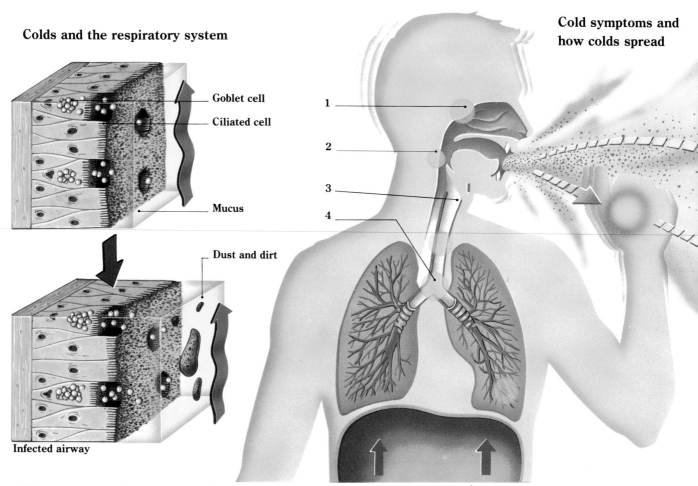

Goblet cell

Ciliated cell

Mucus

Dust and dirt

Infected airway

Lining the nose and throat are goblet cells, which produce mucus, and ciliated cells, which sweep mucus out of the airways. During a cold, goblet cells produce extra mucus, triggering coughing, which removes trapped particles and viruses.

Cold symptoms and how colds spread

Cold symptoms differ, depending on the virus and the affected area of the respiratory system. These symptoms include
1. Nasal cavity: runny or stuffy nose, called rhinitis.
2. Pharynx: sore throat, called pharyngitis.
3. Larynx: coughing and voice loss, called laryngitis.
4. Bronchi: inflammation, called bronchitis.

Types of colds and their complications

Severity of symptoms:
largest equals most severe

Columns: Rhinitis, Pharyngitis, Laryngitis, Tracheal catarrh, Bronchitis, Pneumonia, Malaise, Conjunctivitis

Rows:
Influenza
Common cold
Pharyngoconjunctival fever
Viral laryngitis

The chart at left shows the symptoms produced by different types of colds. While most colds remain in the head and chest, the viruses that cause influenza and pharyngoconjunctival fever produce symptoms such as fever, fatigue, and muscular aches.

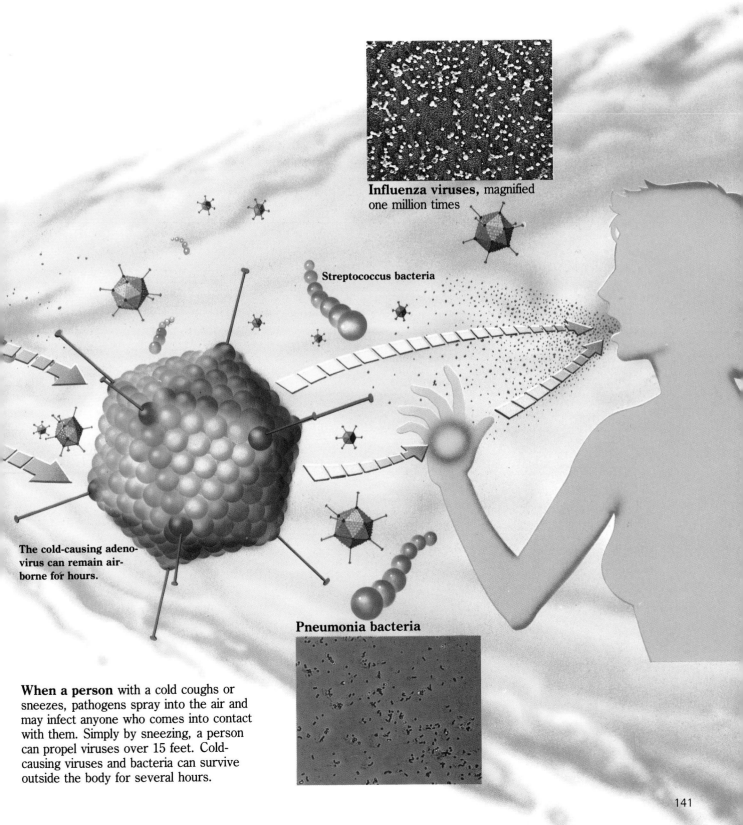

Influenza viruses, magnified one million times

Streptococcus bacteria

The cold-causing adenovirus can remain airborne for hours.

Pneumonia bacteria

When a person with a cold coughs or sneezes, pathogens spray into the air and may infect anyone who comes into contact with them. Simply by sneezing, a person can propel viruses over 15 feet. Cold-causing viruses and bacteria can survive outside the body for several hours.

141

What Is Diabetes?

In a healthy person

Diabetes is a disease in which the body is unable to control the amount of sugar, or glucose, in the bloodstream. This causes hyperglycemia, a dangerously high level of sugar in the blood.

The major factor in diabetes is insulin, a hormone produced by special cells in the pancreas *(right)*. Insulin signals the body's cells to absorb glucose. Working with another pancreatic hormone, called glucagon, insulin also controls the amount of glucose in the blood. When the body produces too little insulin, or when it doesn't respond correctly to insulin, diabetes results *(below)*.

Diabetes can usually be controlled with a low-sugar diet, oral medication, or regular injections of insulin. Even so, the disease takes its toll over time, sometimes causing complications such as blindness and stroke.

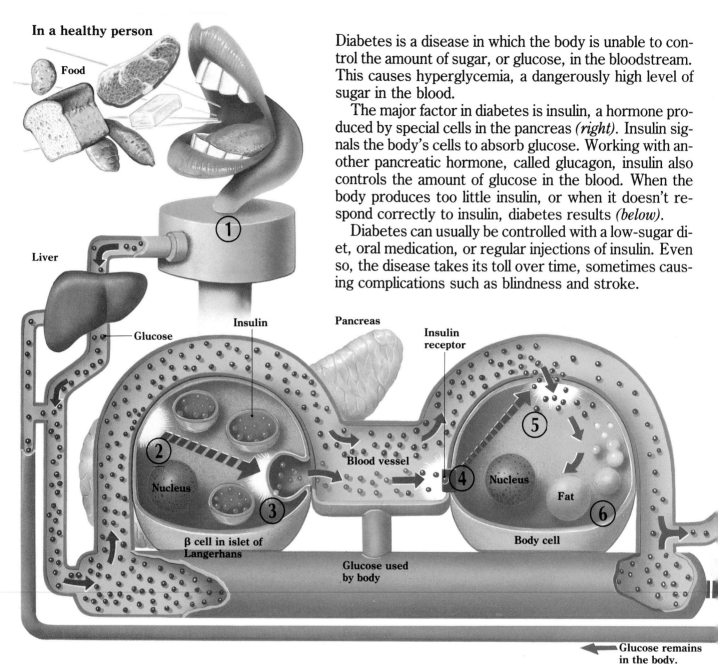

Food
Liver
Glucose
Insulin
Pancreas
Insulin receptor
① ② ③ ④ ⑤ ⑥
Nucleus
β cell in islet of Langerhans
Blood vessel
Nucleus
Fat
Body cell
Glucose used by body
Glucose remains in the body.

In a diabetic

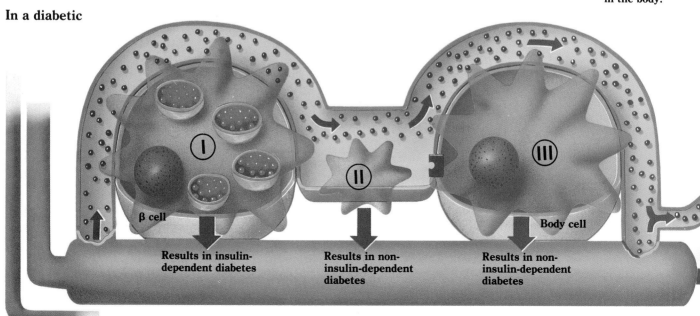

β cell
Ⅰ Ⅱ Ⅲ
Body cell
Results in insulin-dependent diabetes
Results in non-insulin-dependent diabetes
Results in non-insulin-dependent diabetes

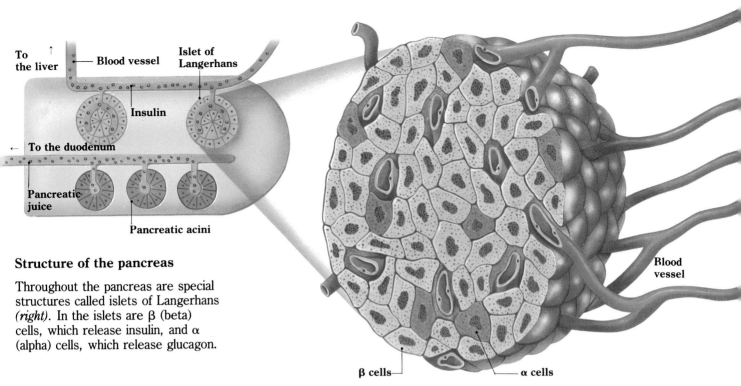

To the liver — Blood vessel   Islet of Langerhans

Insulin

← To the duodenum

Pancreatic juice

Pancreatic acini

Blood vessel

β cells   α cells

Structure of the pancreas

Throughout the pancreas are special structures called islets of Langerhans *(right)*. In the islets are β (beta) cells, which release insulin, and α (alpha) cells, which release glucagon.

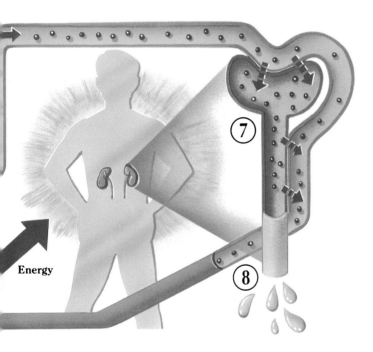

Energy

The function of insulin

1. When a healthy person digests food, the body converts carbohydrates into glucose, causing the blood sugar level to increase.
2. Responding to the increase in blood sugar, β cells in the islets of Langerhans produce insulin.
3. Insulin enters into the bloodstream and circulates throughout the body.
4. Insulin binds with special molecules on the body's cells called insulin receptors.
5. The binding of an insulin molecule with an insulin receptor enables the cell to absorb glucose.
6. The cells break down some of the glucose, using the energy released in the process as fuel. The rest is converted into fat and stored in the cells.
7. The kidneys filter out waste products from the blood and release the products into the urine, while at the same time preventing any glucose from leaving the bloodstream.
8. When the above steps work properly, a person's urine will contain no traces of glucose.

Causes and effects of diabetes

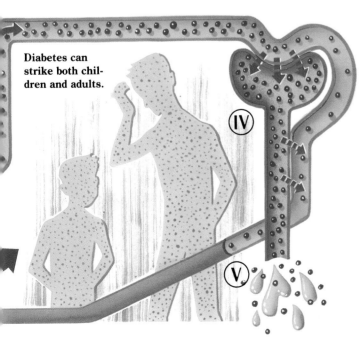

Diabetes can strike both children and adults.

I The β cells may not work correctly, producing little or no insulin. Such a condition is called insulin-dependent diabetes.
II Alternatively, following a viral infection, the immune system may inexplicably begin to produce insulin antibodies, interfering with the action of the insulin produced by the pancreas.
III Another cause is the malfunction of the cells' insulin receptors, making it impossible for insulin molecules to bind to them. Conditions II and III cause non-insulin-dependent diabetes.
IV In conditions I, II, and III, glucose cannot be used by the cells, and it remains in the blood at high concentrations. If left untreated, such high blood sugar levels can cause death in a matter of days.
V Since the kidneys cannot prevent such a large amount of glucose from escaping the bloodstream, the urine of diabetics will contain glucose.

What Is a Heart Attack?

A heart attack strikes when something prevents the heart from pumping enough blood through the body. The most common kind of heart attack is called a myocardial infarction (meaning a blockage of heart muscle), which occurs when heart cells die from lack of oxygen. As illustrated below, this happens when something blocks the flow of oxygen-bearing blood to these cells.

This usually happens in two stages. First, in a process that can take many years, vessels carrying blood into the heart become clogged with plaque, which contains cholesterol—a fatty substance found in food and also produced in the liver. This condition is known as atherosclerosis *(below)*. Lesions, or sores, eventually form in the lining of the damaged arteries. If a blood clot (thrombus) forms at the lesion, the second stage of a heart attack may happen quickly as the clot lodges in and blocks the narrowed blood vessel.

Myocardial infarctions are often fatal since a damaged heart may not be able to pump blood. However, if the affected area of the heart is not too large, the patient usually recovers, although with a weaker heart.

Myocardial infarction

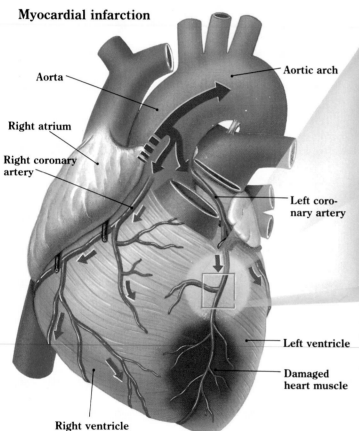

Aorta

Aortic arch

Right atrium

Right coronary artery

Left coronary artery

Left ventricle

Damaged heart muscle

Right ventricle

● **A clogged coronary artery**

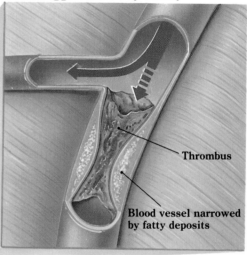

Thrombus

Blood vessel narrowed by fatty deposits

When a clot clogs an artery already choked with fatty deposits *(above)*, blood is prevented from reaching part of the heart. Without oxygen, the tissue begins to die *(black area, left)*.

● **Atherosclerosis**

Arteries have an outer membrane, a middle layer of muscle, and an inner membrane *(right)*. In atherosclerosis, cholesterol builds up between the inner membrane and the muscle layer, where it hardens and thickens the artery's wall. A blood clot may form at the site, or it may be trapped there as it travels through the bloodstream.

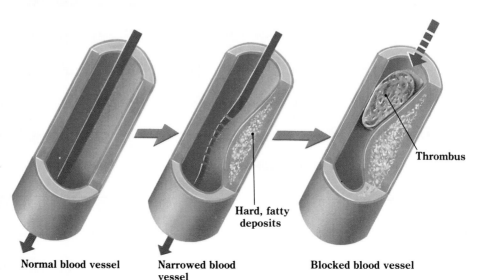

Thrombus

Hard, fatty deposits

Normal blood vessel

Narrowed blood vessel

Blocked blood vessel

Glossary

Agglutinin: An antibody found in blood plasma that causes clumping (agglutination) in incompatible blood types.

Agglutinogen: An antigen on a red blood cell that causes a reaction with an agglutinin.

Ampulla: The wide end of each of the three semicircular canals, located in the inner ear.

Ampullar crest: A structure, located in the ampulla, containing sensitive hair cells that respond to movement of the cupula and notify the brain when the head moves back and forth.

Aneurysm: An inflated, blood-filled weak spot in the wall of a blood vessel.

Angina: Intense pain in the chest caused by insufficient levels of oxygen in the heart muscles.

Antibody: A protein structure in the blood that helps destroy a foreign substance, or antigen, by binding to it.

Antigen: A substance that causes an immune response.

Artery: A blood vessel that carries oxygen-rich blood away from the heart and through the body.

Atrioventricular node: A node located near the tricuspid and mitral valves of the heart that passes impulses from the sinoatrial node to the ventricles.

Atrium: Either of the chambers in the heart that receives blood from the veins and sends it into the ventricles.

Bacterium: Any of a class of microscopic one-celled or noncellular plants that may act as pathogens in the human body.

Blind spot: A small spot in the eye, on the back of the retina, where the optic nerve leads to the brain and where there are no receptors.

Cardiovascular system: The system consisting of the heart and the blood vessels.

Centriole: A structure, located near the nucleus of a cell, that is involved in the early stages of cell division.

Chromosome: The carrier of genes within the nucleus of a cell. There are two types of chromosomes: **somatic chromosomes,** which are regular chromosomes, and **sex chromosomes,** represented as X and Y, which determine the sex of an individual.

Cilia: Short, hairlike structures on the surface of a cell.

Ciliary body: A structure in the eye that produces aqueous humor, supplying the lens and cornea with oxygen and nutrients.

Ciliary muscle: The muscle that surrounds and controls the shape of the eye.

Circulatory system: The organs and vessels that are involved in the transportation of blood and lymph to and from all parts of the body.

Clavicle: The collarbone.

Coccyx: The tailbone.

Connective tissue: The tissue that supports the body and binds tissues and organs together.

Corpus albicans: White tissue that results from the shrinking of the corpus luteum.

Corpus luteum: A structure in the ovary that forms after ovulation and secretes the hormone progesterone. After 14 days, the structure shrinks and is known as the corpus albicans.

Cupula: A jellylike structure in the ampulla of the inner ear's semicircular canals, responsible for detecting any changes in direction.

Dermis: A layer of skin below the epidermis composed of connective tissue.

DNA: Deoxyribonucleic acid; a chain of molecules within a cell nucleus containing the genetic information that determines inherited characteristics.

Endothelium: The membrane lining body cavities and blood vessels.

Enzyme: A protein that triggers and speeds up chemical reactions within cells.

Epidermis: The outer layer of skin, consisting of flattened dead cells in the **corneal layer** on the surface and living epithelial cells in the **basal layer** below.

Epithelial tissue: The tissue making up the skin and the lining of body cavities and organs.

Fibrin: A protein produced when a blood vessel is injured. Fibrin helps to form a network of insoluble fibers that trap red blood cells and platelets.

Fibroblast: A specialized cell that produces connective fibers used to repair damaged tissue.

Gene: A distinct unit of hereditary material, made of DNA, that determines an inherited characteristic.

Granulosa: The bumpy outer layer of an egg cell.

Gray matter: The inner section of the spinal cord, where nerve impulses are transmitted; also the outer layer of the cerebrum. Gray matter contains cell bodies of motor neurons and large numbers of interneurons, which relay impulses from one neuron to another.

Hair papilla: The bulblike base of a hair follicle, where the root is supplied with nutrients.

Haversian canal: A cavity in bone containing nerves and blood vessels.

Hemorrhage: Heavy or uncontrolled bleeding.

Hypodermis: A layer of fat underlying the dermis.

Leukocyte: A white blood cell. The three main types of leukocytes are **lymphocytes,** which are formed primarily in lymph nodes, and become two types, T lymphocytes and B lymphocytes; **granulocytes,** which are formed in bone marrow and turn into neutrophils, eosinophils, and basophils; and **monocytes,**

which are produced in the spleen and turn into macrophages.

Meiosis: Cellular division in which four reproductive cells are produced, each of which contains half the original number of chromosomes.

Membrane: A thin layer of tissue, often covering or lining an organ.

Mitosis: Cellular division in which a cell produces two daughter cells, each containing the original number of chromosomes.

Mitral valve: One of the two valves in the heart that allow blood to flow from the atria into the ventricles. The mitral valve on the left side of the heart has two flaps and is also called the **bicuspid valve.** On the right side is the **tricuspid valve,** named for its three flaps.

Myocardial muscle: Muscle tissue with the characteristics of both smooth and striated muscle; found only in the heart.

Myofibrils: Bundles of fibers making up larger fibers in skeletal muscle tissue.

Nervous system: The system consisting of the brain, spinal cord, nerves, ganglia, and the sense receptors. The **central nervous system** contains the brain and the spinal cord. The sense receptors include the eyes and ears, and the taste, touch, and smell organs. The **peripheral nervous system** contains all the nerves outside the brain and the spinal cord.

Neural tube: The structure in an embryo that develops into the brain and spinal cord.

Neuron: A specialized nerve cell that transmits nerve impulses.

Nucleus: In a cell, the membrane-enclosed structure containing the cell's DNA.

Organ: A group of tissues, such as those making up the heart, that work together to perform a specific function.

Osteoblast: A bone-forming cell.

Osteoclast: A bone-destroying cell.

Osteocyte: A variety of osteoblast that is trapped in cavities inside the bone and surrounding Haversian canals.

Patella: The kneecap.

Pathogen: An agent, such as a bacterium or a virus, that causes a disease.

Plasma: The clear liquid part of blood, making up 55 percent of blood by volume.

Pleural membrane: A membrane covering the outside of the lungs and the inside of the chest cavity.

Pons: A part of the brainstem that serves as a bridge between the two halves of the cerebellum.

Pulmonary artery: An artery that carries oxygen-poor blood from the heart to the lungs, where carbon dioxide is exchanged for oxygen.

Pulmonary vein: The vein that carries oxygen-enriched blood from the lungs to the heart.

Respiratory system: The system consisting of the air passages in the head and neck, as well as the lungs.

RNA: Ribonucleic acid, a chemical that works with DNA to control chemical activities within cells.

Sarcomere: A structural unit of myofibrils; stacks of sarcomeres make up myofibrils, the primary units responsible for muscle contractions.

Sarcoplasmic reticulum: One of two systems of membranes (the other consists of transverse tubules) that separate myofibrils and take part in muscle contractions.

Scapula: The shoulder blade.

Sclera: The outer layer of the eyeball.

Sebaceous gland: A gland in the skin that produces oily secretions to protect the skin and hair.

Sinoatrial node: A small mass of tissue in the right atrium of the heart that sends out impulses to control the pace of the heartbeat; known as the natural pacemaker.

Smooth muscle: Muscle tissue responsible for involuntary muscle movement, such as in the stomach.

Striated muscle: Voluntary muscle tissue that moves on command, such as in the legs. Also known as **skeletal muscle.**

Sulcus: A shallow furrow on the surface of the cerebral cortex.

Thymus: A gland located near the heart that is active only during childhood, when it is involved with the development of the immune system and produces lymphocytes.

Tissue: A group of cells that are structurally similar and perform the same function.

Transverse tubules: One of two systems (with the sarcoplasmic reticulum) of membranes that separate myofibrils and take part in muscle contractions. These membranes serve as a communication pathway between the muscle fiber and the myofibrils.

Vein: A blood vessel that carries blood back to the heart.

Vena cava: One of the two largest veins in the body. The **superior vena cava** returns blood from the upper part of the body to the heart; the **inferior vena cava** returns blood from the lower part of the body to the heart.

Villi: Small fingerlike structures on the lining of the small intestines or in the chorion of developing embryos.

Virus: Any of a group of submicroscopic agents that can cause disease by multiplying within living cells. Viruses typically have a protein coat around a core of RNA or DNA material.

White matter: The outer section of the spinal cord that transmits impulses up and down the cord; also located underneath the gray matter in the brain.

Zygote: A fertilized egg cell that has the ability to develop into an adult.

Index

Staff for
UNDERSTANDING SCIENCE & NATURE

Editorial Directors: Patricia Daniels, Karin Kinney
Text Editor: Allan Fallow
Writer: Mark Galan
Assistant Editor/Research: Elizabeth Thompson
Editorial Assistant: Louisa Potter
Production Manager: Prudence G. Harris
Senior Copy Coordinator: Jill Lai Miller
Production: Celia Beattie
Library: Louise D. Forstall
Computer Composition: Deborah G. Tait (Manager), Monika D. Thayer, Janet Barnes Syring, Lillian Daniels

Special Contributors, Text: John Clausen, James Dawson, Margery duMond, Mark Washburn
Design/Illustration: Antonio Alcalá, Caroline Brock, Nicholas Fasciano, Yin Yi
Photography: Myrleen Ferguson/PhotoEdit, Tony Freeman/PhotoEdit, Carol Harrison, Elizabeth Kupersmith
Research: Jocelyn Lindsay, Jacqueline Shaffer
Index: Barbara L. Klein

Library of Congress Cataloging-in-Publication Data
Human body.
     p.   cm. — (Understanding science & nature)
   Includes index.
   Summary: Uses a question and answer format to discuss the anatomy and function of the human body.
   ISBN 0-8094-9654-2. — ISBN 0-8094-9655-0 (lib. bdg.)
   1. Human physiology—Juvenile literature.
   2. Human anatomy—Juvenile literature.
   3. Body, Human—Juvenile literature.
  [1. Body, Human—Miscellanea.   2. Questions and answers.]
  I. Time-Life Books. II. Series.
QP37.H89   1992
612—dc20   91-36143
                                      CIP
                                       AC

TIME-LIFE for CHILDREN ™

Publisher: Robert H. Smith
Associate Publisher and Managing Editor: Neil Kagan
Editorial Directors: Jean Burke Crawford, Patricia Daniels, Allan Fallow, Karin Kinney, Sara Mark
Editorial Coordinator: Elizabeth Ward
Director of Marketing: Margaret Mooney
Product Manager: Cassandra Ford
Assistant Product Manager: Shelley L. Shimkus
Business Manager: Lisa Peterson
Assistant Business Manager: Patricia Vanderslice
Administrative Assistant: Rebecca C. Christoffersen
Special Contributor: Jacqueline A. Ball

Original English translation by International Editorial Services Inc./ C. E. Berry

First printing. Printed in U.S.A.
Published simultaneously in Canada.
Time Life Inc. is a wholly owned subsidiary of
THE TIME INC. BOOK COMPANY.
TIME-LIFE is a trademark of Time Warner Inc. U.S.A.
For subscription information, call 1-800-621-7026.